Interdisciplinary Unit

Native Americans

CHALLENGING

Illustrator:
Wendy Chang

Editor:
Dona Herweck Rice

Editor-in-Chief:
Sharon Coan, M.S. Ed.

Art Director:
Elayne Roberts

Cover Artist:
Wendy Cipolla-Boccuzzi

Product Manager:
Phil Garcia

Imaging:
Alfred Lau

Publishers:
Rachelle Cracchiolo, M.S. Ed.
Mary Dupuy Smith, M.S. Ed.

Author:
Mari Lu Robbins

Teacher Created Materials, Inc.
P.O. Box 1040
Huntington Beach, CA   92647
ISBN-1-55734-607-0

©1994 Teacher Created Materials, Inc.   Made in U.S.A.

Table of Contents

Introduction

In 1492, two very different cultures came together for the first time on the sandy white beaches of a small island in what are now known as the West Indies. From the beginning, the relationship between the two groups was marked by misunderstanding and miscommunication. One group saw the other as friendly children just waiting to be made into Christians, while the newcomers, in turn, were seen by their hosts as messengers from the gods. Both sides were wrong, and over the centuries to come, this initial misunderstanding grew larger and led to exploitation, war, broken promises, suffering, and many needless deaths.

The initial error the newcomers made was to think that this land to which they had come was India, so their leader named the residents "Indians." After they realized they had not landed in India, they made a second error in believing that they were discovering a new land for the first time, little knowing that the people who "met them at the dock," as Cherokee humorist Will Rogers put it, were the descendants of people who had discovered North America at least 30,000 years earlier. A third error the newcomers made was that these friendly natives had no culture or religion of their own, and, therefore, they must be given those things.

Being accustomed, for the most part, to settling differences in councils or village meetings, and having strong traditions of sharing whatever they had with each other, the native residents of North America did what they could to help their strange new visitors. The natives brought food to the newcomers and showed them how to use the wild game and plants for food and medicine. When the newcomers asked for land on which to live, the natives obliged. After all, there was plenty for everyone. But they did not know how many newcomers there would be, or how hungry for land and minerals they would be. The natives had traditions which said that humans must live in harmony with nature. They had no conception of the belief that nature's resources were to be exploited or that people had a manifest destiny to tame the land and make it their own. And the newcomers thought that the natives had no god, when, in truth, they believed God was in everything.

The newcomers were aggressive, and step by step, year by year, they took over. At first, and for a long time, many of the natives were defeated without the newcomers having to raise a hand. As many as eighty to ninety percent of them died from European diseases for which they had no immunities. And as the settlers kept coming, they pushed the natives out of the way. It was fairly easy to push them. Most of the natives were good warriors, and once they realized they needed to fight for their homelands, they did fight and with growing anger, but in the long run there were just too many to defeat, and the newcomers had better weapons. Many natives were destroyed by alcohol the settlers brought and for which the natives had no physical tolerance. Much of the damage done to the natives was by treaty. The settlers changed their minds frequently about what they wanted from the natives, except usually they wanted more.

To justify killing Indians and pushing them off their land, the newcomers fabricated reasons. The Indians were "dirty," "savage," "godless," and had to be paid back for any fighting they had done. They did not use the land, so it was not right for them to have so much space when there were white men wanting to farm and to look for gold. Then, after the white men settled the Civil War, there were many men left at loose ends. Jobs were hard to find. Some men became professional Indian fighters, and they were proud of it. They believed Indians were not citizens and the only good one was a dead one.

Suddenly in the nineteenth and early twentieth centuries, some of those who had exploited the native people began to say, "Hey! The Indians will all soon be extinct! We had better start learning something about them before they are gone." That is when they learned that the Indians did have cultures and religions. They were people, after all. However, this realization did not stop more treaties from being signed, and it did not stop more land from being taken away. And ironically, in the land where people felt secure having "freedom of religion," the Indians did not get that freedom legally until 1979.

Introduction *(cont.)*

The purpose of this unit is to give the teacher activities which raise the level of understanding about the real discoverers of America and to help them show their students some of the richness which was, and is, in American Indian life. In this unit, these very diverse groups of people will sometimes be called American Indians and sometimes Native Americans. The terms can be confusing, because anyone born in the United States is a Native American, and Indians are people who live in, or come from, India. Most Native Americans/American Indians would prefer to be called by their tribal names (for example, Cherokee, Lakota, Absaroka, Cheyenne, or Modoc, to name a few) because lumping the tribes together suggests that they are alike, which is not the case.

Because folktales and legends tell much about a people and what is important to them, many of the activities are themed around a few characteristic stories of the groups. There are thousands of stories from which to choose, so the ones chosen have been carefully selected, but they represent only a tiny fraction of a percent of the total lore of a region or group. All the tribes had rich languages and rich oral traditions.

Sadly, it has been customary in American education to unintentionally teach racial stereotypes about Native Americans. Mention the word "Indian" and many non-Indians immediately think of a noble savage of the plains, hunting buffalo, living in tipis and scalping his enemies, or a pastoral picture of a colorfully-dressed Navajo sitting at an outdoor loom with red rocks in the distance. The Native American is neither all good nor all bad anymore than the European American is. The reality of the lives of Indian peoples is varied and complex.

This unit will attempt to give the teacher resources to teach students about the wonderful complexity and diversity among the original discoverers of North America and their descendants, showing them as human beings worthy of respect for the qualities of their characters, just as the teachers and students want to be seen themselves.

This unit suggests a wide variety of activities which utilize many different types of learning situations, including the following:

- Cross-curricular activities thematically related to the subject and organized by group
- Activities in language arts, social studies/history, science, math, games, and crafts
- Samples of Native American poetry and oratory
- An annotated bibliography of literature and biographies by and/or about Native Americans
- Activities which teach to written, oral, listening, and kinesthetic modalities
- Suggestions for alternative responses to the literature
- Individual and group activities
- Sources of materials for further reading
- Activities which encourage team-teaching of core curriculum

About the Author

Mari Lu Robbins is a retired teacher who is also part Cherokee. She says, "My father's family came from Tennessee to Indian Territory in the 1800s, and my childhood was spent in Oklahoma. I grew up being proud of my Cherokee heritage. Most of my classmates and friends were also all, or part, Indian, and I did not realize until we moved to California to be near my mother's family that the people with whom I identified were often misunderstood by others. I hope this unit will show some of the wonderful diversity and value of the cultures of the original inhabitants of North America."

Tribal Regions

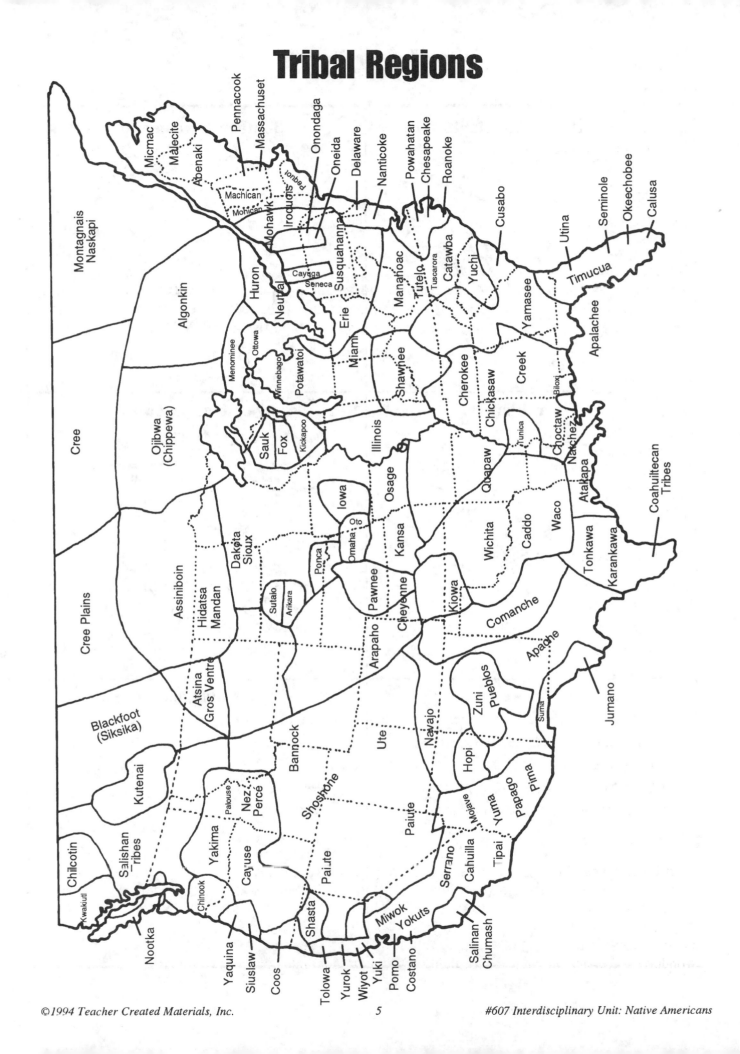

Tribal Regions *(cont.)*

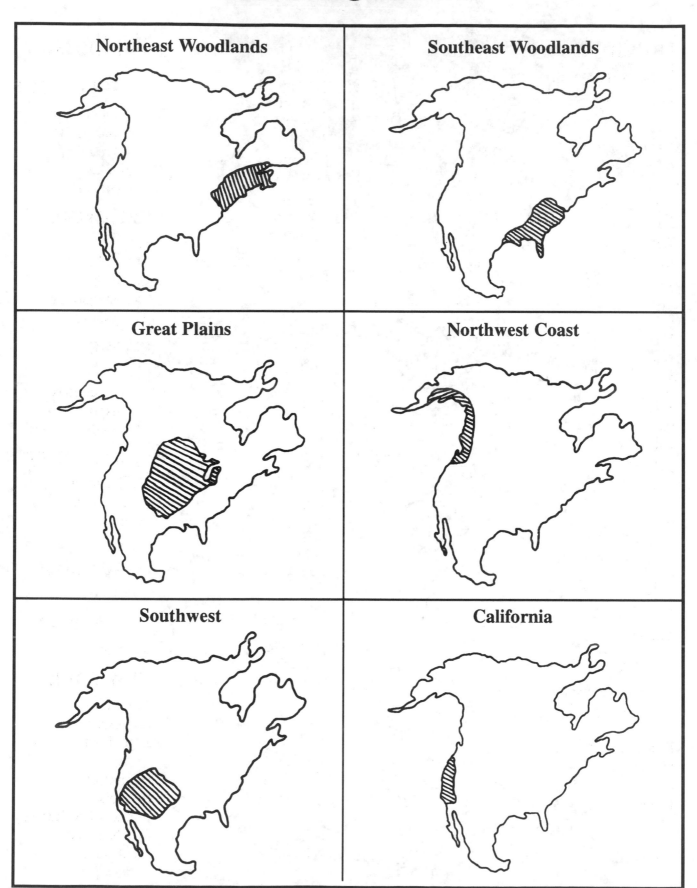

Northeast Woodlands

Southeast Woodlands

Great Plains

Northwest Coast

Southwest

California

Tribal Nations

North and Pacific Northeast

CANADA & ALASKA

Aleut
Athabascan
Bear Lake
Beaver
Bella Coola
Chigmiut
Chuga
Cree
Haida
Han
Hare
Ingalik
Innuit
Kaska
Kwakiutl
Koyukon
Kutchin
Malemiut
Nootka
Salish
Sekani
Slave
Tagish
Tanana
Tlingit

IDAHO

Bannock (Shoshone)
Coeur d'Alene
Flathead
Kootenai
Nez Percé
Paiute
Palouse
Shoshone
Skitswish
Spokan

MICHIGAN

Menominee
Chippewa
Ojibwa
Ottawa

MINNESOTA

Chippewa
Dakota
Sac and Fox
Sioux (Lower, Upper, Shakopee, Satee)
Wahpeton

OREGON

Cayuse
Clatsop
Coos
Deschutes
Kalapoola
Klamath
Modoc
Paiute
Shosoni
Siletz
Siuslaw
Tenino
Tilkuni
Umatilla
Umpqua
Walla Walla
Wasco

WASHINGTON

Chehalis
Chinook
Clallam
Colville
Hoh
Kalispel
Klickitat
Lummi
Makah
Methow
Nespelim
Nez Percé
Nisqually Nooksak
Okinagan
Palouse
Puyallup
Quileute
Quinalut
Sanpoil
Senijextee
Skagit
Skitswish
Skokomish
Spokan
Squaxon
Stillaguamish
Wasco
Wenatchee
Yakima

WISCONSIN

Mahican
Menominee
Munsee
Ojibuwa
Oneida
Potawatomi
Sac and Fox
Winnebago

Northeast

CONNECTICUT

Mashantucket Pequot
Mahican
Paugusset
Pequot
Schaghticoke

DELAWARE

Maliseet
Nanticoke
Nipmuck
Passamaquoddy
Wampanoag

MAINE

Abnaki
Passamaquoddy
Algonkian
Penobscot

MASSACHUSETTS

Massachusetts
Wampanoag
Pequot

NEW HAMPSHIRE

Pennacook

NEW JERSEY

Delaware

NEW YORK

Adirondak
Akwesasne
Algonkian
Cayuga
Hanhasset
Iroquois
Iroquois Confederacy (Six Nations)
Manhatten
Mohawk

Tribal Nations (cont.)

Mohican
Montauk
Oneida
Onondaga
Seneca
Shinnecock
Tuscarora
Wappinger

PENNSYLVANIA

Erie
Munsee
Delaware
Suksquehanna

RHODE ISLAND

Narragansett

VERMONT

Mohawk
Iroquois

Midwest

ILLINOIS

Cahokia
Illinois
Kaskassskia
Kickapoo
Poeria
Shawnee

INDIANA

Miami
Wea
Yuchi

MISSOURI

Shawnee

OHIO

Erie
Shawnee
Wyandot

South

ARKANSAS

Caddo
Quapaw
Nachitoches

FLORIDA

Apalachee
Calusa
Miccosukee
Pensacola
Seminole
Takesta
Timucha

GEORGIA

Chatot
Cherokee
Creek
Okmulgee
Quale
Yamasee

LOUISIANA

Caddo
Chitmacha
Coushatta
Houma
Nachitoches
Natchez
Tunica-Biloxi
Washa

MARYLAND

Nanticoke

MISSISSIPPI

Biloxi
Catawba
Cherokee
Chickasaw
Choctaw
Pascagoula
Yazoo

NORTH CAROLINA

Catawba
Cheraw
Cherokee
Chowanoc
Hatteras
Pamlico
Saponi
Sugeree
Tuscarora
Woccon

SOUTH CAROLINA

Catawba
Coosa
Creek
PeeDee
Santee

TENNESSEE

Cherokee
Chickasaw
Chickmunga
Yuchi

TEXAS

Alabama-Coushatta
Apache (Lipan)
Atakapa
Comanche
Isleta
Karan
Kawa
Kickapoo
Kiowa
Mescalero
Tonkawa
Wichita
Ysleta del Sur Pueblo

VIRGINIA

Chickahominy
Chkowanoc
Manahoac
Mattaponi
Monacan
Pamunkey
Powhatan
Tuscarora
Tutelo

WEST VIRGINIA

Manahoac
Tutelo

Southwest

ARIZONA

Ak-Chin
Apache
Chemhuevi
Chiricahua
Cocopah
Havasupai
Hohokam
Hopi
Hualapai
Kaibab-Paiute
Maricopa
Mohave
Navajo
Paiute (Kaibab)
Papago
Pima
Quechan
Tonto
Walapai
Yaqui
Yavapai
Yuma
Zuni

Tribal Nations *(cont.)*

COLORADO

Arapaho
Cheyenne
Jicarilla Apache
Ute

NEW MEXICO

Acoma
Apache
Conchiti
Keresan
Manso
Mongollon
Piro
Pueblo (numerous)
Tesuque
Tewa
Tiwa Tano
Zuni

UTAH

Bear River
Goshute
Navajo
Pahvant
Shoshone
Ute

Plains

IOWA

Iowa
Mesquakie
Omaha
Sac and Fox
Winnebago
Yangton Sioux

KANSAS

Iowa
Kansa
Kaw
Kickapoo
Kiowa
Osage
oto
Wichita

NEBRASKA

Arapaho
Omaha
Oto
Pawnee
Sioux
Winnebago

NORTH DAKOTA

Arikara
Chippewa
Hankpapa
Hidatsa
Mandan
Sioux (Yankton)

OKLAHOMA

Apache
Arapaho
Caddo
Cherokee
Cheyenne
Chicaksaw
Choctaw
Commanche
Creek
Delaware
Iowa
Kiowa
Kiowa
Kiowa-Appache
Miami
Modoc
Osage
Ottawa

Pawnee
Peoria
Ponca
Potawatomi
Quapaw
Sac and Fox
Seminole
Seneca-Cayuga
Shawnee
Sioux (Kaw, Oto, Missouri)
Susquehanna
Tonkawa
Wichita
Wyandot
Yuchi

SOUTH DAKOTA

Miniconjou
Pona
Sioux (Dakota, Oglala)

WYOMING

Arapaho
Cheyenne
Crow
Gros Ventre
Lakota
Shoshone

West

CALIFORNIA

Achomawi
Atseguwi
Cabazon (Mission)
Cahto
Cahuilla (Mission)
Chemeheuvi
Chumash (Mission)
Coast Miwok
Diegueno (Mission)
Esselen

Hoopa
Ipai
Karok
Kumeyaay Nation
Luiseno (Mission)
Maidu
Mojave
Mono
Morongo (Mission)
Ohlone (Mission)
Paiute
Pomo
Serrano
Shasta
Shoshone
Tache Yokuts
Talawa
Tipai
Tolowa
Tygh
Wailaki
Wappo
Wintun
Wiyot
Yahi
Yokuts
Yuki
Yurok

NEVADA

Gosute
Paiute (Shoshone, Moapa)
Panaca
Shoshone (Paiute)
Washo
Winnemucca

PACIFIC

Hawaiians

Language Groups of North America

One way in which social scientists trace the origins and migrations of native groups is by identifying and classifying their languages. This shows that seemingly different peoples may have been related in the past and may have originated in the same place, although they later became separated. Using this map and the one on page 5, list all the native tribes of one language group.

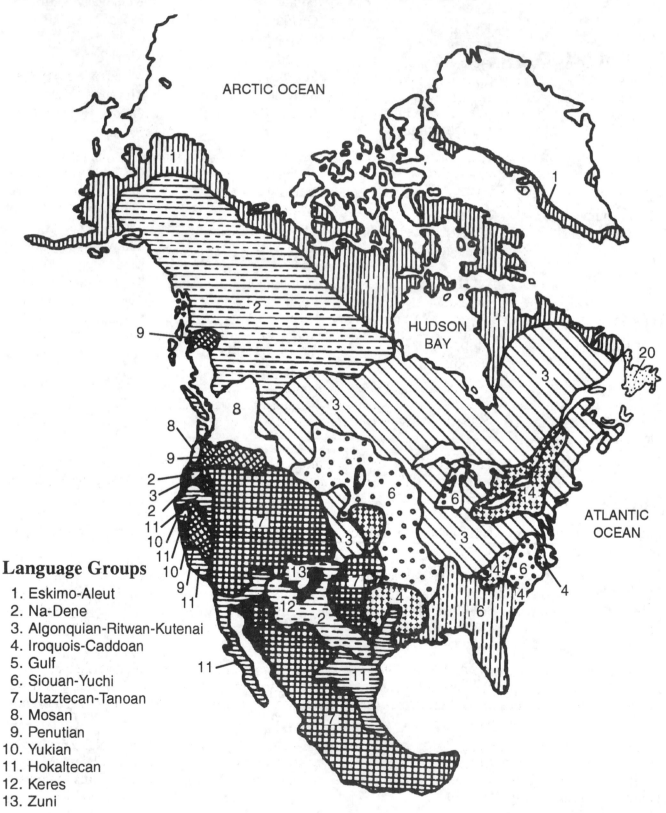

Language Groups

1. Eskimo-Aleut
2. Na-Dene
3. Algonquian-Ritwan-Kutenai
4. Iroquois-Caddoan
5. Gulf
6. Siouan-Yuchi
7. Utaztecan-Tanoan
8. Mosan
9. Penutian
10. Yukian
11. Hokaltecan
12. Keres
13. Zuni

On Being Indian

On a spring day in 1994, an historic meeting took place on the south lawn of the White House. More then three-hundred leaders from all five hundred and forty seven federally recognized tribes met with President Bill Clinton asking for the right to use eagle feathers in their religious ceremonies and asking that the government recognize tribal governments by consulting them when new policies affecting them were issued.

This meeting was a long time in coming, and American Indians are hopeful that, at last, the promises made to them about tribal sovereignty hundreds of years ago will be kept and that the right to live their lives as they choose and to be "Indian" will officially be theirs. What does it mean to be "Indian?"

Ada Deer, a Menominee from Wisconsin who is the head of the Bureau of Indian Affairs, once requested that she not be called "Native American." She prefers to be called American Indian, and that is true of many people who are descendants of the first peoples of the North American Continent. After all, anyone who has been born in the United States is a native American, and American Indian people feel the time has come to express their "Indianness."

There were many differences among the different tribes of North America, and the differences generally reflected the environments in which they lived. Some were farmers who tilled the soil while others were nomads following the game and thinking it wrong to cut into the breast of their mother, the Earth. Some were fishermen with fish a mainstay in their diet, while others ate only red meat and looked down on fisheaters. For some, war was an important part of their culture and the only way a man could make a name for himself, while others were very peaceable, even meek. But among these different tribes with different ways of life, certain beliefs and ideas held true for all or most.

Many of the things the white man thinks of as being typically Indian were really not original with the Indian. Other peoples in the world had bows and arrows, used war paint, and respected *shamans*, or medicine men. Mythical beliefs in the powerful thunderbird, rain dances, and the practice of scalping were all adopted by other peoples as well as the Indian.

Many of the American Indians based their social organization on the clan system and the family, much like people in Africa, Asia, and the Pacific Rim. In these systems, the people of a family or clan traced their roots back to a common ancestor, sometimes named after a totem, which was regarded as a supernatural or spiritual guardian. The clan and the family were responsible for raising and teaching the children, even punishing a child when it was necessary, although few of the Indians ever physically punished a child.

Almost all the different tribes expressed, and still express, a deep spiritual faith in the supernatural. Most of them believed that all living things were linked to them by invisible bonds and that all living things were dependent on each other. Each animal, tree, and manifestation of nature, including the winds, sun, and stars, had its own spirit. That spirit was related to humans, and therefore it was deserving of the utmost respect.

It was believed that a supernatural force filled the world, and some Indians believed that the total spiritual powers of all people were this unseen force. This force shaped and directed all life, and it was called by different names in each group: *wakan* by the Sioux, *manitou* by the Algonquians, and *orenda* by the Iroquois, for example.

Some Indians believed in gods, ghosts, and demons, and some believed that each person had his or her own personal guardian spirit which he or she tried to contact through vision quests or dreams. Many tribes thought there was one Creator who was always with them while others thought of this force as not being interested in daily life.

On Being Indian *(cont.)*

Most Indian tribes believed in *shamans,* individuals thought to have especially strong spiritual abilities or powers. Sometimes these people were called "medicine men," but they did more than try to cure sick people. Because they were able to contact the spirit world, they could call on supernatural help for others. They could ensure that crops or the hunt would be good, that warfare would be successful, or they could bring harm to an enemy. Some of them, like Sitting Bull, also became politically powerful.

Many tribes had two main types of mythologies—the culture hero tales and the trickster tales. Culture heroes are characters credited with teaching the people their way of life long ago while tricksters are jokesters who, in trying to trick others, often trick themselves. Either of these characters may be represented by an animal, like the coyote or the raven, or by a human. Many stories were told to the children by their grandmothers from one generation to the next.

Indian rituals and celebrations usually were cause for dancing, drumming, and singing. Some of these dances were considered sacred, but others were done simply for pleasure. Some songs told of a person's exploits while others simply expressed a thought. All tribes used drums, although there were different kinds. There were drums which sat on the ground, which were held in the hand, and which were hung from poles. Many of these drums could be heard for long distances and were used to send messages. Whistles were also used, as well as flutes and rattles.

Certain ideas were fundamental to the beliefs of most Indians, particularly the idea of land ownership. The Indians did not believe it was possible, or even desirable, for an individual to own land. Land, air, and water were for everyone's use. A tribe might lay claim to a certain area as its hunting grounds, fishing territory, or dwelling, but what they claimed as theirs was held communally by the group.

Many tribes regarded the Earth as the mother of all life and thought the idea of selling one's mother was ludicrous. Because of this, it was important to stay in close contact with the Earth. The Earth could be felt through one's moccasins, and to use steel hoes or plows to cut through the Earth would be to slice open the breast of one's mother.

Indians revered the Earth and even stood in awe of it. They tried to live in such a way that there would be a balance and harmony between humans and nature. They believed that only when things were out of balance would there be illness, pain, or other misfortune. Death was seen as a continuation of life in another world where everything was easier than it had been here, but the term "happy hunting ground" was invented by the white man.

Perhaps the most erroneous idea the white man had about the Indian was that he was a "savage." This was far from the truth. Yes, many of the Indian tribes went to war, but Indian warfare was very different from that of the European American. War consisted of sporadic raids, usually in defense of hunting grounds and for honor, revenge, slaves, or horses. Total war, like that waged against the Indians under Generals Sherman and Custer, was a kind of warfare the Indians had never practiced. In fact, *counting coup*, in which a warrior touched a live enemy and got away to tell about it, was a more honorable feat than killing an enemy.

The days of intertribal warfare are over, for today's Indians realize they have more in common with each other than they have differences. Among today's Indians there has been an attempt in recent years to achieve unity among the different tribes.

On Being Indian (cont.)

The American Indians of the Northeastern Woodlands influenced the white men in ways which are fundamental to "the American way." European ancestors of today's white Americans learned much about individual freedom, personal dignity, representative government, and democracy from those first peoples of America.

America's Indian populations have survived much together: persecution, imported diseases, and the concerted attempts of governments and missionaries to force them to become what they are not, do not want to be, and probably never could be—a redskinned white man.

Many times each year, American Indians now come together at powwows, dances, and other social events to be with each other. They continue to honor their roots and to remember the past while living in the present. There is a new pride and a new sense of dignity in realizing that they have survived and that together they have power—not the power to subdue others, but the power to assert one's self and to be one with the Supreme Power.

The following poem contains the words of the song Sitting Bull sang after he surrendered to the U.S. Army. Both the words of the song and what is left unsaid give a glimpse of how he and his people felt when they knew their entire way of life had been taken away.

Last Song of Sitting Bull

Teton Sioux
A warrior
I have been.
Now
It is all over.
A hard time
I have.

Activities

Like most good poetry, this song says more than its words. That is, there is a great deal of unspoken feeling between the lines. The chief who composed this song had tried for many years to preserve the way of life he and his people had shared for many generations, even leaving their ancestral country and moving to Canada for several years where they hoped to retain their free Great Plains life.

1. In small groups, discuss the following questions:

   • How much do you know about the Plains Indians? (Share what you know.)

   • What could Sitting Bull have meant by the first two lines?

   • What would be hard about having the whole way of life of a large group of people changed against their will?

   • For many years, the U.S. government moved Indians around from one place to another against their will and tried to make them into "red white men." They even forbade them to practice their own religion. Do you think it was right for the government to do this?

   • What kinds of actions might the U.S. government have taken to help the native people adjust?

2. After you have shared your opinions with each other in answer to these questions, think of something in life about which you feel strongly. Write a poem or song about it. You may share it if you like. If it is deeply personal and you hesitate to share it, that is all right, too.

Native American Contributions to American Culture

Americans owe a much larger debt to the American Indians than most of them realize. Almost every aspect of American life has been influenced by the first peoples of America. They have helped to shape the destiny of modern man in such diverse areas of life as agriculture, government, religion, trade, mythology, literature, economics, and arts and crafts.

When the white man first landed on the North American Continent, the Indian supplied him with food. Those early settlers in New England probably would not have survived their first winter had not the Indian people taught them how to use native foods. The Indian people then went on to teach whites how to fish, hunt, and plant foods native to the continent.

The natives helped the newcomers travel over Indian trails and build watercraft. The Indians supplied the whites with furs for clothing. Indian gold and other metals provided the economic means for funding European and American armies, navies, and courts. Americans also owe to the Indians many of the social and political ideas they consider most "American," such as the individual liberties and personal freedoms which are spelled out in the U.S. *Constitution*.

Almost half the crops now grown for the world's food supply were first grown by the Indians. Corn and potatoes were not known to the white man until he came to North America. Among the other foods first grown and/or harvested by the Indians were pumpkins, pineapples, avocados, cacao for chocolate, and many kinds of beans. Cotton was first grown and made into fabrics by the Indians. Many modern medicine sources are native to North America, as well.

American Indian inventions commonly used around the world today include canoes, snowshoes, moccasins, hammocks, kayaks, ponchos, rubber syringes, dog sleds, toboggans, and parkas. Many Indian designs and Indian games have added to American life. Thousands of names for cities, states, lakes, mountains, rivers, and other geographical sights are Indian names. Some words originally Indian include wigwam, succotash, tobacco, chipmunk, skunk, opossum, tomahawk, moose, mackinaw, hickory, pecan, raccoon, cougar, woodchuck, hominy, and hundreds more. Common expressions coming from the Indian include war paint, Indian file, bury the hatchet, paleface, warpath, big chief, and Indian summer.

Although often misinterpreted, Indian mythology and folklore have contributed much to literature, music, art, drama, dance, movies, and television programs. The mythology and folklore of the American Indian is rich and rooted in the past. Only now are non-Indians recognizing the history and vibrancy of this heritage and its importance. The stories of the American Indians explained the universe and how people came to be. They told the way people should behave and how they should worship. The Indians' entire religious, social, and political lives were laid out in their beliefs and mythology.

Indian stories told of creation and of a time before the humans came, and they are as rich and varied as the stories of ancient Greece and Sumeria. There are many reasons in today's modern, "civilized" world, with its water and air pollution, crime, and breakdown of the family, to look back on the Indian beliefs and see in them a wisdom which is eternal.

Other aspects of modern life have also been influenced by Indians. The Boy Scout and Girl Scout movements had their beginnings in Indian life, and only now are non-Indians beginning to realize the need to return to some of the Indian ideas of how land should be used. The whole conservation and ecology movement stems from Indian ideas about nature, and we now know what the Indians knew long ago, that the babies yet to be born have a claim on the land which is equal to our own. We are learning to revere the land, and we know that to "conquer" the land destroys much of what we need for survival.

Native American Contributions to American Culture *(cont.)*

One of the most important ways in which Americans were influenced by the Indians was through the Iroquois Confederacy, from which they took many ideas for government and outlined them in the *Constitution of the United States*. In 1754, long before the United States gained its independence as a nation, Benjamin Franklin proposed a union of colonies similar to that of the Iroquois Confederacy, and in time the structure of the Confederacy indirectly influenced the makers of the *Constitution*. The ways in which the Senate and House of Representatives work out bills in compromise sessions, for example, stems from the ways the Confederacy worked toward the consensus of its members.

Quite possibly the belief most Americans hold most precious is the right to individual freedom. This American belief in individual dignity and individual freedom came, at least in part, from the beliefs of many Indians. In most tribes, an individual was free to be himself, as long as that did not hurt others, even to the extent of being able to leave a battle to do what he thought right or to go his own way in other things. An example of this is in the following situation.

The ideal of manhood was to be a good warrior and hunter. A young man generally could not hope to gain high status in the tribe otherwise; however, he was not coerced into being a warrior or hunter if he did not wish to be one. This even applied to the man who chose to do the work normally done by women or who chose to wear women's clothing.

Pretty-shield, wife of the Custer scout, Goes-ahead, told of one such man in her tribe when she was a young woman. He enjoyed doing women's work and wearing women's clothing, but he was also a brave warrior. When the Crows fought with another tribe, he wore men's clothing in battle, because if he was killed he did not want the enemy to find him hiding behind women's clothing. During peacetime, however, he was free to dress and work the way he wished, and the tribe accepted him as he was. By the same token, women sometimes became warriors.

American lives have been enriched in many ways, not only by the land on which they live, but more so by the people who "met the boat" when the Europeans came, the American Indians. Their lives, beliefs, and accomplishments have contributed many of the best parts of what has come to be the United States.

To gain an understanding of just how much is owed to the Indians, do the following activities.

Activities

1. Imagine that the Americas truly were "new" lands as the early settlers said they were, and that no Indians were there to meet the Europeans when they came to the continent. On the back of this paper, write a description of what the land would now be like without the influence of the native people. Also write how the lives of the people would be different. Consider, for example, such things as the American holiday of Thanksgiving and the U.S. *Constitution*.

2. In each of three columns labeled respectively "Plants," "Arts and Crafts," and "Ideas and Concepts," list some American Indian contributions to American life.

The Myth of the Indian Squaw

Perhaps nowhere has there been more misunderstanding of Indian life than there has been about the place of the woman in Indian society. The white man came to the North American continent with a cultural tradition that placed little value on women except sexually and as housekeepers. When the Europeans saw Indian women working hard, preparing food and clothing and carrying heavy burdens, they saw them through their own cultural eyes. The conclusions they drew were very wrong.

Life was hard for the native people. Tribes divided the work between men and women, and Indian men and women were true partners, doing together what had to be done. Men were the protectors, warriors, and hunters. This was a big job, because they were responsible for providing much of the food and other materials the people needed, and hunting and warring were dangerous. Not only did the men do the work of going after the meat and bringing it back to the village, but they also had to make the bows, arrows, shields, and other things needed for hunting and warring. European American men saw them doing these jobs, and because many of them saw hunting as a sport, not as a necessary job to provide for the people, they concluded that Indian men were lazy and played while the women worked. But the Indian men did the dangerous work of hunting and fighting, staying in the line of fire as their families escaped a battle, and riding into stampeding herds of buffalo. As they did this, the Indian women worked energetically at caring for the welfare of the family. They carried burdens, helped butcher the meat, cooked, tanned hides, and did much of the house building. Nowhere was there an idea that Indian women were "squaws," meaning the slaves of their husbands, as the white man thought they were. In fact, they had a great deal of power, sometimes even more than that of the men, because they were the ones who passed down tribal traditions and beliefs to the children.

Many tribes were *matrilineal,* meaning that family lines were traced through the mother. In these tribes, a child always belonged to the clan of his mother. The father was acknowledged, but he was the head of the families of his sisters, not that of his wife and children. Some tribes were also *matrilocal,* and where this was true, when a couple married, the husband went to live with the family of his wife, so in a sense he was a visitor in his own home. Divorce for a wife was easy. If she wanted a divorce, she merely threw all her husband's belongings outside the lodge, and that was that.

In many tribes the women were able to accumulate much of the family's wealth. With the Navajos, for example, sheep were the basis of wealth, and all sheep were owned by the women. With the Plains Indians and many others, the women owned the lodges and almost everything in them. Filled with many luxurious buffalo robes and other household items, these lodges could be quite valuable. After the horse came, the women also owned horses, sometimes as many of them as the men did, and in many tribes the chiefs were chosen by the women. Pueblo women built and owned the houses, all the furnishings, and all the crops, while the men did the labor in the fields and ran the many religious societies.

Women had a great deal of influence with their husbands when it came to making major decisions about almost everything, and there are many reports of women who went to battle with or without their husbands. The Sioux, Cheyenne, and Crow all have stories of women warriors going into battle to avenge the death of a brother. One story tells of a woman who went into battle with no weapon except a coup stick. She rode her horse straight into the midst of the fighting, pointing her coup stick at the enemy. The warriors immediately turned and ran from her, believing that her medicine was so strong they did not want to fight against her.

Other stories tell of women fighting to the death alongside their husbands. When Dull Knife and Little Wolf led their people on their long journey back to Montana, several of the younger women stayed behind with the men and fought with them as the older people and children were taken by others to safety. Life was often difficult for everyone, and sometimes it took courage just to stay alive. When a woman needed to help fight, she did so, and she was admired for it. Women were often the true rulers of a village, as well, spurring the men into doing their duties and holding them back from acting rashly.

The Myth of the Indian Squaw *(cont.)*

When the white men came to North America forcing tremendous change on Indian life, the change was in many ways harder for the men than it was for the women. Forced with their families onto reservations, men had most of their traditional occupations of hunting and warring taken from them, and with those occupations went much of their sense of manhood. Left with much idle time and few responsibilities, many of them drank the liquor they bought from the white traders. However, when there was a chance to work as a scout for the army, or when the United States went to war, they were able, at least temporarily, to fill their ancient roles as warriors.

Throughout the times of change, however, women still had their homes to care for and their children to raise. Except during wartime, the women were hired by whites before the men, usually into clerical or domestic jobs, so the women had greater exposure to white culture and learned more quickly to move between the cultures. Part of this greater mobility for the women was due to the special schools, usually boarding schools, most Indian children had to attend once the Indians were on the reservations.

For many years the Indian schools forced their students to learn the white culture and language, often forbidding them to speak their native languages at school. Boys were taught farming skills and the girls were taught clerical and homemaking skills. For the boys who had been raised as hunters, being made to learn how to farm was an exercise in futility, for very few of them wanted to become farmers. For many men, farming was sacrilegious, because they saw it as cutting into the body of Mother Earth. For the women, however, learning clerical and new homemaking skills allowed them to become stenographers, secretaries, and domestics. While these were not usually high-level jobs, they did give women early opportunities to adjust to white culture, unlike the farming skills taught to boys. Thus, women were able to gain in self-confidence more readily than men.

Modern times have seen Indian women succeed in a number of areas, including the professions. The Bureau of Indian Affairs has seen a woman, Ada Deer, a Menominee from Wisconsin, as its head, and the Cherokee Nation has elected Wilma Mankiller as Principal Chief. Gail Small, lawyer and member of the Northern Cheyennes, while running for the Montana State legislature in 1984 was able to quintuple the number of voters on the Cheyenne reservation and is active in working for Indian rights. Angela Russell, Crow, is a member of the Montana State Advisory Committee to the U.S. Civil Rights Commission. Marge Anderson is chairwoman of the Mille Lacs Ojibwe in Minnesota. LaDonna Harris, Commanche, heads Americans for Indian Opportunity. Cassadore Davis, Apache and Chairperson of the Apache Survival Coalition, at the age of seventy took on the University of Arizona and the Vatican in opposition to plans for turning a sacred Apache site, Mount Graham, into an observatory. Teresa Wall, Salish and Kootenay, is a member of the tribal council of her reservation and works to protect tribal rights. President of the Little Bighorn Community College is Janine Pease Windy Boy, Crow, who has also been national president of the American Indian Higher Education Consortium. Other native women serve as judges, lawyers, doctors, nurses, national park rangers, professional musicians, artists, and in many other occupations, and they still raise their families, often in quite traditional ways.

There is an old Indian saying that one should not criticize the way another lives until that person has walked a mile in the other's moccasins. If the white man who stormed his way onto the North American continent had taken the time to really learn something about Indian life, he would have discovered that the women he called squaws were not the drudges he thought they were. He would have learned that what the Indian valued most were brave men and good, sensible women who raised their children to be honest, generous, and hard-working members of their people. There is nothing to look down on about that!

The Myth of the Indian Squaw *(cont.)*

Activities

1. In small groups, brainstorm the ways in which the people you know teach "girls to be girls" and "boys to be boys" from babyhood on. What kinds of clothing does one wear as opposed to the other? What colors? Are there things that girls like and things that boys like? What are some differences between how boys and girls are "supposed" to act? List everything you can think of, then come back together as a class and discuss what you have decided. Do you think it is right to teach children these things? Do you think things should change? Why?

2. According to law, girls and boys are supposed to have "equal access" to school subjects and activities. This was not always true. For example, girls used to have to take homemaking classes while boys had to take woodshop or metal shop, and girls used to have to play games like basketball with "girls' rules," which were easier, while boys played the "real rules." Is this still true? Survey your parents and other people, both adults and students, asking the following questions to see how many of them think girls and boys are, or should be, taught differently in school. Tally the answers you get, then write a paper discussing the results.

   • Do girls and boys have the same opportunity now to learn the same things?

   • If a girl takes woodshop, should she be expected to complete the same projects as a boy?

   • If a boy takes cooking, should he be expected to complete the same projects as a girl?

   • How do you think people would react to a boy wearing a dress in school?

   • How do you think people would react to a girl wearing pants in school?

   • Can men make good preschool teachers? Why?

   • Can women make good telephone linemen? Why?

   • Do you think the United States will someday have a woman president?

The Myth of the Indian Squaw *(cont.)*

3. In groups, research to identify each of the following Native American women. Then, individually research one of the women or another of your choice and report back to the class in an appropriate way on the woman you have studied.

• Maria Campbell

_____

• Wilma Mankiller

_____

• Ada Deer

_____

• Sacajawea

_____

• Pocahontas

_____

• Beverly Hungry Wolf

_____

• Buffy Sainte-Marie

_____

• Cynthia Parker

_____

• Maria Tallchief

_____

• Sarah Winnemucca

_____

• Nancy Ward

_____

• Suzette and Rosalie La Flesche

_____

• Ella Deloria

_____

• Leslie Silko

_____

• Janet Campbell Hale

_____

• Marie McLaughlin

_____

• Mourning Dove

_____

Iroquois Confederacy: Seed for the U.S. Constitution

When the Europeans first came to North America, they brought with them many prejudices, including the idea that they were the only advanced people on earth. Because of this belief, they felt it was their responsibility to bring "civilization" to the native "savages." The Europeans, however, soon learned many things from the native people. First, they were shown many plant foods they had never seen before, such as corn, beans, squashes, and tomatoes. The people who introduced these plants to the newcomers probably saved their lives during the early, bitterly cold months. But the new residents learned much more from the native people than new foods to eat.

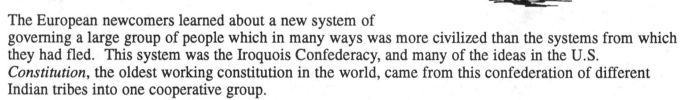

When the newcomers first came, they said that the Indians had no government and no laws, but they were wrong. The Indians governed themselves by a system of family relationships and obligations. From babyhood every member of the group learned the rules which were to be followed. Their leaders did not rule. They advised, resolved disputes, and tried to satisfy the wishes of their people. Everyone had the opportunity to speak out on an issue, and everyone came to agreement before any action was taken.

The European newcomers learned about a new system of governing a large group of people which in many ways was more civilized than the systems from which they had fled. This system was the Iroquois Confederacy, and many of the ideas in the U.S. *Constitution*, the oldest working constitution in the world, came from this confederation of different Indian tribes into one cooperative group.

The Iroquois Confederacy had its birth long ago in the northeastern part of what is now the United States. At the time, there was a great deal of warfare among the different tribes, and it seemed that all the warriors did was go to war to avenge actions taken against them in an endless cycle of warfare and killing. It is said that two men, a Huron named Deganawidah and an Mohawk named Hayenwatha (or Hiawatha) first proposed forming an alliance of tribes that would agree to live side by side in peace.

Deganawidah, a holy man, had a vision of Five Nations being united under a symbolic Tree of Peace. He said that the tribes must stop fighting and live in harmony by forming a government of law. He said that the people should consider courage, patience, and honesty as the most important human characteristics and that they should always put the future welfare of their people ahead of anything else. He said, "Carry no anger and hold no grudges. Think of continuing generations of our families. Think of our grandchildren and of those yet unborn."

Hayenwatha heard what Deganawidah said and became very moved by it. He began to travel from one tribe to another over the area which is now New York state, spreading the idea of a confederation. One by one, the leaders of five large tribes agreed to observe the Great Law of Peace.

The Mohawk first accepted the idea. They sent messengers to the Oneida, who agreed to make peace. Soon the Onondaga, the Cayuga, and the Seneca of the Northeast Woodlands joined with the others, and later the Tuscarora, who had fled their former homes in the Carolinas, also became members. This League of Six Nations agreed to stop fighting among themselves and cooperate with each other for a common defense. Each tribe kept control of its own tribal affairs, but the tribes united together in matters that had to do with other tribes and later with foreign countries.

Iroquois Confederacy: Seed for the U.S. Constitution *(cont.)*

The Mohawk, who lived on the eastern borders of the area, were called the Keepers of the Eastern Door. The Seneca, who lived in the western part of the territory, were called the Keepers of the Western Door. The Onondagas were the Firekeepers, and confederacy meetings were held in Onondaga territory in what is now Syracuse, New York, which was near the center of Iroquois country. Every year, usually in the late summer or fall, each tribe sent a delegation of chiefs to the great council. Fifty chiefs would meet together, although other people were free to attend the council meetings. All decisions were reached after lengthy deliberation by the chiefs, and decisions were made by consensus. That is, everyone had to agree. Each tribe had one vote equal to each of the others.

The chiefs who came together each year had usually been chosen by his or her people because of courage, hunting skills, and speaking ability. Some were chosen for other reasons such as being able to heal the sick or being considered to have a very high spiritual position. Each chief was expected to serve as an example, and one who acted unwisely or rashly soon lost prestige with the people. There were no police, no jails, and everyone was expected to act in ways which benefitted the whole tribe.

The members of the confederation spoke of each other as brothers. They symbolized their league as a bundle of arrows which become stronger by being united. The idea was that it was easy to break one arrow, but if a group of them were held together, they were much harder to break. The confederacy worked together for many years.

Activities

1. In small groups, brainstorm the similarities between what you have learned about the Iroquois Confederacy and what you know about the U.S. *Constitution*, then put those similarities into a list. Use this list to write one or two paragraphs beginning with the sentence, "The founding fathers of the United States drew on what they knew about the Iroquois Confederacy when they wrote the U.S. *Constitution*."

2. Research one of the following people and write a short biography of that person.

   - General George Rogers Clark
   - Metacomet ("King Philip")
   - General John Sullivan
   - Ely S. Parker
   - Tecumseh
   - Joseph Brant
   - Squanto
   - Pocahontas
   - John Eliot
   - Pontiac

People of the Longhouses

The English Puritans came to the shores of northeastern North America in the early seventeenth century to find a large population of people whose ancestors had arrived many centuries earlier. The Puritans thought the Indians, as they called them, were heathens, and they set about showing the natives how to live and worship. The natives, however, had a flourishing civilization of their own.

One of the native groups present at the arrival of the Puritans we now know as the Iroquois. The Iroquois lived in villages of twelve or more longhouses, each of which housed about fifty people. A village was surrounded by a high wall of upright logs which had been driven into the ground and tied near the top. This wall served as a kind of fortification to protect the villagers as they went about their daily lives.

The longhouses were built like arbors with very long poles driven into the ground and arched across to bend down to the other side of the building. The Iroquois tied these poles together with basswood bark. Other poles were entwined crosswise with the upright poles and covered from top to bottom with the barks of fir and cedar trees. Openings about two feet (60 cm) wide were left at the ridge for its entire length to allow smoke from the fires to escape, but the structures were weatherproof. The houses were sometimes as big as one hundred and thirty feet (39 m) long by twenty four feet (7.2 m) wide and twenty feet (6 m) high. These longhouses were something like early apartment houses in structure. A hallway ran down the middle, and living quarters were entered from the hallway. Some of the individual units had their own firepits, although occasionally two shared a fire.

The core of Iroquois life was the family which included grandparents, aunts, uncles, cousins, and in-laws as well as parents and children. All of the members of a family lived near each other. The inhabitants of one house were members of several families related to each other. Everyone in the family helped raise and train the children. A baby went to the fields in a cradleboard with its mother when she worked. The cradleboard was hung from a tree branch, and the baby could then watch its mother from its leafy perch. Children took part in all the daily aspects of life, and they were expected to act in ways which would help the other members of the family. They learned early to respect and care for the older people in the family.

Part of being a family member meant being a member of a clan. Clans were groups of people who traced their origins back to a common ancestor, and a clan was identified by a certain animal as its symbol, such as the Wolf Clan or the Turtle Clan. The people traced their lineage through their mothers, so a person would belong to the same clan as his or her mother. A person could not marry someone from his or her own clan. When a young man married, he moved into the longhouse of his new wife's family. This system made it possible for a person to be sure of lodging when travelling, because the clan in another village would always take that person in. It also ensured that blood lines would continually be strengthened.

The women named and raised the children, and they were in charge of running the household affairs. Children were usually raised with affection, and they were seldom punished or scolded, although they might be shamed into behaving correctly. The education they received was the responsibility of their parents, who taught them the skills they needed to become responsible adults. Stories were often used to explain things, and they were taught to live in harmony with nature and with other members of the group.

People of the Longhouses *(cont.)*

Young girls learned the skills they would need when they became women and mothers. Boys were taught to be food hunters and warriors so they could be good providers and protectors for their families when they were men. Many of the games the children played were ones which allowed them to practice adult skills. Girls played with wooden or cornhusk dolls, and boys competed in races and games of skill.

Because the people of the longhouses were farmers, their lives also revolved around the seasons. Men and women supported each other in daily quests for foods with women doing most of the growing of crops and men hunting and fishing. Much of what was caught was preserved for winter when food supplies were scarce. In spring, crops were planted. Corn, beans, and squash grown in summer were such an important part of the diet they were often called the Three Sisters. Other crops were grown as well, some to be eaten fresh and some to be dried and stored for winter use. Some of their methods of agriculture we now know to be excellent ways of taking care of the Earth.

In the fall, the women harvested the plants and dried them, and the men hunted, mostly for deer. Hunting trips would sometimes last several days, but when the men returned home, the women finished butchering the meat, cutting it into long strips to smoke it and preserve it for winter. The people also gathered wild foods such as berries, fruits, and wild rice.

Clothing was made from animal skins which the women tanned with bone or wooden awls and thongs until they were soft and pliable. Men generally wore shirts, leggings, and a loincloth, all of which were made of deerskin. In the summer, when the weather was hot and muggy, they sometimes wore only the loincloth and moccasins. The women always wore dresses belted at the waist with skirts reaching down to the knees to meet their high moccasins.

Both men and women liked their clothing decorated. Before the Europeans came, they embroidered their clothing with dyed porcupine quills, and after the Europeans came, they decorated clothing with the glass beads brought by traders. Both men and women wore necklaces, earrings, and bracelets made of copper, shells, and other materials. The people of different tribes wore their hair in different ways. Some men plucked out all their hair except for a scalplock. Others wore their hair in braids or brushed straight back from the forehead. Both men and women tattooed their faces and bodies.

People of the Longhouses *(cont.)*

Activity

Follow the directions below to make a model longhouse.

Materials:

- shoebox lid
- thirteen ⅛" (.3 cm) diameter wooden dowels or sticks approximately the same length as the lid
- water
- a pan to soak the dowels in
- brown construction paper cut into strips

Directions:

1. Soak six dowels in water until they are soft enough to bend.

2. Arch the dowels over the lid and secure them inside as shown, spacing them evenly approximately two inches (5 cm) apart the entire length of the lid. This forms the frame.

3. Weave the other dowels crosswise in and out of the frame supports.

4. Beginning at lower edges of the frame, weave strips of construction paper over and under the dowels until the entire structure is covered. Leave smoke holes at the top. Leave openings for doors at each end.

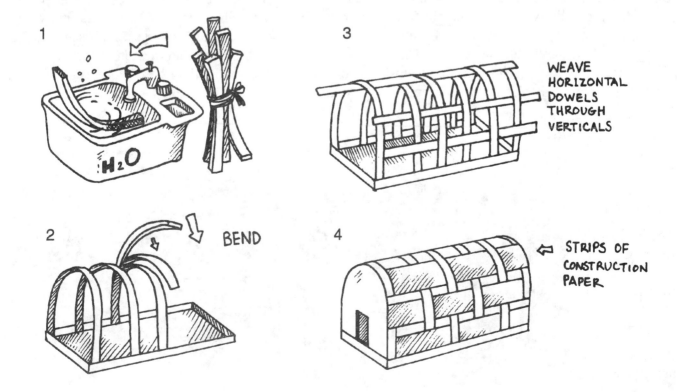

1

2 BEND

3 WEAVE HORIZONTAL DOWELS THROUGH VERTICALS

4 STRIPS OF CONSTRUCTION PAPER

H₂O

Folktales of the Northeast Woodlands

Read these stories told by Native Americans of the Northeast Woodlands. Complete one or more of the activities which follow.

Corn Mother
(Penobscot)

Long ago before there were any people, the All-maker lived on earth. Then one day a young man was born from the foam of the waves and was given life by the wind and warmed by the sun. This young man appeared to the All-maker calling him "Uncle," and he lived with the All-maker and became his main helper. Together these two created all manner of living things.

One day as the noon sun was shining, a drop of dew fell on a leaf and was warmed by the sun, creating from the green, living plant the warmth and the moisture a lovely young girl.

"I am love," the young girl said. "I nourish and I give strength. I am the mother of all men."

The youth, now named Great Nephew, thanked the All-maker above for having sent the maiden to him, and he married her. In time, the maiden had a son, and she now was called First Mother. The All-maker taught humans all they needed to know in order to live a good life. He then went away, far to the North, but he will return at anytime that he is needed.

The people increased and became many, living by hunting for their food. After a time, however, they discovered that game was becoming scarce, and as this happened, the people began to starve. First Mother took pity on them. The little children came to her and said, "We are starving," and she wept, because she had nothing to give them.

She said to them, "Be patient. I will think of something to make for you to eat," and she continued to cry to herself.

Her husband did not want to see her cry, and he said to her, "What can I do to stop your weeping?"

"There is only one thing," she replied. "You must kill me. If you do not, I will go on weeping forever."

The husband went far to the North to see the All-maker and asked what he should do. "You must do as she asks," he was told, so the young man went home, and now he was weeping.

When he arrived at his home, First Mother told him, "Tomorrow at noon is the time for you to do it. After you have killed me, have two of our sons take me by the hair and drag my body over the empty patch of earth which you see there. Have them drag me back and forth until my flesh has been torn from my body and become part of the earth. Then you must gather my bones and bury them in the middle of the clearing. When you have finished, leave this place, and do not return for seven moons. When you return, you will find my flesh given out of love which will nourish you and feed you forever."

The husband and his sons did as First Mother asked them to do, weeping all the while, and when they returned to the place after seven moons, the earth was covered with tall, green tasseled plants. The fruit of the plants was corn, and they knew that this corn was the flesh of First Mother. They followed her instructions and did not eat all of it, saving some to put back into the earth. In this way, her body renewed itself every seven moons.

First Mother's husband told all the people, "Always remember to take good care of this plant, for it came to us from the goodness of her flesh. Remember her and think of her when you eat, because she has given you life.

Folktales of the Northeast Woodlands *(cont.)*

Glooscap Fights the Water Monster

(Passamaquoddy, Micmac, Maliset)

Glooscap is a great hero. He is a spirit, medicine man, magician, and creator of all animals and people. He lives at the southern edge of the world when the people do not need him.

When he first made the animals, he made them too big. The first squirrel was as large as a whale and once attacked a huge tree. "You are too destructive," Glooscap told him and remade him small. The first beaver also was as large as a whale, building a dam that flooded the country. "You are too destructive," Glooscap told him, and remade him to his present size. The first moose was so tall it hit the sky and trounced on everything in its path. "You ruin everything," and he tapped the moose to make it small. However, the moose refused to follow orders, so Glooscap killed him and recreated him in his present size.

In one of the villages he made, the people were very happy. They hunted and fished, and the children played. Each person loved and cherished the other. This village had just one spring, and it flowed with cool, clear water. But one day the spring began to run dry, sending out only a small, thick, slimy ooze to satisfy the people's thirst. All year it stayed this way, and the people began to despair. The council decided to send a man to the source of the spring to learn why it had dried up.

The man walked a long time and came to another village. The people here were strange with webbed feet. The man asked for a drink of water, but the people said, "We cannot give you water unless our chief tells us it is all right. He wants to keep the water for himself."

The man walked to the head of the spring until he came to the home of the big chief. The big chief was frightening to look upon, and he filled up the valley from one end to the other with his body. He had dug a huge hole for himself, and in it he stayed, fouling the water, making it poisonous so that green, stinking mists came up off its surface. His huge yellow eyes stuck out from his face, and his body was swollen and covered with giant warts. He looked at the man and said, "Little man, what do you want?"

"My people need water. Our spring has run dry because you are keeping all the water. We would like to have some of it."

The monster blinked and croaked:

> *Do as you please,*
> *Do as you please,*
> *I don't care,*
> *I don't care,*
> *If you want water,*
> *If you want water,*
> *Go elsewhere!*

The man said, "But, please, we need water.
We are dying of thirst." The monster replied:

> *I don't care,*
> *I don't care,*
> *Don't bother me,*
> *Don't bother me,*
> *Go away,*
> *Go away,*
> *Or I'll swallow you up!*

Folktales of the Northeast Woodlands *(cont.)*

Glooscap Fights the Water Monster *(cont.)*

And the monster opened his mouth wide so the man could see inside the many creatures the monster had swallowed, and the man fled from him in terror. He returned to his village and reported to the people, "Nothing can be done. The monster will kill us all if we complain."

So the people went to Glooscap saying, "He knows everything!"

Glooscap came immediately and prepared himself for war. He painted his body red and made himself twelve feet tall. He wore huge clamshells for earrings and put a hundred black eagle feathers and a hundred white eagle feathers in his hair. He painted yellow rings around his eyes and twisted his face into a snarl. When he stamped his foot, the earth trembled, and he strode forth with the thunder and lightning all about him and a dozen eagles circling his head.

When he reached the village of the webbed-footed people, he said, "I want clean water for the people downstream," and then he heard:

> *Ho! Ho!*
> *Ho! Ho!*
> *All the waters are mine!*
> *All the waters are mine!*
> *Go away!*
> *Go away!*
> *Or I'll kill you!*

"You slimy piece of trash!" Glooscap cried. "We'll see who will be killed!" and he started fighting the monster.

They fought so hard that the mountains shook and the swamps burst into flames. The earth split wide open, and mighty trees broke into slivers. The monster opened its horrible, big mouth to swallow Glooscap, and Glooscap made himself as big as a tree. He seized his flint knife and slit the monster's belly. From the wound the water flowed in a giant stream like a rushing river and flowed past the village and on to the sea.

"There is your water!" Glooscap said to the people, and he picked up the monster and squeezed him in his mighty hand until the monster was nothing but a small bullfrog which he threw into the swamp. Since that time, the bullfrog's skin has been wrinkled because Glooscap squeezed him so hard.

Folktales of the Northeast Woodlands *(cont.)*

Little Brother Snares the Sun
(Winnebago)

Long ago people had little power. The animals were the chiefs, and they hunted, killed, and ate the humans instead of the way it is now. After time had passed all the people had been killed except one girl and her little brother. The two spent all their days and nights in hiding with the girl going out only to hunt for plant foods for them to eat.

The boy, whose name was Little Brother, was quite small for his age, so Big Sister took care of him. One day as she left to find food in the forest, she gave Little Brother her bow and arrow to keep him busy while she was gone.

"Do not let yourself be seen," she told him. "Watch for the snowbird. When he looks for grubs in that dead tree over there, shoot him with one of these arrows."

Big Sister left, and Little Brother waited for the snowbird. When it came, Little Brother shot an arrow at him, but he missed and the bird flew away.

"Don't feel badly," she told the boy. "Tomorrow he will come again, and you will hit him."

Next day, it was just as Big Sister had said. The snowbird came, and Little Brother shot it dead with one of his arrows. When Big Sister came home, he proudly showed her the bird.

"Sister," he said, "I would like you to skin the bird for me and stretch its hide. Tomorrow I will shoot another bird, and each day another until I have killed enough for you to make me a feather robe."

"I do not know what to do with the meat," Big Sister said. Until this time they had eaten only berries and roots.

"Make it into soup," Little Brother told her, so that is what she did.

For ten days in a row, Little Brother shot snowbirds until he had enough bird skins to make a feather robe for him to wear.

By this time, Little Brother had given a lot of thought to something which puzzled him, so one day he said to his sister, "Why do we never see other people? Are we the only people in the world?"

"Other people may live somewhere," she answered, "but we cannot go out to look for them, for if we did we would surely be caught and eaten by some animal."

Little Brother could not contain his curiosity, so after his sister left the following morning to look for plant foods, he went out determined to see whether there were any other people in the world. After awhile he became tired, so he lay down to rest and soon fell fast asleep. When he awakened, Sun had grown very hot on his body, and his feather robe had burned and shrunk around him.

Little Brother was angry. He shook his fists at Sun and shouted, "Just you wait! I will repay you for this!" and he left to return home. He cried and told Big Sister about how Sun had ruined his feather robe. He fasted for ten days, lying all the time on his right side. Then he fasted for another ten days, lying on his left side. Then he arose and asked Big Sister to make him a net with which to snare Sun.

First she made him a noose from a piece of dried sinew, and then she went out and gathered some secret things with which she was able to fashion a very strong cord. Little Brother ran the cord through his lips, wetting it many times until it was the length and strength he wanted. When Sun had gone down through its hole and it was dark, he went there and set his snare, then waited for Sun to rise and show its face.

Folktales of the Northeast Woodlands *(cont.)*

Little Brother Snares the Sun *(cont.)*

As soon as Sun came up through the hole, Little Brother caught him in his snare, and because of this, there was no Sun shining that day or the next. The animals were afraid. They called a council and discussed the matter for a long time. Finally they sent the largest animal, Dormouse, to bite through the cord. This animal was then the largest of all the animals, but even she was afraid of Sun.

Despite her fear, Dormouse agreed to do her best, and she went to the place where Sun rises each day. As Sun had struggled to get out of the snare, he had become even hotter. Dormouse came near to Sun to gnaw the cord, and when she did, the hair on her back was singed, but she did not allow this to stop her from doing what she had come to do.

She continued to gnaw at the cord until, at last, it broke, and Sun was free to rise into the sky again. But the heat of Sun had shrunk Dormouse until she was the size you see her today, and her eyes were damaged so that she can no longer see well. This is the reason we now call Dormouse "Blind Woman."

Because Little Brother was able to snare Sun, however, the animals realized that he was the most intelligent of all the living beings and that he had the greatest power, and since that time people have been chiefs over all the animals. Now people hunt animals instead of the other way around.

Activities

1. Folktales are often intended to teach a certain lesson. For example, in Aesop's fable "The Tortoise and the Hare," the moral is that good effort and persistence are more important than physical strength or speed. In one sentence per story, tell the lesson you think each tale is trying to teach.

   a. "Corn Mother"
   b. "Glooscap Fights the Water Monster"
   c. "Little Brother Snares the Sun"

2. Glooscap is a type of character called a *culture hero*. A culture hero is shown as being bigger than life, able to accomplish great feats impossible for ordinary people. What can the following culture heroes do that a person usually is not able to do? (You may need to research to find your answer.)

   a. Paul Bunyan
   b. Pecos Bill
   c. Sal Fink
   d. Atlas

3. In groups of three to five, write a dramatization of one of these folktales and present it to the class.

4. Compile an illustrated book of folktales.

5. Find a folktale from another part of the world and tell it to the class. Then compare this folktale to one of the Native American ones you have just read. How are they alike? How are they different? Do they both teach a lesson? Could you do something to the folktale you have brought to class to make it sound like a Native American folktale? What would that be? Do you think folktales from around the world come from common needs all people have? What might those needs be?

6. Write down a story you have heard at home. Tell it to the class.

Migration Math

Contrary to popular thought, Native Americans of the past did not always remain in the same locations in which the Europeans found them upon first arriving. In fact, there was a great deal of moving around and migrating from one place to another, and groups of people sometimes traveled many hundreds of miles to settle in a new location. Most of the moves probably were due to changes in climate or in the availability of game. The horse did not come to North America until it was brought by the Spaniards. Most natives did not have horses until the eighteenth century, so most migration was on foot, sometimes with dogs and travois as carriers of clothing and the few living essentials.

Activity

When migrating from one place to another, many necessities had to be taken into consideration, such as food, drinking water, and shelter. Solve the following problems to gain an understanding of some things needed by the migrators. Remember, there were no convenience stores or shops and no restaurants along the way.

1. If each person needs about two quarts (two liters) of fresh drinking water each day, how much water would be needed daily for the following:

    6 people
    12 people
    45 people
    317 people

2. If a freshly-killed deer contains enough meat to feed 18 people for three days, how many deer would be needed to feed 216 people for fifteen days?

3. If one-half cup (125 mL) of berries will provide enough vitamin C in one day to prevent one child from getting scurvy, how many cups (L) would be needed for 79 children?

4. If one adult can walk 12 miles (19 km) in one day without becoming too exhausted, how long would it take for that person to walk 348 miles (551 km)?

5. If bad weather, sick children, and the elderly keep the people from covering more than 6 miles (9.5 km) in one day, how long would it take them to cover the same 348 miles (551 km)?

6. If one skin from an adult deer contains enough leather to make 11 pairs of adult-sized moccasins, how many deerskins would be needed to make 209 pairs?

7. If an adult male goes through 27 pairs of moccasins in one year, how many pairs of moccasins would need to be made for 117 adult males each year?

8. If it takes 7 deerskins to make a simple shelter for 6 people to take on a long journey, how many deerskins would be needed to shelter 342 people?

9. If a large dog can carry 29 pounds (13 kg) of living necessities on his travois, how many dogs would be needed to carry 348 pounds (156 kg) of supplies?

Garden Math

Like many of the other Native American groups, the Indians of the Northeast Woodlands were farmers who raised mainly corn, beans, and squash. Good farming requires a lot of planning, and the farmer needs to know how much room each plant takes so he can plan his garden efficiently. The following are typical spaces needed for each vegetable.

corn: 6 plants to a "hill" of one square yard or meter

squash: 3 plants to a "hill" of one square yard or meter

beans: 3 inches or 8 centimeters apart in rows 3 feet or 1 meter apart

Determine the answers to the following questions for a village of thirty people. You may use graph paper to help you visualize the problem and its answer. You may round your answers.

1. a. Corn was eaten on the cob, roasted, ground for corn meal, or dried for later use in stews and soups. If each person ate an average of two ears of corn per day for the year and three ears grew on each plant, how many plants would need to be planted each year?

   b. How many hills of corn would you need to plant?

2. a. Squash lasts longer than most vegetables and can be eaten for six months of the year. If each person ate one squash every day for six months and each plant produced 12 squash, how many squash plants would need to be planted for the six months? (Figure on 183 days per six months.)

   b. How much land would be needed in square yards or square meters?

3. a. Beans would have been eaten fresh and also dried for later use so they could be eaten all year. If each person ate an average of one pound (1 kg) of beans each day for the entire year, and each plant produced one pound (1 kg), how many bean plants would be needed for the entire year?

Challenge: If you saved approximately one fourth of the corn kernels and beans to use for seeds, how many additional corn, squash, and bean plants would you need to plant?

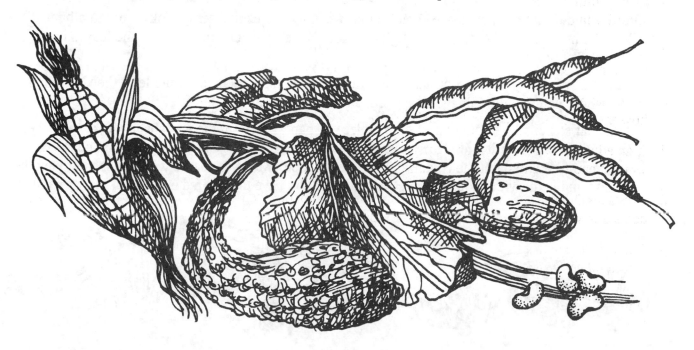

What Makes an Indian Summer?

Many people think the prettiest time of year is the autumn during what is often called "Indian Summer." This is the time of year when the sun shines beautifully on trees dressed in a riot of reds, golds, and oranges. Did you ever stop to wonder why the trees lose their green colors and change to the brilliant colors marvelled at in the fall?

Contrary to what is often thought, frost is not what brings about color change. Many of the plants will change color before the first frost, and some trees even turn color while summer is still in the air. A severe drought, for example, will cause many trees to change color early while trees which are well fed and nourished may change late.

The factor determining when trees turn color is a weather pattern of warm, sunny days followed by sudden drops in temperature to cool nights. During the summer, leaves manufacture starches, sugars, and proteins which are distributed by chlorophyll, the green coloring matter in leaves. The change in the weather slows this process, and the chlorophyll breaks down.

When the chlorophyll breaks down, it becomes colorless and allows the colors which are already present in the leaves to become visible. Yellow leaf colors are caused by chemicals in the leaves called carotinoids. (Notice the same word root as in the word "carrot?") Anthocyanins are the chemicals in the leaves which cause reds and purples.

The warmer days combined with cooler evenings will cause the most brilliant colors to appear. Because of this, if a person begins traveling in the north of North America or Europe and travels south over a period of weeks, that person can "follow" the color trail. The reason for this is that the weather tends to get cooler earlier in the year in the North than it does in the South. Of course, if a person lives below the equator, in Australia for example, the opposite will be true. Can you think of the reason this is so?

Activities

Here are some things you can do with autumn leaves, besides rake them.

1. Press some of the prettiest leaves you find between the pages in a scrapbook or photo album. Hold them down with a few drops of glue or some clear contact paper. When the leaves dry, the color will stay.

2. Make leaf prints by painting poster or acrylic paints on the underside of the leaf, then "printing" it onto where you want the image to appear. Blot with a paper towel.

3. Make leaf stencils by tracing a leaf onto a piece of paper. Cut out the leaf shape. Take the paper with the leaf cut from it and place it over white or colored paper. Choose a paint that contrasts with the paper color and paint the color within the leaf shape. Move the paper with the shape to another position and paint with another color. Repeat until you have the desired number of leaves painted.

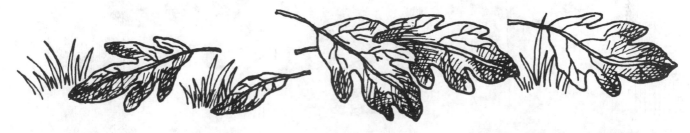

Genetic Tracing of the First Americans

Note: Before reading this lesson, find the definitions of the words shown in bold letters and record them.

For almost as long as European Americans have been in North America, debates have gone on about the possible origins of the Native Americans. Now scientists are beginning to learn the answers to questions such as, "From where did the Native Americans first come?" and "How did they get to North America?"

Early European settlers thought of some explanations, most of which said more about their own racial and religious prejudices than about those early peoples. One explanation was that the natives were uncivilized savages who had not progressed as much as the Europeans had and, therefore, were inferior to them. Those who believed this **theory** (and that included most of the newcomers) thought these "**primitive**" peoples needed to be conquered and taught the "right" ways to live and to believe. One popular theory with some fundamentalist religious immigrants was that the natives were "the lost tribes of Israel."

Today, a group of scientists using the latest in instruments which scientifically measure the ages of plant materials, cells, and bones by measuring the energy-producing structures of the **DNA** in their **genes**, can tell us approximately how old **relics** are. The scientists who do this work are sometimes called **molecular archaeologists**. This is what they have learned.

The first peoples, called by scientists "Paleo-Indians," came to this continent in four major waves of immigration from Asia. These waves of immigration are labeled A,B,C and D. (See page 34.) Three of them, A,C, and D, came across the Bering Land Bridge which existed between modern Siberia and Alaska before the ocean rose to submerge it. These people spread throughout the American continents and **diversified** into many different tribes.

Scientists are not in total agreement as to the exact date of these migrations. **Carbon dating** of the remains of campsites in Pennsylvania show evidence of human **habitation** as long as 33,000 years ago, but examination of the DNA of the earliest skeletal remains found so far can be dated to only 14,000 years ago. The people who came in the A, C, and D migrations are genetically related to the natives of Siberia, and all of these people were derived from an even older group in Southern Asia.

The B migration is thought to have come over on a different route, probably by sea from Southeast Asia, because these people carry a different genetic makeup than do the other groups. They share this **genetic** makeup with populations in Southern Asia and Polynesia, and they are thought to have migrated between 6,000 to 12,000 years ago. A third major migration occurred 5,000 to 10,000 years ago. This was the Na-Dene group which settled in the Northwest United States and Western Canada. This group only carries genetic history A.

When the first Americans came to North America, they were fully developed human beings. They looked very much like the Native Americans of today. They lived in closely knit family groups and shared beliefs about magic and the supernatural. They spoke human languages, and over time the number of languages grew to over two thousand.

The parts of the genes that scientists look at to study how long a people has been present are the **mitochondria**. The genetic coding in the mitochondria is represented by the letters ATCG. There are 16,569 "base pairs" of these letters in mitochondria. "Reading" the ways in which the pairs are arranged is similar to the way a checkout counter in the supermarket "reads" the bar code on a package of food. Scientists read the changes which have taken place over thousands of years to determine how old a population is. Scientists believe that changes in the mitochondria DNA of human cells correspond with **ethnic heritage** and movement to different geographic areas.

Genetic Tracing of the First Americans *(cont.)*

The map below shows how and when the ancestors of the Native Americans first came to North America.

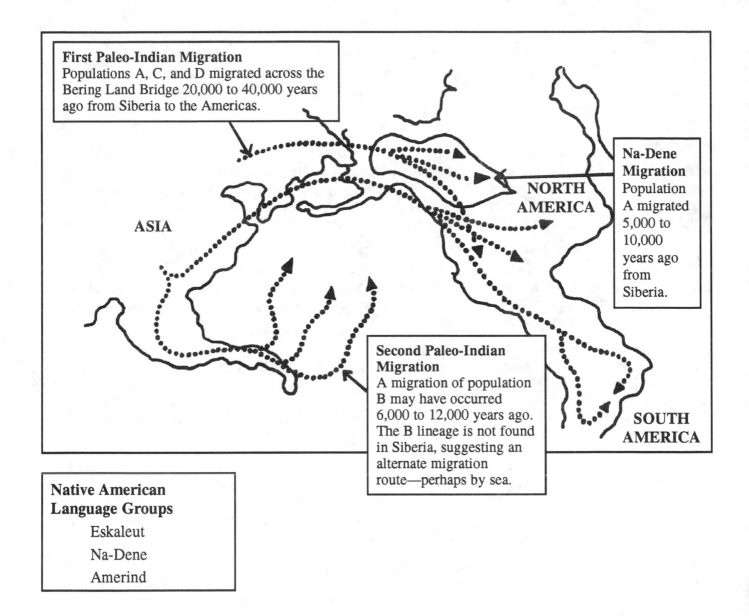

First Paleo-Indian Migration
Populations A, C, and D migrated across the Bering Land Bridge 20,000 to 40,000 years ago from Siberia to the Americas.

Na-Dene Migration
Population A migrated 5,000 to 10,000 years ago from Siberia.

ASIA

NORTH AMERICA

SOUTH AMERICA

Second Paleo-Indian Migration
A migration of population B may have occurred 6,000 to 12,000 years ago. The B lineage is not found in Siberia, suggesting an alternate migration route—perhaps by sea.

Native American Language Groups
Eskaleut
Na-Dene
Amerind

Genetic Tracing of the First Americans *(cont.)*

This whole field of study brings up many questions about the origin of life. In the book and movie *Jurassic Park*, scientists brought dinosaurs back to life from extinction by using the ancient DNA in a process called "cloning," but actual cloning of a whole creature is still science fiction. This is the way scientists work with DNA in real life.

1. They identify the specimen from which the DNA is taken.

2. They grind up the specimen and add water to make a "soup" of DNA fragments, taking special care not to contaminate the mixture with DNA from other specimens.

3. Chemicals are added to separate the DNA from everything else, and the mixture is strained through an ultrafine filter and combined with chemicals which allow the scientists to identify the DNA.

4. The DNA fragments are put through a special machine which makes many identical copies at the molecular level.

5. The copies are put through a "genetic sequencing" process which breaks the DNA into its basic elements. This gives a result similar to a supermarket bar code.

6. Scientists then compare the sequence with others that they know, hunting for similarities. The differences between an old gene and an existing one can show how something evolved over history. This also shows how one form of life is related to others.

Activity

To get an understanding of how very small particles can be extracted from a substance, do the following experiment to remove iron from instant hot cereal.

1. Check the ingredients of a small pack of hot cereal (any kind) to make sure it has been enriched with iron.

2. Pour the contents of the pack and a small magnet into a self sealing plastic bag.

3. Seal the bag and shake it for several minutes.

4. Remove the magnet and look at it closely. Do you see the small pieces of iron which stuck to the magnet? Using special chemicals, DNA can also be extracted from cells.

A Corny Story

Question: How does a boy corn get together with a girl corn?

Answer: It isn't easy! The answer lies in the corn silk, that fine, stringy stuff that is hard to wash off corn on the cob and gets stuck in your teeth. Like other plants, corn needs both male and female cells in order to reproduce. This is how it works.

Corn has both male and female cells. Corn silk belongs to the female part of the corn, and its job is to snag the pollen produced by the male flowers and guide it to the egg. The eggs are hidden far down inside the ear of corn. When fertilized they will become the developed kernels.

The male parts of the corn plant, called the *stamens*, are in the *tassels* at the top of the plant. These cells are loaded with *pollen sacs* which eventually open and release their pollen. The female parts are called the *pistils*, and they are the small, undeveloped *kernels* on the ear which need to be fertilized if they are to produce mature kernels. The ear of the corn is the female *flower* of the plant.

The corn plant reproduces when the stamens in the tassels send off their pollen and the corn silk grows out of the ear to snag the pollen. There is a corn silk which leads from outside the top of the ear to each single kernel, and this corn silk catches the pollen and carries it down inside the ear to its kernel.

When the grain of pollen lands on the silk, it sends out a tiny pollen tube which grows down inside the silk to the waiting kernel, fertilizing its egg. After fertilization, the kernel fills with a starchy substance called the *endosperm* which nourishes the plant if it ever germinates. When you eat corn, the endosperm is what fills the kernel with a sweet, milky liquid that nourishes you instead of a new corn plant. The tiny, undeveloped kernels at the tip of the ear of corn are ones which have not been fertilized. They became ready for fertilization after the pollen from the tassels had already been used.

Activities

1. Draw and label the parts of a corn plant with the italicized terms in the paragraphs above.

2. A colorful craft can be made during the fall when "Indian corn" is available. Indian corn is the colorful variety available in shades of red, gold, and blue. Use its kernels to make a necklace. Break off the kernels from the cobs and soak them in water for a day or so. Remove them from the water. Use thread and a tapestry needle to string the softened kernels until the necklace is long enough to slip over your head when tied.

Racket Games

The Native Americans took games very seriously, and they had many games of skill and of chance. Many myths and folktales concern the playing of games, and sometimes when an important decision proved difficult to make, it was decided by the results of a game. The main reason for playing games, however, was to develop muscular power and speed, for these qualities were crucial to a people who often had to depend on physical strength or speed for survival in a harsh environment.

One of the most universal games was a form of racket ball, usually played only by the men, which is sometimes called lacrosse. Many different native people played a version of this very exciting and strenuous game which the Passamaquoddy called *E-bes-qua-mo'gan*, or "game of ball."

In this game, a ball made of animal hide about 3½ inches (8.75 cm) in diameter was used. It was moved about by rackets approximately three feet (.9 m) long and made of a flexible wood bent into three-fourths of a circle at one end and interwoven with thin strips of hide similar to the mesh on a tennis racket. (See illustration.) Each player carried a racket, and the game was played on a level playing field which varied in length but could be as long as one-half mile (.8 km) with goals marked by two rings or holes set at each end.

The players formed in a circle, the size of which depended on how many people were playing. Each player held a racket stick, and two teams formed. One man, who was not playing, spat on one side of a wood chip, then threw it into the air as the players called out "wet" or "dry," and whichever way the chip landed determined which side began the play.

The ball was never touched by hand but once thrown in motion was kept going by the use of the rackets. The object of the game was to get the ball into the goal of the opposite side, and it was a rough, no-holds-barred exercise for all involved. There were few rules. Most of the players wore little clothing, and many ended up being hurt during the game. The players considered injuries to be part of the game, so they had no anger or resentment toward other players when someone got hurt.

Activity

In small groups, brainstorm and list all the games you know of which involve getting a ball from one end of the playing field to another. Make another list of all the games you know of which involve using a stick or a racket. Choose one of the games to teach to the rest of the class. You may need to make a model playing field to help explain your game.

ball and racket

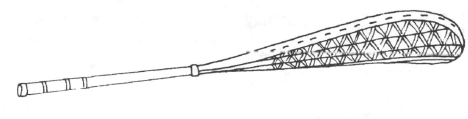

Vegetable Dyes Are Hard to "Beet"

Before they were able to purchase glass beads from the white man, many Native Americans dyed porcupine quills. They used these quills to embroider colorful designs on their clothing, moccasins, and storage cases. The dyes they used were all made from natural sources such as plants, vegetables, and certain substances which occurred in the soil.

You, too, can make many different colors of dye from vegetable sources. Follow the directions below.

Materials:

- newspaper
- paper towels
- plain white paper
- white 100% cotton fabric
- white cotton-blend fabric
- ³/₄ cup (190 mL) warm water
- raw carrot, beet, and red cabbage
- measuring cup

- metric ruler
- food grater
- three small plates
- scissors
- 3 zipper-seal sandwich bags
- 6 plastic cups
- laundry detergent

Directions:

1. Wear protective clothing to prevent staining your good clothing and cover your work area with newspaper. Ask an adult to grate ⅛ cup (30 mL) each of the carrot, beet, and red cabbage onto separate plates.

2. Place each vegetable into a separate plastic bag with ¼ cup (65 mL) warm water. Seal tightly. Gently knead or roll the sealed bags with your hands for 2–3 minutes until the water is colored.

3. Open the corner of a bag and pour the colored water into a cup. Repeat this process with the other bags.

4. Cut paper and the two kinds of fabric into three strips about 1¼ inch (3 cm) by 6 inches (15 cm). Mark the cotton strips with a notch to distinguish them from the cotton blend strips.

5. Place one strip of each material into each of the cups of dye and soak overnight. On the next day, remove each strip from the dye and place them on clean paper towels to dry. Which dye worked best?

6. Now fill three clean cups with warm water and separately swirl the strips in the water for one or two minutes. Which of the dyes stays longest? Did any of them fade or run?

7. Add laundry detergent to the water and slowly agitate the strips in it. Do you still have color on the materials? Use the chart below to record your data.

DYE	Color stays.	Color fades in water.	Color fades in detergent.
Carrot			
Beet			
Cabbage			

Carve an Apple Doll

The Crow Indians had a saying they used to describe a person who was very old. It was, "The man (or woman) is so old, his skin crackles and tears when he moves about."

Have you ever looked at the skin of a very old person? After people have lived for a very long time, some changes usually take place in the way they look. The force of gravity tends to push down on the skin and muscles of the body so that over time old people may acquire wrinkles as marks of their experience in living a long life. To some, these wrinkles look like an apple looks after it becomes old.

You can make an apple doll depicting a very old person with skin that seems to "crackle and tear." To do this, follow the directions below.

Materials:

- large apple
- bowl of salt water or lemon juice deep enough to cover the apple
- pencil or straight, pointed stick
- craft knife
- pieces of colored paper or fabric for clothing
- long-necked bottle

Directions:

1. Peel and core the apple.

2. Carve a face in one side of the apple to suggest a nose, eyes, and mouth.

3. Soak the apple in salt water or lemon juice for approximately one-half hour.

4. Dry the apple gently with paper towels.

5. Spear the apple from below with the pencil or pointed stick.

6. Place the apple on top of the long-necked bottle with the pencil down inside.

7. Let the apple dry for three or four weeks. As it dries, it will gradually take on the appearance of an old person.

8. Make some simple clothing which will cover the bottle and glue it on. Now your doll is complete!

Quiz

1. List three important things you have learned about the natives of the Northeast Woodlands.

   _____

   _____

2. Who were Deganawidah and Hayenwatha, and how did they affect the government of the United States? _____

   _____

3. Describe the family life of the Iroquois._____

   _____

4. Why would the Natives of the Northeast Woodlands have stories about corn, calling it "Corn Mother?" _____

   _____

5. Who was Glooscap and what did he do? _____

   _____

6. What measures would you need to take to help your family survive a move on foot from one place to another? _____

   _____

7. What would you need to know to plan a garden which would feed your family for an entire year?

   _____

   _____

8. Why do leaves turn their colors in the fall? _____

   _____

9. Name some differences between Indian sports of long ago and the sports you play or watch today.

   _____

   _____

10. On the back of this page, explain what you know about how the Native Americans first came to North America.

Natives of the Southeast Woodlands and How They Lived

The natives of the Southeast Woodlands were blessed by nature with a beautiful and bountiful country. When the white man arrived in the early 1600s, the forests, which were teeming with deer and other wildlife, stretched from the Atlantic Ocean to the Mississippi River. All the people, including the ones later called the *Five Civilized Tribes*, lived in villages of several hundred people with complex systems of laws and traditions. The countryside was rich with many kinds of nuts, berries, birds, and animals, and the rivers were filled with fish.

A boy living in this area looked forward to becoming a hunter and a warrior in manhood, and his training with the bow and arrow began early. He learned to hunt in a group or alone, and he especially enjoyed getting his quarry at close range for this showed greater skill and bravery than did shooting an animal from a distance. He had to get close to this prey without alerting it to his presence. He used blowguns and darts as well as bows and arrows to kill smaller animals like alligators and turtles. He fished in the many rivers and streams of his country. War was the most important way for him to gain honor and prestige among his people; therefore, to gain honor by killing and running risks was his greatest aim in life.

A girl also learned to do the things that she would do as an adult. She learned to cook and prepare the deerskins and other animal skins which she would then make into clothing for herself and her family. She learned to prepare the ground and plant gardens of beans, squash, corn, and other domestic plants. She cared for the maturing plants until her crops were ready to be harvested. Then she preserved meat and plants for the winter. The tools she used in the garden were digging sticks and hoes of wood, bone, and stone. Her sewing tools were bone awls and needles.

Housing for the Southeast native centered around the village meeting house. The home was roofed with a thatch of reeds, grass, cane, or bark, and many tribes used open-sided summer houses similar to the ones seen in the Caribbean or the South Pacific with roofs and floors but no walls. The more permanent houses were walled with reeds, cane, or grass, and then plastered with mud like the wattle and daub houses in medieval England. Whitewash was applied to the dried wall to help protect it from the rain.

Like villages in the Northeast, the villages here were surrounded by log fortifications called *palisades*. An open square was in the middle of the village. The chief's house was at one end of the square, and the town meeting house was at the other. This house was used as a clubhouse, dance hall, or as the meeting place for the village council. The chief was the most influential person in the village, and he headed the village council and was in charge of handling village matters.

Another chief was the war chief. His job was to lead the warriors when it was decided to fight. He also handled the supervision of dances and games and policed the town. The war chief sometimes acquired great power. His high place in town affairs was signified by special feathered robes. All chiefs were allowed to have more than one wife, if they wished to do so.

The center of family life was the clan, which was named after an animal such as the bear clan, the deer clan, or the eagle clan. The clan into which a child was born was that of his mother. This meant his mother's brothers would be the ones who served in the capacity of "father" and head of the family. A child's own father would serve as the head of his sisters' families in the same way.

Natives of the Southeast Woodlands and How They Lived *(cont.)*

This clan system is what is known as a *matrilineal* system. The "family line" passed through the mother. A Cherokee mother, for example, would always have children who were considered Cherokee whatever their father's lineage. Even when a Cherokee mother married and had children with a man who was not Cherokee, the child was Cherokee like his mother and her clan. The clan system was also *matrilocal*. When a couple married, the husband went to live with the family of his wife, and she or her family owned all the property where they lived. A husband was almost like a visitor in his own home, but he was family head in the homes of his sisters.

According to Southeastern native thought, the world was created by the Great Mystery above, but there were many spirits to which he gave reverence. The spirits of the animal tribes, plant tribes, and water and air tribes were all important. They were not worshipped in the Christian sense but were prayed to and given gifts of tobacco, beads, and other things. Then there were the Little People. These were the small trickster beings who sometimes helped, sometimes tricked, and always lurked in fun just around the corner. One could not see them, but they could hear one and see what he was doing. They especially liked to come around after dark and listen to people talk or move things (like tools) so a person had to look for them in the morning. However, one was never to look upon one of the Little People. If one did, that person would surely die.

Ceremonies and dances were very popular, especially the Green Corn Ceremony. This celebration took place as soon as the corn began to ripen. At this time, everything was made new. The old was thrown out. Houses were cleaned, old clothing and pottery were thrown away, leftover food discarded, and fires were put out. Prisoners were freed. Men drank a mixture called the *black drink*, an emetic made from the leaves of a local plant, so their bodies would be cleaned from the inside out. Everyone danced, sang, and drank for days until a purifying bath brought it all to an end.

Clothing worn was similar to that of other native groups. Men wore moccasins and breechcloths of skin, fiber, or cloth. Women wore skirts of buckskin or fiber, and both men and women wore buckskin leggings in the cold weather. For special occasions, the men wore feathered crowns on their heads. Some men shaved or plucked the hairs from their heads, leaving a scalplock as a challenge to the enemy. Women always wore their hair long. Almost everyone wore tattoos—the more, the better. The men wore paint when they went on the warpath. Everyone wore jewelry and ornaments of feathers, bones, shells, and beads.

Women sometimes wove a highly prized cloth from nettle, silk grass, and mulberry bark. They made cradleboards from the swamp cane, and they also made split cane and wicker baskets. The men hollowed out cypress logs and made them into canoes which they used to traverse the streams and rivers.

War was taken very seriously by all the natives of the Southeast. They fought for personal glory, slaves, and revenge. If a village thought its people had been wronged by another group, it was the signal to go to war. The warriors prepared for battle by fasting, drinking the black drink, and smoking the war pipe. No one was immune from the slaughter which thereafter occurred, and a village would be ambushed at dawn, its thatched roofs set afire and its inhabitants massacred. The men of the invaded village were seldom captured except to be used as the subject of public torture, but women and children were usually captured and adopted.

Natives of the Southeast Woodlands and How They Lived *(cont.)*

When the white men came, they were befriended by many native groups. The Cherokee in particular often intermarried with whites, and by the early nineteenth century had developed laws and customs based on those of their new neighbors. By the time of the removal in 1838, when the Cherokees and others were forced on their Trail of Tears to Indian Territory, many of the natives were living lives very similar to those of the Southern whites. They planted cotton on their own plantations and owned black slaves. Many went to Christian churches and sent their children to schools run by white missionaries.

The natives of the Southeast Woodlands were not treated well by their white conquerors. The removal of 1838, especially, was a terrible time for the Five Civilized Tribes. Fifteen thousand Cherokees were forcibly moved over a thousand miles, many without notice. They were not even allowed to take clothing, food stores, or personal belongings, and four thousand are estimated to have died from cold, disease, and starvation. Some Cherokees managed to escape the removal, however, by hiding out in the Great Smoky Mountains of their homeland. Later they were given permanent permission to remain there, and other small groups escaped as well. But wherever one ended up living, that person's life was changed forever.

Activity

Have each student research one of the following topics. They can each complete an original project and give an oral report to the class, also explaining how the subject fits into the history of the United States.

- John Ross
- Doublehead
- Major Ridge
- Cherokee Nation (modern)
- Chickasaw Nation
- Creek Nation
- Seminole Nation
- Choctaw Nation
- Andrew Jackson
- Will Rogers
- Wilma Mankiller
- Indian Territory
- Indian takeover of Alcatraz (1969)
- General Allotment Act of 1887
- Indian schools
- *Ramona* by Helen Hunt Jackson
- Bureau of Indian Affairs
- Trail of Tears
- The Little People
- The Great Smoky Mountains

Wilma Mankiller

Sequoyah and His Syllabary

The North American natives were fascinated by something the white man had that they did not have: his "talking leaves," which is what some called the books and written documents with which the whites communicated. Although the natives had rich systems of language and a long heritage of oral literature, none had a written language apart from the pictographs with which they left messages on cave walls or rocks.

A half-blood Cherokee named Sequoyah, whose English name was George Guess, realized that being able to write and read gave the white newcomers a great advantage, socially and politically, over his people. So, he set out in 1820 to analyze his own language and develop a system of writing for it. He listened carefully to how he and his people spoke and decided that the Cherokee language could be broken down into eighty-six syllables based on sound. The process of inventing a written alphabet, called a syllabary, took several years of trial and error.

He first attempted the almost impossible task of designing a pictograph for every word in the language. When he realized this would be extremely difficult, he returned to his discovery of the eighty–six sounds in the language and designed a symbol for each of these sounds. Simply by memorizing all these symbols, he thought any person who could speak the language would be able to read it.

The new system was not perfect. It lacked a means of punctuation, and the symbols were complicated and could be easily distorted. At the time, there were three distinct dialects in Cherokee, which made it sometimes difficult to translate. Nonetheless, within a very short time, thousands of Cherokees were literate in their own language and were writing letters and passing notes to one other.

Sequoyah soon convinced the tribal chiefs that their language had been put into written form, and the council put all their laws into the Sequoyan Syllabary. English remained the official language of the land, however, although only about 15% of the Cherokees spoke it at that time. Sequoyan, as it was called, could be learned in one day by the people, and it greatly advanced their ability to communicate and transact business. However, it did deter some Cherokees from learning English, because they thought since they now had a written language of their own, they would not need to learn English.

Within a very short time, the Cherokees had crossed the dividing line between preliteracy and being literate. It was a tremendous accomplishment. Before long, the Cherokee community had its own newspaper, the *Cherokee Phoenix*. By 1825, most Cherokees could both read and write, and many of them were bilingual and biliterate in Sequoyan and English.

Activities

1. Written language is a kind of code, a system of symbols which can be used to communicate and send messages. There are many different codes, and new ones are being invented all the time. Study the Cherokee syllabary on page 45.

2. Use logic to solve the code on page 46.

Sequoyah and His Syllabary *(cont.)*

This chart illustrates the syllabary, or alphabet, invented by Sequoyah. The large figures show the characters, or letters, and the figures following the larger ones show the pronunciation of each in the Cherokee language. Would it be possible for you to use Sequoyah's code to write a message to a friend?

Cherokee Alphabet

D *a*	R *e*	T *i*	Ꭷ *o*	Ꮃ *u*	i *v*
Ꮝ *ga* Ꭴ *ka*	Ꮆ *ge*	Y *gi*	A *go*	J *gu*	E *gv*
Ꮏ *ha*	Ꭾ *he*	Ꭿ *hi*	Ꮀ *ho*	Ꭱ *hu*	Ꮴ *hv*
W *la*	Ꮁ *le*	Ꮈ *li*	Ꮊ *lo*	M *lu*	Ꮅ *lv*
Ꮉ *ma*	Ꮺ *me*	H *mi*	Ꮄ *mo*	Ꮋ *mu*	
Ꮎ *na* Ꮏ *hna* Ꮐ *nah*	Ꭺ *ne*	Ꮒ *ni*	Z *no*	Ꮕ *nu*	Ꮔ *nv*
Ꮖ *qua*	Ꮙ *que*	Ꮗ *qui*	Ꮚ *quo*	Ꮘ *quu*	Ꮢ *quv*
Ꭴ *sa* Ꮝ *s*	Ꮄ *se*	Ꮎ *si*	Ꮅ *so*	Ꮃ *su*	R *sv*
Ꮮ *da* Ꮃ *ta*	Ꮖ *de* Ꮦ *te*	Ꮧ *di* Ꮨ *ti*	V *do*	Ꮪ *du*	Ꮫ *dv*
Ꮬ *dla* Ꮭ *tla*	L *tle*	C *tli*	Ꮲ *tlo*	Ꮰ *tlu*	P *tlv*
Ꮳ *tsa*	Ꮴ *tse*	Ꮭ *tsi*	K *tso*	Ꮷ *tsu*	Ꮵ *tsv*
Ꮹ *wa*	Ꮺ *we*	Ꮻ *wi*	Ꮼ *wo*	Ꮽ *wu*	6 *wv*
Ꭴ *ya*	Ᏸ *ye*	Ꭶ *yi*	Ꭾ *yo*	Ᏻ *yu*	B *yv*

Sequoyah and His Syllabary (cont.)

Try to solve this code so that you can read the message. Two letters have been given to help you. Dashes indicate new words. **Hint:** This is a quote.

Code

			24									
A	B	C	D	E	F	G	H	I	J	K	L	M

					14							
N	O	P	Q	R	S	T	U	V	W	X	Y	Z

Message

"
21 8 19 9 8 25 23 21 8 6 25 21 12 8

14 2 3 13 13 19 6 6 21 22 21 12 19 9 26

7 3 8 25 3 8 9 8 25 24 21 19 21 8 24

22 25 21 22 6 25 14 9 12 25 21 24

17 3 14 2 3 8 9 8 25 17 25 25 5 ."

13 25 11 15 9 19 21 2

The Trail of Tears

It was not the only forced march made by American Indians, and it certainly was not the last, but for many people The Trail of Tears came to represent the entirety of inhumane treatment suffered by the native people at the hands of the United States government. The reality of the march, also known as the Trail Where They Cried, completely contradicted the reasons given by the army and Indian agents for making an entire people leave their ancestral homes to go where they did not want to go.

From early colonial days, the majority of Cherokees had embraced the ways of the white newcomers. They had intermarried with whites and adopted their laws which they wrote into their own constitution. They worked hard and were prosperous, some of them owning large plantations. They had a written language of their own and a newspaper which most Cherokees could read. Fields of corn, potatoes, beans, and cotton stretched out for miles from their townships, and their cotton industry gave them an economic base which rivaled that of their white neighbors. They owned horses, hogs, and poultry even before the Revolution. In many ways, they were far more civilized than many of the whites and had a higher literacy rate.

But one treaty after another took more and more land away from them. In 1798, the Treaty of Tellico between the Cherokees and the U.S. government promised that the remaining 43,000 square miles (111,800 square kilometers) of tribal land would belong to the Cherokees forever. However, within twenty-one years, their lands had shrunk to one-third that size, and the government wanted to build roads across what was left. The new white settlers wanted the rich, fertile soil in which almost any crop could grow, and they wanted the minerals, like gold, which lay under the soil. By 1815, 3,000 Cherokees had ceded their lands under governmental pressure and moved to Arkansas, and two years later 4,000 more did the same. Then in 1828, many of those in Arkansas were persuaded to move even further west to what was to be Indian Territory, now the state of Oklahoma.

When gold was discovered in Cherokee land in Georgia, the Cherokees were not the ones to profit from it. After all, they were not citizens of the United States; they were Indians. Then Andrew Jackson was elected President in 1828, and even though a Cherokee had once saved his life, he needed the support of the frontiersmen who wanted Cherokee lands, so he was determined to move the Cherokee and all the other tribes known as the Five Civilized Tribes (Cherokee, Choctaw, Seminole, Creek, and Chickasaw) west to Indian Territory. Educated Cherokees went to Washington, D.C. to try to persuade Jackson to change his mind. The men in Washington, however, some of whom were almost illiterate, claimed the Cherokees were savages and primitives, living on roots, herbs, and disgusting reptiles.

In 1830, the Removal Bill was passed by a narrow margin. Not all whites thought the Indians should be removed. Men like Noah Webster, John Adams, Sam Houston, and Davy Crockett defended the Cherokees, but their efforts did no good. The government of Georgia harassed the Cherokees, and the federal government did nothing. A missionary, Samuel Worcester, who had worked for years with them was arrested and imprisoned. He appealed to the U.S. Supreme Court which declared all the Georgia legislation against the Cherokee null and void, but President Jackson defied the court and told its members to try to enforce their decision.

The Trail of Tears *(cont.)*

Heartened by this, Georgia placed the Cherokee under martial law, forbidding them to assemble, and the federal government pressured them to relocate. Finally, Major Ridge, a Cherokee chief, signed the Treaty of Echota, ceding all eastern Cherokee lands. Sixteen thousand of the seventeen thousand Cherokees still in Georgia, Alabama, Tennessee, and South Carolina signed a petition repudiating the treaty, but the die was cast. The Cherokee were forced to give up 8,000,000 acres of land for about fifty cents an acre. Speculators turned around and sold 40-acre plots in the areas where gold had been found for $30,000. However, most of the Cherokee still refused to leave their homes.

Martin Van Buren was elected President, and General Winfield Scott was ordered to use his 7,000 men to force the Cherokee west. On May 17, 1838, the troops began their assignment. Twenty-three stockaded detention camps were set up throughout the Cherokee Nation, and each day armed troops went out and rounded up all the Cherokees they could find. Many Indians lost most of their household goods since they were taken from wherever they were found. They were taken from their fields, interrupted at meals, and stopped on the road. Women were taken from their spinning wheels, and children were taken from their play. Many left with only the clothing on their backs, and as soon as they left their homes, looters who were waiting in the bushes broke into them and took everything there.

Three hundred Cherokees hid in the Smoky Mountains, however, and their descendants still live there on land now called the Qualla Reservation. Every year they put on a pageant of the Trail of Tears so that no one will ever forget.

All told, 13,000 Cherokees were forced west to Indian Territory in 1838. Given scanty and spoiled rations by contractors who wanted to make a profit off the Cherokees' misery, and weakened by the pneumonia, tuberculosis, smallpox, and cholera which quickly spread in the makeshift campsites, the weak, the very young, and the old quickly died. About 4,000 people died before the ordeal was over. The wife of Chief John Ross, sick with pneumonia, gave up her only blanket to a child who was cold, and she soon joined the list of dead. On the trail, not one family was spared the loss of at least one loved one.

The Trail of Tears *(cont.)*

The last group reached the Territory March 25, 1839. They were welcomed by the Cherokee settlers already there, and the survivors of the Trail of Tears began building new homes and starting their lives anew. Yet, it was not all sweetness and light between the "old" settlers and the new, and political struggles sometimes became quite bitter. Chief John Ross worked hard to reunite the two main factions of settlers, and by 1846 the Cherokees turned their new land into a progressive nation with a new constitution. All land was held in common, and everyone could use it for grazing or farming as long as no one infringed on the rights of others.

By 1843, the Cherokees had eighteen public schools, and in 1851 seminaries were opened for young ladies and young men. Some of the top scholars were sent to major universities such as Princeton to complete their educations. The Cherokee schools were better than the neighboring ones for whites.

The Cherokee Nation established regular courts and peace officers, including mounted rangers called the Lighthorse Police who maintained peace in the Territory. Cherokee towns were connected by flatboats and steamers, roads were built, and towns were started. The farms and ranches made the Cherokee self-sufficient, and long before the Civil War, they had regained much of their former prosperity. They published the first newspaper in Oklahoma, *The Cherokee Advocate*, and the first periodicals, *The Cherokee Messenger* and *The Cherokee Almanac*. The Chisholm Trail was named after a famous Cherokee trailmaker, and the Cherokee worked to make peace between all the Indians in the Territory. Until the Civil War started, things had been looking up for the Cherokees, but what happened then is another story.

Activities

1. Every year the Cherokees have pageants depicting the Trail of Tears. To ask about the annual pageants, write to the Educational Director of the Cherokee Nation, Tahlequah, Oklahoma. Also research to learn everything you can about the Cherokee Nation. Then, as a group or class, write and produce your own Trail of Tears pageant.

2. Make a triptych, which is a three-paneled picture like the one shown in the illustration. In the left panel, show the Cherokees as they were when they lived in their ancestral homes in the Southeast Woodlands. In the right panel, show them as they were on the Trail of Tears. In the center, show them as the strong, intelligent people they are today who have triumphed over adversity.

3. Read a biography of a famous Cherokee like Will Rogers, Sequoyah, John Ross, or Wilma Mankiller. Using information you get from that biography, do a one-man show for the class portraying the person you have studied.

Effigy Burial Mounds

On a high bluff overlooking the
Mississippi River along the eastern edge of
Iowa, there stands a fascinating group of ancient
Indian burial mounds. There are many groups of burial
mounds throughout the Mississippi River Valley, but these particular mounds are shaped
like marching bears, ten of them, each about three feet (.9 m) high and as long as eighty to
one hundred feet (24–30 m).

The ancestors of the people who built the mounds came into northeast Iowa about 12,000 years ago.
They were hunters who pursued and killed huge mammals like the giant mammoth and forms of bison
which are now extinct. They used darts tipped with leaf-shaped stone points and they hurled these darts
with spear throwers. Remains of these ancient people have not been found, but evidence of their
presence has been found in the forms of dart points. Archaeologists have also found an ax, adz, and
gouge which have been radiocarbon dated from a date just a little later.

The oldest of the mounds were built about 2,500 years ago by a group of people now called the Red
Ocher Culture. They were named after the burial bundles covered with red ocher, a natural dye, which
were found in an excavated mound. Other relics found included large chipped blades, straight-stemmed
and corner-notched spear and dart points, and spherical copper beads. The spear thrower was still the
principal weapon.

Pottery has also been found in the mounds. The earliest was crude and thick, and it contained a lot of
coarse pieces of crushed rock. Later pottery was thinner and decorated with wide, indifferently applied
incised lines.

Several of the excavated mounds have been dated from the Hopewellian period which lasted from about
100 BC to 600 AD. The people who lived in the area during this time already were part of a trading
system which extended from the Rocky Mountains to the Gulf of Mexico to Lake Superior.
Archaeologists can determine this because they have found mica from the Rocky Mountains, seashells
from the Gulf of Mexico, and copper from Lake Superior.

The people of the Effigy Mounds were probably supplanted by another group of Indians, the Oneota
Culture, about 1300 or 1400 AD. These people seem to have come from the south, and they were
known as the Ioway for whom the state of Iowa is named.

The first white men to explore northeast Iowa were Louis Joliet and Father Marquette. They did so in
1673, but as far as can be determined, the mounds were not discovered until 1881 when Theodore H.
Lewis and Alfred J. Hill began to survey the mound groups which can be found throughout the
Mississippi Valley and southern United States. Unfortunately, some of the mounds were destroyed
before the area was made part of the National Park Service. A monument was built in 1949.

Effigy Burial Mounds *(cont.)*

Activity

You are going to make an archaeological dig. This activity takes a great deal of planning on the part of the teacher, but it can be a productive and exciting learning experience for the students. It will be easier to plan and make if several teachers prepare it together. Follow these steps.

Teacher:

1. The easiest way to proceed would be to plan on having a load of sand delivered. If the school already has a sandbox, so much the better. Just use brightly colored tape to mark it "off limits" while the project is under way. Use as many objects as you can conveniently label and bury. Make a list so you will know when the students have dug up all "artifacts."

2. Gather a large group of objects: seashells, pieces of cast-off jewelry, old kitchen implements, old dishes or pottery, and objects of all kinds which are in some way part of daily life. Try to include some items not easily identifiable, such as small parts from something larger.

3. Be sure to spread out the objects enabling more students to dig for them. Cover the objects and bury them under the sand.

4. Serve as supervisors as the students dig.

Students:

1. Choose a recorder to list, label, number, and describe each artifact as it is excavated.

2. Tape off the dig area into squares. Each of the squares will be the area of one student so that everyone can have a turn at digging.

3. Carefully sift through your area for artifacts. It helps to have a piece of screen to sift your sand through. Use a small brush because artifacts will be quite small and you may miss them otherwise. As you discover an artifact, take it to the recorder to label, number, and list.

4. When time runs out, check with your teacher to see how many artifacts have not yet been found.

5. On your return to class, determine the purpose of each artifact and record that purpose. If you cannot determine the purpose, try to guess what it might have been by examining the artifact closely. Record everything in writing: description, number in order found, and possible usage.

Cherokee Fables

Read these three fables told by the Cherokees. Then, complete the activity which follows.

How Rabbit Stole Otter's Coat

Long ago the animals had coats of many different colors and textures. Some had long hair and others had short hair. Some had lovely, decorated tails, but others had no tails at all. One day, a quarrel began between some of the animals because each thought his or her coat was the best looking. They called a council to determine which had the prettiest coat of all.

Some said that Otter had a very fine coat, indeed, but no one knew for sure because they hardly ever saw him. They sent for Otter who lived far away up the creek and seldom came to visit, but they were certain he would come if he was invited.

Rabbit wanted to win the contest. So always being the Trickster, he decided to figure out a way he could trick Otter out of his coat. He asked around until he learned the trail Otter would take to get to the council meeting, and secretly he went ahead on the journey which took four days until he met Otter. As soon as Rabbit saw Otter, he saw that Otter's coat of soft, brown fur was, indeed, the most beautiful coat to be found among any of the animals, so he resolved to get it.

When Rabbit saw Otter, he said in his most friendly manner, "I am so glad to see you! The council members sent me to accompany you to the meeting because you live so far away and they were afraid you would get lost."

Otter thanked Rabbit, and together they traveled all day toward the council ground. That night, Rabbit chose a resting place, knowing that Otter was a stranger to the area. In the morning, they continued their journey. In the afternoon, Rabbit began to pick up wood and bark which he placed on his back.

"Why do you pick up wood and carry it on your back?" Otter asked him.

"I wish for us to be comfortable and warm when we stop tonight," Rabbit replied, and that evening the two stopped and made camp for the night.

After supper, Rabbit took a stick and whittled it down to form a paddle. Otter asked him, "What are you doing that for?"

"I have good dreams when I sleep with a paddle under my head," Rabbit said.

After whittling the paddle, Rabbit began to cut down the bushes and clear a trail down to the river. Again, Otter questioned Rabbit about what he was doing.

"Sometimes it rains fire in this place," Rabbit answered, "and the sky looks as though it might do that tonight. Go to sleep, and I will stay awake and watch. If the fire comes, I can shout for you to jump up and run into the river."

So Otter went to sleep, and Rabbit stayed awake. After awhile, the campfire burned down to embers. Rabbit called to Otter, but he was sound asleep and did not answer. Again Rabbit called to Otter, but Otter did not budge, so Rabbit filled the paddle with red hot embers, threw it into the air, and called out, "It's raining fire! It's raining fire!" The embers fell all around Otter, and he jumped up and ran to the river, where he has lived ever since.

Rabbit took Otter's coat and put it on, leaving his own behind. When Otter appeared at the council, the animals were so glad to see him, but Otter kept his head down in shame with one paw over his face. The animals wondered why Otter was so bashful, and when Bear pulled Otter's paw away from his face, he saw Rabbit wearing Otter's coat.

Bear hit at Rabbit and tried to catch him, but he only managed to pull off Rabbit's tail before Rabbit got away. That is the reason Rabbit now has only a little short stub of a tail.

52

Cherokee Fables *(cont.)*

Why Possum's Tail Is Bare

Possum used to have a long, bushy tail. He was very proud of his tail and would brush it every morning and sing about it at every dance. Rabbit, who had no tail, was jealous of Possum, so he decided to play a trick on Possum.

An important council meeting was planned, and there was to be a big dance afterwards. Rabbit was entrusted with the responsibility of letting everyone know about the dance, so he stopped over at Possum's house and asked him if he was planning to attend the dance.

"Oh yes," Possum replied. "I cannot miss the dance. I must show off my beautiful tail so everyone can admire me!"

Rabbit promised to make sure that Possum got the best seat in the place and that someone would comb and dress Possum's tail. Possum was very pleased by this and agreed to come.

Next, Rabbit went to Cricket, an excellent haircutter who is called "the barber." Rabbit told Cricket to go to Possum's house the morning of the dance and gave him instructions on how to dress Possum's tail. Cricket did as Rabbit told him and the following morning showed up bright and early at Possum's house.

"I am here to help you get ready for the dance," he told the pleased Possum who stretched himself out and closed his eyes while Cricket dressed his tail. He had tied his tail with a red string to keep it in place until the dance. Of course, all the time Cricket had been cutting Possum's tail without Possum knowing.

That night Possum went to the dance, and sure enough, the best seat in the place was waiting for him. When his turn came to dance, he loosened the red string from his tail and stepped into the middle of the floor. The drummers began to drum, and Possum began to sing, "See my beautiful tail."

Everyone shouted, and Possum continued, "See what a lovely color it is."

They shouted again, and Possum sang, "See how my tail sweeps the ground."

The animals shouted again, and Possum, who was pleased to no end, sang, "See how fine the fur on my tail is."

Possum suddenly realized that everyone was falling onto the floor in laughter and that they were laughing at him. He looked down at what had been his beautiful tail, and he saw that there was not a hair left on it. It was as bare as the tail of a lizard. He was so surprised and ashamed that he fell on the ground helpless, a stupid grin on his face. And that is what Possum does to this day when he is taken by surprise.

 #607 Interdisciplinary Unit: Native Americans

Cherokee Fables *(cont.)*

How Terrapin Beat the Rabbit

Everyone knew that Rabbit was a great runner and that Terrapin was very slow. However, Terrapin was a great warrior, and he was also very boastful. He and Rabbit were continually having arguments over who could move faster. Finally, they decided to have a race, and they set the day and the starting place. They agreed to run across four mountain ridges, and the one who came in first at the end would be the winner.

Rabbit was very sure of himself. He told Terrapin, "You know you can't win. You can't run. You'll never win over me, so I'll do something for you. I'll give you the first ridge, and you'll only have three ridges to cross while I cross over four."

That night Terrapin told his family about Rabbit's boasting, and they sent for all their terrapin friends. He asked them for help. He said he knew he could not outrun Rabbit, but he was tired of Rabbit's boasting. He explained his plan to his friends, and they agreed to help him.

On the day of the race, the animals all came to watch. Rabbit was with them, but Terrapin was already far ahead on the first ridge, as they had agreed. The grass there was so tall the animals could barely see him. The signal was given, and Rabbit started off with his long jumps across the mountain. But before he got to the next ridge, he saw Terrapin crossing the ridge ahead of him.

"How did he get there so quickly?" he thought to himself, but he kept on going. He got to the next ridge, and the same thing happened again. He saw Terrapin crossing the ridge ahead of him.

"What's going on here?" he thought, and he jumped his longest jumps trying to catch up, but there was Terrapin again, a ridge ahead all the way.

Rabbit was getting tired by now, and he was nearly out of breath, but he kept running as hard as he could. When he got to the third ridge, he saw Terrapin crossing the fourth ridge and winning the race.

Rabbit could not even finish the race. He fell over, crying out loud, just like he always does when he gets too tired. The prize was given to Terrapin, and everyone wondered how he had won. But Terrapin never told anyone his secret.

It was easy, because everyone knows that all terrapins look alike. He had simply posted one of his friends on each of the ridges, and he, himself, waited at the fourth ridge, coming in at the end of the race to answer any questions put to him.

Now, when the young men are getting ready for a race, the leader boils many rabbit hamstrings into a soup. He sends someone at night to pour the soup across the path along which the other racers will come. In this way, they will become tired just as Rabbit did and lose the race. Of course, it is not easy to do this, because the other team is always watching out for this.

Cherokee Fables *(cont.)*

Activity

These stories you have just read are *fables*. Fables are stories in which animals talk and act like people. They teach a lesson called a *moral*. Can you tell what the moral of each of these fables is? What about the morals of other fables you have read?

The fable is a universal kind of story, which means that most cultures of the world (from the ancient Greeks, and probably before, to the present time) have had fables as part of their oral and written literature. Fables are amusing stories to read. They make us smile while at the same time showing a human failing or weakness in the character of an animal. Fables tell us, "You had better be careful! If you do such and such a thing, you will get your come-uppance, just like Rabbit does!"

To review, the qualities a tale must have to be considered a fable are:

1. Animals talk and act like people. This is called *personification*.

2. The story teaches a lesson.

Now, complete one or more of the following:

a. Compile a book of fables. Illustrate it like a picture book. Read it to a young child or lower grade classroom.

b. Make a poster advertising the race which is going to take place between Rabbit and Terrapin. Be sure to include the time and place the event is going to take place.

c. Make a film strip of one of the stories. Use permanent marker pens on blank film or on long strips of paper such as would go into a cash register. You can purchase these at many stationery or office supply stores.

d. Collect several fables from cultures other than Native American and put them into an illustrated book, or collect fables from other groups of Native Americans.

e. Make puppets and a puppet theater, then dramatize one of the stories to present to other classrooms.

f. Prepare a news story to present on the "evening news" about what happens in one of the stories. Make it as exciting as possible to attract your listeners' attention.

g. Rewrite a story and change its ending.

h. Find another famous story about a race between a rabbit and a terrapin and write a paper comparing the two. How are they alike? How are they different?

i. Rewrite one of the stories telling it from a different viewpoint. For example, the story "Why Possum's Tail Is Bare" can be told from the viewpoint of Possum.

j. Write a story from the viewpoint of an ecologist. What would he think of ruining a natural beauty like the possum's tail or of cutting down the natural vegetation as Rabbit does to beat Otter?

Mystical Numbers

Do you have a lucky number? Do you have an unlucky number? Many people would say "yes" to both these questions, and the Native Americans were no exception.

Most native peoples considered four to be a mystical number. That is, they believed the number four held special powers. The number four represented the four cardinal directions: north, south, east, west. All the rituals of a people would involve this number. For example, when a baby was being named, he would be raised overhead four times as the name was bestowed. When smoking with incense or the sacred tobacco, the smoke would be wafted to the four directions. Any action included in a ritual was done four times.

Many people of the world have thought of certain numbers as being magical or mystical. The Mayans of ancient Mexico and Central America believed that each of the first thirteen numbers represented a god, and the Babylonians had sixty gods, each of which was represented by one of the first sixty natural numbers. They designated the importance of each god by where he appeared in numerical position, number one being the most important.

The Cherokee had two mystical numbers, four and seven. Just as it did for other native peoples, the number four represented the four directions. The mystical shape of the circle came from these directions because one went around in a full circle from one direction to the other until the circle was closed.

The number seven had many meanings, the most important being it was the actual number of tribal clans. It also was the number of the heavens. The story went that when the Great Mystery above created the world, he made a heaven about as high as the tops of the mountains. This heaven was too warm, so he made another which was also too warm. He continued making heavens, one over the other, until he had made the seventh. This one was perfect, and there he decided to live forever. The ceremonial number of repetitions in rituals is seven, and seven stands for the four cardinal directions in addition to "above," "below," and "here in the center."

Activity

Take a survey of your neighbors, parents, teachers, and anyone else you would like, asking them the following questions. Bring your results back to class and compare them with those of your classmates.

1. Do you have a lucky number? If so, what is it?

2. Do you have an unlucky number? If so, what is it?

3. Would you fly on Friday the thirteenth?

4. Would you stay in a hotel room numbered 1313?

Storing Food

In the days before refrigerators, freezers, canned goods, and supermarkets, it was much more important to be able to store food than it is today. One's life could literally depend on the stores of food one had set aside for one's family. Some believe that even today people should keep emergency food supplies on hand, because when an emergency hits, such as a flood, hurricane, or earthquake, one might be unable to get to the store for food, and water supplies might be limited.

Solve the following problems for a family of four. Assume 30 days per month.

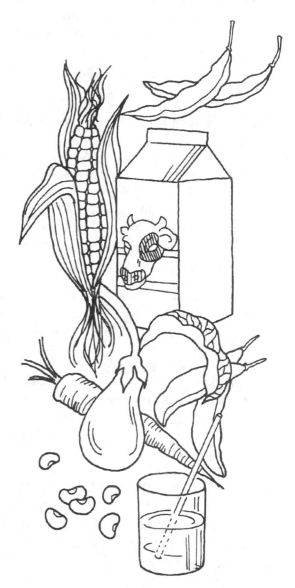

1. If each person needs 2 liters of water per day, how many liters of water would need to be saved for one month's supply?

2. One person consumes ½ pound (225 g) of bread per day. How many pounds or grams of bread would be needed for each person for a month? For the family for a month? For the family for a year?

3. Each person needs 5½ cups (1375 mL) of fruits and vegetables per day. How many cans of fruits and vegetables containing 2 cups (500 mL) would need to be saved for each person for one month? For each person for a year? For the family for one month? For the family for one year? Solve in cans first and then in cups or liters.

4. Each of the two children in the family needs 2 cups (500 mL) of milk each day. How many cups or liters of milk would be needed for the children for one month? For one year?

5. If powdered milk is used instead of fresh, and ¼ cup (60 mL) is added to ¾ cup (180 mL) water to substitute for 1 cup (240 ml) fresh milk, how much powdered milk will be needed for two children for one month? For one year?

6. If 1 cup (250 mL) dried beans will make two servings of cooked beans, and each person eats two servings per day, how many cups (mL) will the family need to save for one month's supply? For one year's supply?

7. How many people will each get a 1 cup (250 mL) serving from 7 gallons (280 liters) of water?

8. How many people will each get one serving of 1 cup (250 mL) cooked dried beans from 10 quarts (10 liters) dried beans?

9. How many servings of liquid milk will each of the two children get from 20 quarts (20 liters) dried powdered milk?

   #607 Interdisciplinary Unit: Native Americans

Stewards of the Land

The great Cherokee culture hero was Ke-na-ti, the Great Hunter, and his wife was Se-lu, the Mother of Corn. In an early story of Ke-na-ti, his two mischievous sons followed him one morning to see where he got the wonderful meat with which their plates were filled each day. As they watched, he opened a door to a huge cave, letting out one deer. He shot the deer, closed the door, put the deer over his shoulders, and carried it home.

The boys thought, "Aha! That looks like fun! Let's open the door and shoot some for ourselves!"

They opened the door to the cave and began shooting at the animals running out. They were having so much fun that the time passed rapidly, and suddenly, no more animals came from the door to the cave. They were all gone. Ke-na-ti had, by now, come back looking for the boys, and when he saw them standing at the cave's open door, he realized what they had done.

"You have been very foolish," he told them. "Because of your foolishness, from this day on, man will have to work hard for his food. He will have to look very long before he finds an animal to shoot, and he might never find one."

Because the natives depended on the wild game they could find for food, this story served to teach Cherokee youngsters how important it is to take care of the land and its resources and never to waste them. The natives of North America were horrified when they saw how their new European neighbors wasted the land and its resources. They believed the land and every living thing, both the animal tribes and the plant tribes, had been placed here by the Great Mystery above. It was a sacrilege to harm or misuse them.

When a Southeast Woodlands native hunted, he followed a certain procedure. Before he shot his arrow or his gun, he bowed his head and asked permission of the animal to take its life so that he and his family could eat. After he had killed the animal, he stopped and thanked it reverently before cleaning and butchering the meat. He and his family would use almost every part of the carcass for food as well as the skins for clothing. Neither he nor anyone he knew would have considered wasting that which was intended to give them life.

When a mother gathered corn and beans or any other plant food, she thanked Se-lu. She took care to see that a plot of land was not overplanted, and she treated the foods she gathered with respect, knowing there are a limited amount of resources. She wasted nothing, knowing that all living things depend upon each other. The earth flourished for many thousands of years under the **stewardship** of the North American natives, yet much of the earth where they lived is threatened today.

Stewards of the Land *(cont.)*

Scientists now realize that the Earth's natural wealth is slipping away, just as the animals of the story slipped away when the cave door was opened. Man is reproducing at a rapid rate and overpopulating the earth. Wild plants and animals, the very basis of our food, are being destroyed in many places today. People are using up or changing many of the natural habitats which shelter the wild creatures who have lived here for millions of years, and they are doing it so quickly that by the early twenty-first century, one–fourth of the world's existing plant and animal species may have vanished forever.

The main reason this is true is the loss of **habitat**. Each year a forested area the size of Pennsylvania is cleared of its trees in the rain forests of South America. At least half the world's species of plants and animals live there. When the forests are cut down, the animals and people who live there die or move from their homes to a strange place for which they are unprepared, and the plants which are killed no longer produce the oxygen people need to breathe. In the developed countries of the world, thousands of square miles of natural habitat are converted to urban and agricultural uses. Pollutants are released into the soil and air, and water becomes poisoned by chemicals and garbage.

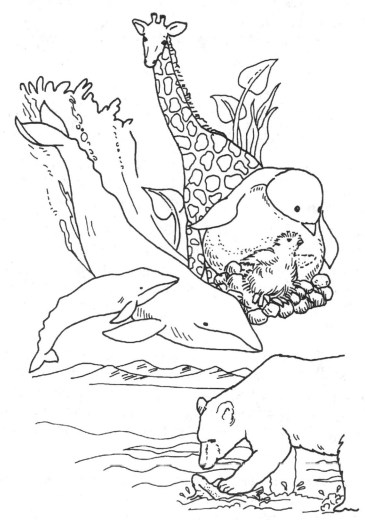

The consequence for man and the Earth's other living things is a changing **biosphere**. The relationships between the different **species** of the world took many millions of years to develop, and those relationships are threatened. Many species have already disappeared. For this destruction to stop, we must all change our thinking about how to use the resources we have. All life is interconnected.

The North American natives thought of the Earth as their mother and of all living things as their brothers. They acknowledged long ago what scientists are recognizing now: humans must live in harmony on the earth. Nearly all the food we eat, including all of that which we buy in the supermarket, originally came from wild sources. Resources for wild animals are also important. For example, commercial fishing relies on natural water systems which are clean and uncontaminated. And one–fourth of all medicines in our medicine cabinets contain natural substances.

We depend on our wild resources, and they depend on us.

Stewards of the Land *(cont.)*

Activities

1. Find the definitions of the words in boldface on pages 58–59. Write the definitions and then write a paragraph using the words.

2. Sometimes students think that they do not have the power to do important things, but this is not true. Everyone has the power to make a difference in our world before it is too late. In groups of three or four, list the ways you and your families can have a positive influence on preserving our natural resources.

3. The Bureau of Land Management is a governmental agency in the United States which is responsible for identifying endangered species and safeguarding them. Find where the nearest office of this bureau is, and learn what they do in your area to protect natural resources.

4. UNESCO is an agency of the United Nations which operates a type of protected area called a biosphere reserve. There are 311 biosphere reserves in 81 countries of the world. Forty-seven of these reserves are in the United States. Contact either the United Nations or your nearest National Park Service, which is part of the Department of the Interior, to learn of any biosphere reserves near you.

5. Visit a nearby recycler to learn how your class can encourage recycling in your school. Some schools place special bins in certain areas or in each classroom for storing discarded papers and aluminum cans until they can be picked up. Other schools have recycling drives or contests to see which class can collect the largest amount of recyclable materials during a specific time.

6. Make a poster urging others to recycle paper, aluminum, and plastic.

7. *Consumer Reports* recommends that everyone does the following to cut down on the amount of trash.

    a. Avoid buying new things whenever possible. "Use it up, wear it out, make it do."

    b. Buy products which use as little packaging as possible. Buy large containers and use the contents to refill a smaller container you already have.

    c. Buy products which use recycled materials whenever possible. This encourages manufacturers to use more recycled products.

    d. Recycle whatever you can in your community.

8. Go through your home with your family and list the ways you recycle or use recycled products. Bring the list to class, and share it with your classmates. Has someone in the class discovered a way to recycle which you have not thought of?

Build a Seminole Summer House

The Seminole Indians lived in Florida where it is warm most of the year. Like the people in the warm climates of the South Pacific and the nearby Caribbean, the Seminoles did not require enclosed shelters. The people could enjoy the fresh air and cooling breezes in the shade of their summer house.

To build a model Seminole summer house, follow these directions.

Materials:

- sticks or dowels about ¼" (.6 cm) thick
  - four 10" (25 cm) long
  - two 11½" (29 cm) long
  - six 6" (15 cm) long
  - seven 12" (30 cm) long
  - twenty 3½" (9 cm) long
- flat pieces of wood 6" (15 cm) long
- box approximately 10" x 15" x 1" (25 cm x 37.5 cm x 2.5 cm)
- grass, straw, or raffia
- string or other lashing material
- glue

Directions:

1. Make a 6" x 12" (15 cm x 30 cm) platform by lashing two 12" (30 cm) and two 6" (15 cm) sticks at the corners.

2. Glue the flat pieces of wood onto the sticks. This makes the flooring. Set aside.

3. Construct the building frame as illustrated. Lash all junctures together.

4. Place blobs of clay at the ends of the frame as shown. Place the frame in the box.

5. Add the platform to the frame about 2½" (6 cm) up. Lash it in place.

6. Glue the flat pieces on for the roof. Cover with tied bunches of grass, straw, or pieces of raffia. Lash on the remaining 3½" (9 cm) sticks for triangular roof supports.

7. Glue any place which needs extra reinforcement.

8. Fill the box with sand so that the platform is about 1½" (4 cm) above the surface.

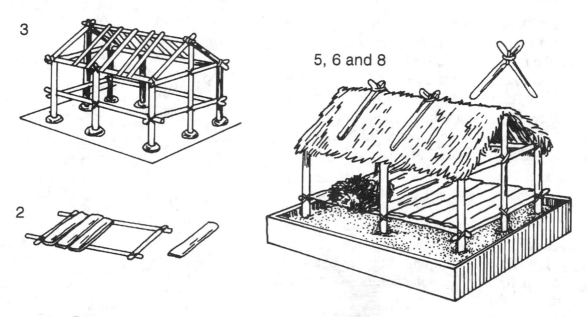

Cherokee Cooklore

Have you ever thought about the amount of work it took to keep a family fed before the days of modern appliances and supermarkets? A mother might spend most of her day growing, preserving, and cooking food for her family, and what time she had left was probably spent making and repairing clothing and moccasins. It is very easy today to take for granted the conveniences we have, and it is probably much more fun to read about how it used to be than it was to have lived it.

In 1949, Aggie Lossiah, the granddaughter of Chief John Ross, made public some of her Cherokee recipes made by the old ways of cooking. She cooked these foods over an outdoor fire.

Here is a menu for what would have been a feast long ago:

Yellow Jacket Soup
Baked Squirrel
Succotash
Bean Bread
Sassafras Tea

Yellow Jacket Soup

Hunt for ground-dwelling yellow jackets either in the early morning or in the late afternoon. Gather the whole comb. Place the comb over the fire or on the stove with the right side up to loosen the grubs that are not covered. Remove all the uncovered grubs. Now place the comb over the fire or on the stove upside down until the paper-like covering parches. Remove the comb from the heat, pick out the yellow jackets, and place them in the oven to brown. Make the soup by boiling the browned yellow jackets in a pot of water with salt and grease added, if you like.

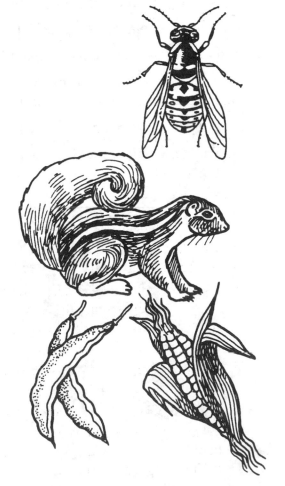

Baked Squirrel

Dress a freshly killed squirrel with its skin on. To do this, singe off the fur in the fire and then scrub the skin with ashes from the fire. Wash the squirrel well on the inside and outside. Rub the squirrel inside and outside with lard. Bake it over the fire or in the oven until it is well-browned. Cut the squirrel up and put it in a pot, add a little water, and cook it until the meat is done. Add a little meal to thicken the gravy. Cook until the meal is done.

Succotash

Shell some corn. Skin it with wood ashes and lye. Cook corn and beans separately and then together. If desired, you may put in pieces of pumpkin. Be sure to add the pumpkin in time for it to get done before the pot is removed from the fire.

62

Cherokee Cooklore (cont.)

Bean Bread

Skin the corn with wood ashes. Sieve the ashes and put them into an iron pot over the fire. Let this boil until it is thick enough to bubble. Take the corn off the fire. Go to the branch. Wash the corn in the running water in a sieve by letting the water run through it until it is clean. Let it drip until all the extra water has dripped off. While the corn is still damp, pound it into meal by using an old homemade corn beater. To make bean bread, boil dry beans in plain water until tender. Pour the boiling beans and some of the soup into the cornmeal and stir until mixed. Have a pot of plain water boiling. Mold the bread flat in your hand and wrap it in corn blades. Tie with a stout reed. Drop this into the boiling water, cover, and boil until done. Do not put any salt in Bean Bread or it will crumble.

Sassafras Tea

Gather and wash the roots of the red sassafras. Do this in the early spring before the sap rises. Store for future use. When ready to make tea, boil a few pieces of the roots and serve hot. Sweeten if desired.

Activities

1. Make up a menu of foods you are more familiar with than these old Cherokee foods but that are still similar to the ones in the Cherokee menu. Find the recipes for them or list where you can find them ready made. Demonstrate to your classmates how you would change the old foods to new ones of your own.

2. Answer these discussion questions.

   a. How would you go about getting the foods in these old–time recipes? Could you buy any of them in a store?

   b. If you were lost in the deep woods somewhere, how would you survive? What foods would you eat? How would you know which ones were safe and which ones were not? What implements or tools would you need to help you obtain food? How long could you go without food?

   c. What do you think Mrs. Lossiah meant by the terms branch, sieve, and corn blades? How can you tell?

   d. Write a story about how you dressed the first squirrel you obtained on a hunt.

   e. What other animals besides a squirrel do you think a Southeast Woodlands native might have hunted for food? Can you name any foods which the early Native Americans first introduced to the European newcomers?

Make a Corn Doll

Native American girls from many parts of the country loved to play with cornhusk dolls. Sometimes called harvest figures, they represented the corn spirit that ensured a plentiful harvest. They are easy to make. To make one yourself, follow these directions.

Materials:

- fresh or dried cornhusks
- water
- string
- soft cotton

Directions:

1. If you are using dried husks, soak them in the water to soften them.

2. Place cotton in the center of a piece of husk, and tie it down to make the head.

3. Make arms by rolling one piece of husk and tying it near the ends for hands. Slide the arms through the husk under the head.

4. Tie around the husk with the string to make the waist.

5. Arrange five or six husks around the waist and tie them in place. Carefully fold them down to make a skirt. Cut the skirt straight across the bottom for a girl doll. Divide the skirt in two and tie each half at the ankles for a boy doll.

6. Let the husks dry completely. The doll is ready!

4

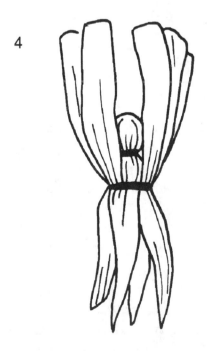

5

Native Americans in the Civil War

From the first battle which took place among European Americans in North America, through to the French and Indian War, the American Revolution, and the Civil War, Native Americans were on the battlefield fighting with and against the white man. Unfortunately for them, the ones who fought on the losing side were often punished by the whites on the winning side.

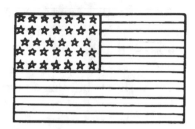

In no war was this more true than the Civil War in which large numbers of natives fought on the sides of both North and South. The Indians were actively recruited by both sides of this bloody war, and it is now estimated that about 20,000 actually served, most for the South. Five hundred were reported to be at Harper's Ferry stationed with the Confederates, and newspapers had a field day reporting that "bloodthirsty Indians" were there armed with tomahawks, scalping knives, and rifles. These false reports led to a federal investigation.

The Union army was at first reluctant to allow natives in their midst. When the first native, a Chippewa chief from Minnesota, tried to enlist in the Union army, he was refused because Secretary of War Simon Cameron said that "the nature of our present national troubles forbids the use of savages..." The issue of whether or not to allow natives in the army led to editorials such as the one in the *Detroit Daily Tribune* entitled "Shall the Indians Be Armed?" This pointed up the fears many Americans had that allowing Indians to serve would be setting a dangerous precedent. Of course, at that time African Americans were not allowed to enlist in the military either. The Civil War was intended to be a white man's war until both sides realized it was going to be harder to win than they had anticipated.

While the Union was still trying to decide whether the Indians had a place in the war, the Confederacy established a Bureau of Indian Affairs. Leaders of the Confederacy wanted to gain control of an area, now known as the state of Oklahoma. This land had been set aside as Indian Territory and had been settled by the five groups of Indians called the Five Civilized Tribes. These tribes—the Cherokee, Chickasaw, Choctaw, Creek, and Seminole—had long adopted the white man's forms of government, religion, and commerce, and in the South had lived alongside their white neighbors. Some of them were even slave holders. Many had intermarried with whites for decades, and some had become wealthy.

The people of the Five Civilized Tribes had in 1838 been robbed by the government of their lands in the Carolinas, Tennessee, Alabama, and Georgia and been forced to march their Trail of Tears over one thousand miles to Indian Territory. When the Civil War broke out, about 74,000 Indians lived in Indian Territory, most of them from the southern tribes. Most of the Chickasaws were slaveholders, and most of the mixed-blood natives were as well. They distrusted the federal government more than they did the Confederacy. The federal government had not kept its promises to them to protect them from raiding by Plains tribes, and when federal forts were abandoned by the Union army in 1861, the forts were left for the Confederacy to protect.

The Confederate government in 1861 sent Albert Pike to Indian Territory to negotiate an alliance with the tribes. He went bearing gifts of money and promises of free trade, fishing rights, and the right to sue and be represented in court. The Indians of the territory had never been given these by the federal government, so it was easy for Pike to convince most of them to ally themselves with the South.

Native Americans in the Civil War *(cont.)*

About 10,000 Native Americans served in 25 separate units of the Confederate army, all of them from the Five Civilized Tribes except for a group of Osage. Most were mounted units riding their own horses, but they were poorly equipped by the Confederacy and often given obsolete weapons which had been discarded by the Union years before. By treaty, these troops were not required to serve outside the territory, but large numbers of them fought in some principal battles.

At the Battle of Pea Ridge, Pike led nearly a thousand Cherokee, Chickasaw, Choctaw, Creek, and Seminole warriors against the Union. They were successful at first, but when some of them started to loot, their military discipline broke down and they were forced to flee for their lives. This battle saw the largest concentration of Indians in any battle of the war. Formal federal charges were filed saying that several Union soldiers had been scalped and mutilated, and although the Cherokee Council issued a formal statement denying this charge, such rumors continued to circulate.

The Union army managed to get into Indian Territory, and soon war became a guerrilla effort. Stand Watie, a Cherokee, was the main leader of these troops, and he was to become the only Native American to attain the rank of Brigadier General in the Confederacy during this war. Other Indians served with various white units east of the territory. Some Choctaws had avoided being removed to Indian Territory and still lived in Mississippi. Several hundred of them served in the 1st Mississippi Choctaw Battalion. Their main job was to track down deserters in the swamps of Mississippi.

Some Cherokees had also escaped the removal and hid in the Great Smoky Mountains rather than obey the orders of the federal government to move to Indian Territory. At the beginning of the war, about 2,000 Cherokee, the Qualla Band, lived there. Four companies were recruited for the North Carolina regiment and became known as the "Thomas Legion." They fought mainly in the mountains of North Carolina and Tennessee. They practiced their native customs while in the army. They consulted an oracle stone to see whether or not someone would survive, and they played stickball games when they were in camp.

In 1861, the Union army finally decided to enlist Indians, and more than 7,000 pro-Union Indian women and children sought refuge in Kansas. They were harassed all the way by Confederate Indians because their men signed up for the North. In 1862, three regiments were formed for duty in the Territory. A company of Omahas and Pawnees was raised in Nebraska, and eventually Native Americans were recruited in nearly every state. It was said that more than one-fifth of the Penobscot tribe volunteered.

More than 600 Iroquois and a company of Chippewas enlisted as well. These troops were reported by a medical officer to be the healthiest and most physically fit of all the Union soldiers, excellent marksmen, and the best scouts.

Native Americans in the Civil War *(cont.)*

The Native American to receive the highest honor in the Union Army was Ely S. Parker, a Seneca, who was secretary to General Ulysses S. Grant. When General Robert E. Lee surrendered to Grant at Appomattox, ending this bloody war, Parker was the one chosen to write the official document of surrender in his own handwriting. This happened before the advent of typewriters or computers when all documents were laboriously written by hand. Ely S. Parker was said to have the most beautiful penmanship of anyone; therefore, he got the job. In pictures of the signing, Parker can be seen standing behind General Grant.

Ely S. Parker

The last Confederate military command to surrender was that of Stand Watie's band of Cherokee guerrillas. They surrendered on June 28, 1865.

The Civil War left Indian Territory in chaos. Towns, farms, and schools had been destroyed, and the people were destitute. Some of them migrated to Mexico in frustration and bitterness. The terrible Reconstruction era would prove to be much harder on the Indians who served in the Confederacy than it was on their white neighbors, and they lost even more land than they had previously lost.

The Native American veterans of the North returned home to the same prejudice, poverty, and discrimination they had left at the war's beginning. They found it difficult to get pensions, and their war-related wounds were treated at home by tribal medicine men not covered by government pensions.

Why had they joined? Probably they had joined for the regular pay, clothing, and food just as their poor white neighbors had. There also was the matter of the warrior spirit. It was a way for young men to show their courage because all the old ways had been taken from them. It was one last chance for a young Indian man to prove his manhood.

Activity

Have a formal debate on the following situation. One side will argue in favor and one side will argue against. You will also need a timekeeper and judges.

Put yourself back into the year 1861. A terrible war has broken out between the Northern states and the Southern ones. Tempers are high because no one in the country can escape the effects of what will happen. Every man is needed, and a suggestion has been made that Native Americans should be taken into the army to fight alongside the whites.

Should Indians be included in the army to fight with white men? To prepare yourself for the debate, learn as much as you can about the war. Use all your best reasoning ability to develop a strategy for your debate which will be true to what you know about the war's history.

Quiz

1. List three important things you learned about natives of the Southeast Woodlands._____

   _____

   _____

2. Describe the family life of the natives of the Southeast Woodlands._____

   _____

   _____

3. What were the jobs of the head chief in a village?_____

   _____

4. How was writing with Sequoyah's syllabary different from writing with English letters? _____

   _____

   _____

5. How long have people lived in the Mississippi River Valley, and how do we know?_____

   _____

   _____

6. Who won the race between Rabbit and Terrapin, and how did he do it?_____

   _____

7. What number did most Native Americans consider sacred, and what did it stand for? _____

   _____

8. Of what importance were games and sports to the Southeast natives? _____

   _____

9. Compare the house of the Seminole Indians to that of your own._____

   _____

10. On the back of this paper, describe the skills a young native of the Southeastern Woodlands would have been expected to learn.

The General

The general was dashing and romantic, a Victorian lady's dream, and he made sure everyone knew it. Known as the "Boy Wonder" for his exploits in the Civil War, George Armstrong Custer became a general when he was twenty-three. He stayed in the army after the war because that was the place a young man could make a name for himself, and he had ambitions. Who knew what heights he might attain, especially as he had come so far already?

He was no ordinary general. He wore custom-made uniforms of buckskin and velvet, and he delighted in having his portrait taken. Writing about his daring in his popular book *My Life on the Plains*, and including in his entourage a sixteen-piece band to play "Gary Owen" every time he and his troops left the fort, all that he did was flamboyant and exciting. America had its boy general, Indian fighter, and romanticist all wrapped up in one blond, blue-eyed package.

Almost everyone forgot that the general had graduated last in his class at West Point. At least he had graduated. Most people did not know that he had once been suspended for leaving his post to make a long visit to his sweet little wife, Libby. He did not publicize that.

Yet, not everyone liked the general. Ullyses S. Grant, for one, did not like him. Neither did his fellow officers or the men who served under him. They found him arrogant and self-serving. The desertion rate in his charge was much higher than that under other generals. And how many other generals kept a large pack of hunting hounds at the fort and had a ballroom built so he and his wife could dance to the music of their own band?

Then there was the matter of the Battle of Washita. The general often remarked to his scouts and fellow officers that his seventh cavalry could whip any bunch of Indians in the entire West, but Washita was the only battle he had ever won against the Indians—if you could call it a battle, that is. It was more of a massacre. At dawn one day in 1868, he and his men surprised a peaceful village of Cheyenne who were camped with their chief, Black Kettle. Black Kettle's group did not consider themselves to be at war, and their chief was on good terms with the Great Father, the President. Custer attacked them anyhow.

The cost to the Cheyenne at the Battle of Washita was high: over one hundred men, women, and children were killed, eight hundred horses shot, and all the tepees, clothing, and food destroyed—everything they had. The great Indian fighter ordered babies and old people killed. The general claimed he had won a victory, but the Cheyenne knew it had been a tragedy. That was in 1868.

The General *(cont.)*

This was the same general who came to the valley of the Little Bighorn in June, 1876, looking for Indians. If he had come a few days earlier, or a few days later, the story of the battle would probably have been much different. The Sioux and Cheyenne who gathered together in the valley were not there to stage a war. They were a little concerned that General Crook, whose troops had been routed by the warriors of Crazy Horse several days earlier, would return, but they did not give much thought to the possibility that the one they knew as "Long Hair" would come looking for them.

Generals Terry, Gibbon, and Custer had agreed to smash the Hunkpapa Sioux village of Sitting Bull and planned to meet for an early morning attack on June 26. Custer was to wait to attack until all three forces could meet. He had several Crow and Arikara Indian scouts with him who tried to point out that the group of Indians was huge, "more of them than there are bullets in your soldiers' guns." But Custer could not see the danger. All he saw was his chance to gain glory and honor, and instead of waiting until the time was right for his meeting with Terry and Gibbon, he divided up his men and charged down to his death. All of his men died with him, their bodies spread for miles across the countryside.

No member of Custer's Seventh Cavalry lived to tell the tale of exactly what happened that day. By the time the army came to collect its dead, all of the bodies except one had been mutilated and most of them were scalped. It was said that none of them, except perhaps Tom Custer, the general's brother, were recognizable.

For years, the popular press, Buffalo Bill's Wild West Show, and Hollywood put forth a picture of a gallant officer on top of a hill making his "last stand" against a murderous horde of savages. But that is not quite the way it was. The story told at the monument marking the site of the battle was that Custer was killed near the top of the hill, surrounded by his men. No one knows for sure, but many years after the battle, Pretty–shield, the wife of Custer's Crow scout, Goes-ahead, said that her husband had seen Custer die. The story Goes-ahead told his wife was that Custer, known to the Crows as Son-of-the-morning-star, rode down to the river valley ahead of his men just as he always did. His interpreter, Mitch Boyer, and his flag bearer rode on each side of him. Just as he got to the water's edge, Custer was shot along with the other two. Total confusion then broke out as Indians "swarmed across the river like bees from a hive." Gunsmoke and dust flew up until one could not see one's hand in front of one's face, but it only lasted, at most, half an hour. When the smoke cleared, Custer and all his men were dead. According to Goes-ahead, Custer was the first one killed.

Buffalo Bill

Whatever really happened, Custer became an instant hero to a public hungry for tales of courage and daring. It is not even known for certain exactly how many soldiers died that day, and skeletons have been found near the remnants of rotted uniforms as recently as the 1950's. For the rest of her life, Custer's wife, Libby, did her part to polish Custer's stature in the public eye, and Buffalo Bill reenacted the popular version of Custer's last stand in arenas from America to Europe.

Why didn't Goes-ahead tell the public his story of how Custer died? Who knows? Anti-Indian feeling was very high at that time, and the buffalo were gone. Crow Indians had to feed their families, and working for the army was a way for many of them to do that. Maybe he had learned from Custer that the white man did not want to hear what he knew, and maybe he found it safer just to tell the white man what the white man wanted to hear. Perhaps the story will never be known in its entirety.

The General *(cont.)*

Time has not dealt kindly with Custer, in any event. For over a century, the site of the battlefield was called the Custer Monument. But in 1991, because of new information which had come to light over the years, Custer's name was taken off the monument, and it was renamed as a monument to the Battle of the Little Bighorn. The battle was the last important one with the white man which the Indians won. Within a few short years, the buffalo were gone and the Indians were on reservations. Now, the site of the battle includes a veteran's cemetery.

Activity

Choose the scenario from 1–4 below that you think was likeliest to have happened given the following facts (which are the ones we know in certainty).

   a. General Custer and all his men were killed on June 25, 1876, in a battle with Sioux and Cheyennes at the Little Bighorn River. There were no survivors from his troops. There were Sioux and Cheyenne survivors, and Crow scouts who survived, but none of the scouts except Curly claimed to have seen the battle. The exact number of Indians killed that day is unknown.

1. Rain-in-the-face, a Hunkpapa Sioux chief, bragged in later years that he had killed Custer on the hill and that he had killed Tom Custer, the general's brother, then cut out his heart and eaten a bite of it. Rain-in-the-face had once said that someday he would kill Tom Custer and eat his heart, and he claimed to have kept his promise. But Rain-in-the-face was known to be a bragger, and he often told white people stories which were not true to make himself look big and brave.

2. Goes-ahead, one of Custer's Crow Indian scouts, said that Custer was shot and fell into the water at the edge of the river, a good half mile or more downhill from where tradition says he died. Goes-ahead said that the Crow scouts then left and made their way back to their village. Goesahead did not tell this story to anyone in the army or to the public. He also said that Curly, a seventeen-year-old scout on his first sortie with the army, got sick and ran away as soon as he saw what was going to happen.

3. Curly claimed to be the only survivor of the battle. He said Custer was killed on the hill, but the Sioux who heard him say this said that he could not have seen what happened because he was a coward and had run away. Nonetheless, Curly's story was widely publicized at the time.

4. Libby Custer said her husband was a great hero who died fighting with his troops.

   Now, decide which account is true, and write an account for the newspaper telling the true story of what happened at the Little Bighorn River on June 25, 1876. Be sure to include who, what, where, when, and why the event happened as you say it did.

Dull Knife, Little Wolf, and the Long Way Home

The Northern Cheyenne, Dull Knife and Little Wolf, did not want to go to Indian Territory far from their native home in the Black Hills, but the white man wanted their land. Gold had been found there, and in the Moon When the Ponies Shed, nearly 1000 Northern Cheyenne left their beloved Black Hills for Indian Territory.

They thought the treaty they had signed in 1868 promised they could stay on the reservation with the Sioux at Fort Robinson, but the Indian Bureau now told them the treaty said, ". . . or on a reservation set apart for the Southern Cheyenne." The reservation was in Indian Territory. They had been promised by General Crook that they only had to go down and look around, and if they did not like what they saw, they could return home. The buffalo were almost gone, and they were becoming dependent on the Great Father for food, so they said, "Okay, we'll go look."

They traveled for almost one hundred sleeps, and on August 5, 1877, they arrived at Fort Reno on the Cheyenne-Arapaho reservation. It was customary for the Cheyenne to provide a feast for guests, and when the newcomers from the north arrived, the Southern Cheyenne provided what hospitality they could. It amounted to a little watery soup and nothing else.

The Northerners were appalled. They had been told this was a better place for them than their home, yet now they learned that the place to which they had come had no wild game, no clear water, and the rations given by the Indian agents were too little to satisfy the rumbling bellies of the Southerners already there, much less an additional nine hundred. Beside that, the weather was almost unbearable with hot, humid summer skies, mosquitoes, and dust blowing in the wind.

Little Wolf told the agent that they had taken a look and now were ready to go back. They did not want to stay in this barren place. The agent told them that was not possible unless the Great Father in Washington gave his approval, which was not going to happen. "Wait," the agent said. "We are bringing up a whole herd of cattle from Texas for you to eat." They waited.

When the cattle came, they were only able to make soup from the meat because it was so tough they could not eat it otherwise. Then the people started to become sick with fevers, chills, aching bones, and malaria. When Little Wolf and Dull Knife complained, the agent came and agreed that the people were starving and in a very bad way. They had been promised they would be fed, but the only food they had been given was tough, stringy beef and contaminated flour. There was no medicine for those who were sick with the shaking disease. They were not even allowed to hunt buffalo until the winter, and when they did, all they found were rotting carcasses and ghostly heaps of bones left by white hunters who only wanted the hides. So they killed coyotes and ate them, and when those were gone, they started killing their dogs for food. Some people even wanted to eat the horses, but they decided to save those in case they were able to go back north. Finally the chiefs decided: they would return home, permission or no.

Dull Knife, Little Wolf, and the Long Way Home *(cont.)*

On September 9, Little Wolf and Dull Knife told their people to pack and get ready to leave. Two hundred and ninety-seven men, women, and children left their tipis standing and started north. They did not have enough horses for everyone, so they took turns riding and walking. They traveled without stopping for three days, and after crossing the Cimarron River 150 miles (240 km) north of Fort Reno, they stopped in a sheltered canyon to rest. The blue soldiers caught up with them and tried to talk them into returning, but Little Wolf said, "We are going north."

The soldiers began firing, but the Cheyenne had chosen their position well and had the soldiers trapped. Gradually the Cheyenne slipped away, leaving warriors to cover for them until all had gone, but they did not get away easily, and the soldiers followed. Whenever they could, the people took fresh horses, leaving their worn ones behind.

Ten thousand soldiers, ranchers, cowboys, and settlers all joined to pursue the fleeing Cheyenne. Five times they were caught by soldiers, but each time they managed to slip away. They kept to the roughest country so the soldiers could not use their big guns. After six weeks their clothing and blankets were in tatters, they were short of horses, and thirty-four people were missing, most of them dead from the white man's bullets. The people were weak from hunger and exhaustion. Some wanted to head for Red Cloud's agency, which was closer than home, but Little Wolf said no.

The group split up, some following Little Wolf north, the rest following Dull Knife toward Red Cloud's agency. In a driving snowstorm, Dull Knife's group was surrounded by soldiers. "We only want to go to Red Cloud," he said. "He is no longer where you thought he was," the blue soldier chief said. "He is now at Fort Robinson in Dakota. We will take you there."

Dull Knife's group had no choice but to go with the soldiers, but they did not trust them so they dismantled their weapons and hid them. The women hid them under their skirts and tied the small pieces to their clothing as though they were ornaments. The next morning, the soldiers told them to turn in their weapons. They turned in old, broken ones. When they arrived at Fort Robinson, they were given a barracks, blankets, and food. Everything seemed all right. Then a new commander came.

The new commander was named Wessells, and he did not believe in putting up with any nonsense. When orders came to send the Cheyenne back to Indian Territory, he said they had to go. Dull Knife refused. He said if they tried to make them go back, his people would kill themselves. The War Department told them to go immediately. Dull Knife said no. Wessells gave them five days to decide to go during which time they would not receive food, water, or wood for their stoves.

So the people huddled in their unheated building, trying to keep the little ones warm in the January cold. Snow fell each night, and they scraped it off the window sills for water, but they had nothing to eat. After five days, Wessells summoned Dull Knife to his office. "Will you go now?" he asked. Dull Knife said no. Wessells told him to let the women and children out so they would not suffer. Still Dull Knife said no. "We will die here together," they all said. Wessells left, and the soldiers put iron bars and chains over the doors.

After dark, they took up some planks and pulled out five gun barrels. They put the guns back together and painted their faces. The women put their things under the windows. They shot the guards and poured out of the building, grabbing the guns of the dead guards as they passed.

Dull Knife, Little Wolf, and the Long Way Home *(cont.)*

More than half the warriors were killed in the first hour. By morning the soldiers had recaptured sixty-five women and children and herded them back to Fort Robinson. Only thirty-eight made it out. Several days later the soldiers found thirty-two more, but by the time they got back to the fort, only nine were still alive.

Dull Knife and five others had not been found by the soldiers, and toward the end of January he and his party made it to the Pine Ridge reservation where Red Cloud was. In the meantime, Little Wolf and his small group of followers spent the winter in concealed pits which they had dug in the banks of Chokecherry Creek. At last, the soldiers found them there, and they were taken to Fort Keogh, where they spent the rest of the winter.

Many people—labelled "bleeding idealists" by the masses—thought this treatment was terrible. These were people being treated this way, not dogs. They thought it was disgraceful to do such things to women and children. Finally, after many months, the women and children still at Fort Robinson were brought back to Red Cloud's

Red Cloud

agency at Pine Ridge where they joined Dull Knife. Sometime later they were given a reservation on the Tongue River in Montana where the people were allowed to be together again. By the time this happened, there were not many of the people left, and they feared that soon there would be none, soon no one would remember their names or what they had done.

But they were wrong. People do remember, and they do recall their names. The Cheyenne still live in Montana. The name of Dull Knife is known to all of them. The people survived, and no one forgets the bravery of those who said, "I would rather die than leave my home, the place where my father and his father lived before me."

Activities

1. On the map on page 75, trace the route taken by Little Wolf, Dull Knife, and the people.

2. Divide a piece of paper in half crosswise, and draw a line down the middle. On the left side of the page, draw a picture of how the people looked when they were in Indian Territory. On the right side of the page, draw a picture of how the people looked when they got their reservation in Montana. Then write two paragraphs explaining your pictures.

Dull Knife, Little Wolf, and the Long Way Home *(cont.)*

Cheyenne Indian Region 1846-1879

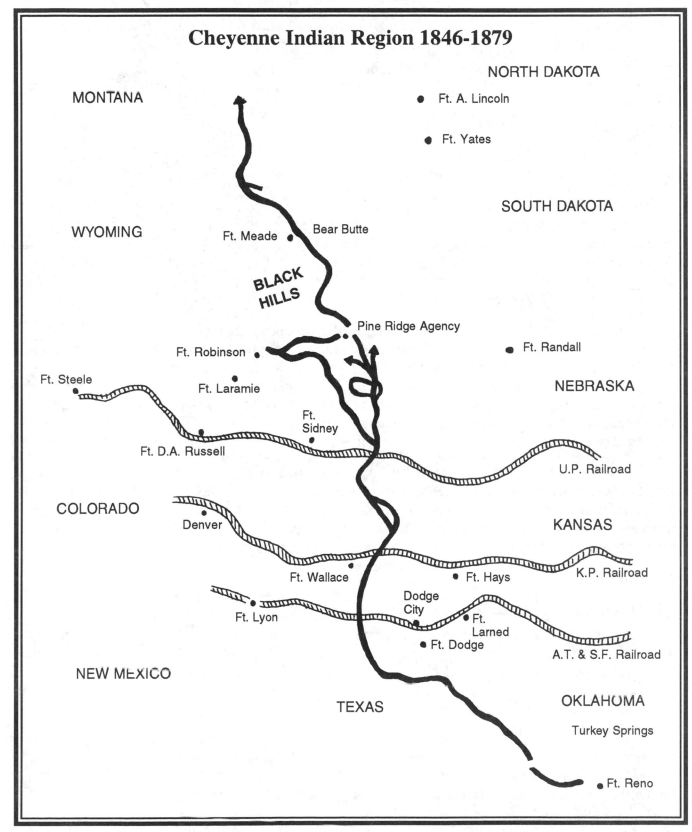

The Buffalo Hunters

For many years, the natives of the Great Plains depended on the buffalo, or bison, for their lives. However, this had not always been so. Long ago before anyone could remember, the people were farmers, hunters, and gatherers of wild foods. That was in the days before they came to the bountiful plains teeming with the wonderful walking array of raw material for meat, clothing, and shelter called the buffalo.

For many generations the people lived on the plains. The Absaroka, called Crow Indians by the white man, believed the Great Spirit, Maker of All, had made their country first and then created them to live on it because the Great Spirit had put it in just the right place for them.

Young boys and girls spent their childhoods learning to do what they would do when they were grown. The boys learned about making war, stealing horses, hunting the buffalo, and all the ways a man could gain prestige with his people. The girls learned about tanning buffalo hides into soft, warm robes and garments, making snug tipis, cooking and preserving the tasty, fat meat of the buffalo, and growing up to be a good woman.

What a marvel this buffalo was! Its meat was plentiful with good, fat ribs to roast over the fire. Its hide, when worked and softened by the women, could be made into beautiful robes, beaded moccasins, and shields to protect the warriors when they went to war. The hide could also be tanned and sewn to make cozy tipis which provided cool, restful shade in the summer and warm, weather-tight shelters in the coldest winter. The buffalo's bones could be carved and honed into useful tools for tanning the robes and digging wild roots to supplement the meat diet.

Hunting the buffalo was not always as easy as it was after the horse came. The horse was not native to North America, and before the people got it from those in the south, they had to resort to clever ways of tricking the buffalo into going where they could be easily killed. One way the hunters did this was by having the people line up in a big V-shaped position pointing toward a cliff. Then, the people would wave blankets and yell to scare the buffalo and get them running toward the cliff. Since the buffalo were not very smart, once they began stampeding in a certain direction, they wouldn't shift directions, and over the cliff they would go to their deaths.

Sometimes, instead of having people stand on the sides, the hunters would light little fires in a V with handfuls of sweet sage and let the fires direct the buffalo toward the cliff as the hunters yelled at them from behind. The women would wait near the bottom of the cliff where the buffalo were falling and begin butchering the animals as they fell, finishing off the ones not yet dead by knocking them in the heads. They would work quickly to cut up some parts to roast for the evening meal and keep the tongues and other parts to dry and save for the days when no buffalo were near. They would cut off the hides carefully and scrape off the fat underneath, and then they would soak them in liver and brains to soften them before tanning.

Before the people had horses, the tipis were not very big. Then, they would make a tipi from only about fourteen hides because that made as big a load as a big dog could drag on a travois. After the people got horses, they could have much larger and more luxurious tipis because a horse could pull a bigger load than a dog.

76

The Buffalo Hunters *(cont.)*

Being able to move easily was important when you traveled frequently to follow the buffalo herds. After they had the horse, the hunters could go right up to the buffalo. A good hunter could send an arrow straight through the animal's body, killing it with one arrow, and sometimes be able to retrieve the arrow for use at another time.

The good times ended when the white men began coming in droves. At first, there were only a few white trappers and traders coming into the country. Most of the native peoples befriended the white men and helped them find good places to trap beavers. Some of these white men would live with the Indians for awhile, marrying their women and adopting the life of their new compatriots. But after awhile, the white men came in bigger and bigger numbers until there were more of them than there were buffalo. These white men did not kill just so they could feed and shelter their families. They hunted the buffalo for its hides which they could sell for big money in the East, and sometimes they shot the buffalo just for fun. The good meat, even those delicious fat ribs, was left on the prairie to rot because there were more of them dead than the wolves and coyotes could eat.

In 1870, by the white man's calendar, there were an estimated 15,000,000 buffalo roaming the Great Plains. Five years later, there were only 1,000,000, and soon there were none. The missing ones had all been killed. Some of the old Indians thought someone was hiding the buffalo, that he had managed to put them all into a big hole or cave somewhere, and that if the people could just find that hole, they would again have their food and shelter supply. How could the plains be full of them one day and most of them be gone the next?

But the giant herds of buffalo were gone for good, and the people of the Great Plains did not know what to do. How could they provide for their families? Even the deer and the antelope were in short supply. Finally, their only recourse was to let the government feed and shelter them, so they reluctantly went to the reservations to accept what food they could get from the Great White Father, although not everyone gave in at first.

The Great White Father wanted the men to plant crops and become farmers. How could they do this? The Earth was their mother! They could not cut into their mother's body! So some tried to fight the Great White Father's blue soldiers, but in the end they all had to go the way of the soldiers or die. The young men no longer had their traditional ways to gain prestige with their people, and the young women after awhile forgot how to build a buffalo–hide tipi or make one so snug and tight it fit like a leaf tipi— the tiny tipis young girls practiced making from leaves before they could graduate to the real things.

It was a hard time for the people. To have their whole way of living taken from them in so few snows was very difficult. It took many more snows to adjust to another way, but the people were strong and they did adjust.

Activities

1. Imagine that you are a young man or woman of the Great Plains. The buffalo you have been raised to think of as your main source of food and shelter have suddenly disappeared. Write about the way you feel and what you will do. Where will you go? How will you gain prestige and honor with your people?

The Buffalo Hunters *(cont.)*

2. The buffalo-hide tipi was one of the simplest, but also most beautiful, homes ever devised by man. A large group of tipis sitting next to a clear stream, smoke coming up from the holes at the top, formed a scene which caused a plains native to say, "My heart was as light as breath feathers as I looked out over my village."

   To make a model tipi, follow these directions.

Materials:

- white or light-colored heavy fabric
- approximately eighteen 18" (45 cm) sticks or wooden dowels
- cord

Directions:

1. Use the pattern below to cut fourteen to eighteen "buffalo hides" from the fabric.

2. Stand the sticks or dowels on end, sloping them together near the top and tying them with cord.

3. Work with the hides until you can get them to fit together, making a cover in one piece by sewing or gluing them together to form a tipi when wrapped around the outside of the sticks. Remember to leave a hole at the top for smoke to escape. Also, two sticks should be loose so they can be moved to open or close the "ears" of the smoke hole at the top of the tipi.

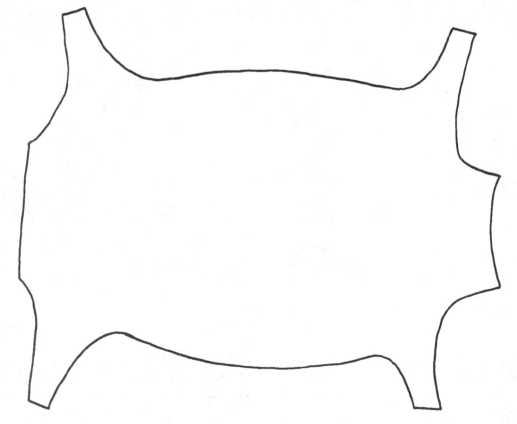

Hero Stories of the Great Plains

One can tell much about a people and what is important to them by hearing their hero stories. These three stories are examples of those told by the natives of the Great Plains.

Orphan Boy and the Mud Ponies
(Pawnee)

Long ago before the people had horses, dogs were the only animals who helped the people by carrying burdens for them. At that time, there was a poor boy who did not have any family or anyone to care for him. He spent much of his time going from one tipi to the next, trying to get some food to eat, but everyone he went to would chase him away, saying "Go away from here! You have no family. You are nobody. Stop pestering me!"

All except one. The chief was a kind man, and sometimes when the Orphan Boy came to him, he would give food to the child. The chief felt sorry for Orphan Boy, and at times he even gave him moccasins or leggings to protect the boy's legs and feet from the cold. There were those who would criticize the chief for this, but he said to them, "Tirawa, the Great Spirit, knows about this boy. He will watch him as he grows up, and someday he may be a great chief." The people laughed at the chief for saying this, although not to his face for that would have been unkind.

Orphan Boy had a dream. He saw two ponies drop down from heaven for him. These ponies were very clear to him in his dream. He could see their manes and tails and the way they were shaped. When the people broke camp in order to move to another campsite, he tarried behind and, with mud, made shapes which looked like the ponies in his dream. Then he placed the ponies in his robe and ran ahead to follow the people. Just before he got back into camp, he placed the mud ponies outside the village.

Early each morning he visited his ponies. He would take them down to the creek and pretend that they were drinking, and he would take them to grass and pretend that they were eating. He did this for many moons, and when the people returned to their permanent village, he continued to do this, watering and feeding his ponies.

One night the boy had another dream. He dreamed that Tirawa had opened up the heavens and dropped two ponies down for him. He heard Tirawa singing, and he remembered the song. He went out onto the nearby hill and sang the song. The people heard him singing and wondered where he had gotten the song and what it meant.

While Orphan Boy was singing, he heard a voice say to him, "This song was given to you by Tirawa. Tirawa will also give you a dance. Go tonight to see your mud ponies, and you will find that they have become real. You will become a great chief."

Orphan boy did as Tirawa told him. He ran to where he had hidden the mud ponies, and when he got there, he saw them big and alive with graceful manes and tails. He caught the ponies and took them to the village, and the people were amazed because they had never before seen horses. The boy grew up to become a great chief, and he always cared for the ones who had no families of their own.

Hero Stories of the Great Plains *(cont.)*

Sweet Medicine Shows His Power
(Cheyenne)

A woman got married. When her second child was born, she named him Sweet Medicine. She soon noticed that this boy could do things which other children could not. When he was yet a baby, he could understand everything that was said around him, and after he learned to talk, he said to his father, "Father, next time you go on a hunt, bring back for me a yellow calf. Skin it, taking the whole skin in one piece, because I want a yellow robe to wear."

The boy had the power to make his father do what he wished him to do, so the next time the father went on a hunt, he brought back a yellow calfskin for his son. The boy was happy, and he asked his mother to dress it for him and make it into a robe. He wore this robe inside out, and he wore it until he had grown too big for it. Then he said to his father, "Father, next time you go on a hunt, kill for me a yearling calf, and skin it like you did the other one."

His father did as his son asked, and the boy's mother made for him a robe with the head still attached. And again, several years later when he had outgrown this robe, Sweet Medicine told his father, "Father, next time you go on a hunt, kill for me a two-year-old calf the color of coal, because I wish to have a black robe."

When Sweet Medicine had about seventeen snows, there was going to be a big medicine dance. The people with great spiritual power were all going to be at the dance. The young man told his father, "Father, I wish to go to this dance. I, myself, wish to dance."

"Son," the father said to Sweet Medicine, "the people who will be at this dance are people with great spiritual power. They will show what they can do with their power. You are only a boy. You can do nothing."

"I wish to go, and I will wear my new buffalo robe. I will carry your bow with its string around my neck."

The father asked, "Son, why are you going to wear the string around your neck?"

The young man replied, "I am going to break my neck. My buffalo robe must be painted red. Please paint me as I tell you."

The father painted his son all over with red paint, and Sweet Medicine painted the bowstring red. His father asked him, "Son, what shall I do if you break your neck?"

Sweet Medicine said, "After I have pulled my head away from my body, it will fall to the ground while my body remains standing up. Take my body and lay it with my head next to it, pointing east where the sun comes up. Then cover me with my robe."

The father took Sweet Medicine to the lodge where the dance was to be held. A number of people were watching. They saw Sweet Medicine coming with an eagle feather in his hair. "See! Sweet Medicine is coming!" they all said.

The father said, "My son wishes to dance," and the men inside let Sweet Medicine come into the lodge, and he sat on the right side.

After the dance began, Sweet Medicine stood up to dance. The men watching remarked that Sweet Medicine was the best dancer of all. They had another smoke and another dance.

Hero Stories of the Great Plains *(cont.)*

Sweet Medicine Shows His Power *(cont.)*

As Sweet Medicine was dancing, he kept time with his bowstring in both hands. They all sat down, and then they got up for a third time to dance. Sweet Medicine continued to keep time with the bowstring around his neck. Suddenly, his head fell to the ground. His eyes were open, and he looked at the people. His body remained standing up with the bowstring in his hands. The people were very frightened, as you can imagine. They called out to one another, "Sweet Medicine has broken his neck!"

Everyone sat down, and the dancing stopped. Sweet Medicine's father took the body and lay it on the ground with the head in place, toward the east where the sun rises. After a short time, Sweet Medicine stood up facing the sunrise. He took his robe in both hands, shook it lightly, and as soon as he stopped, a wind whistled in from the north. The people were amazed because they knew he had called the wind, and it came to him.

Sweet Medicine went over to sit on the right side of the door. He rubbed his bowstring down four times. Then the people feasted.

Sweet Medicine Foretells the Future
(Cheyenne)

Sweet Medicine lived with the people for a very long time. He lived for four or five generations. Even after the other people had grown old and died, Sweet Medicine still lived on. In the summer he was a young man, and when fall came he began to dry up like the grass dried up, and he began to look older. In the winter, he was a very old man, but he would become young again as soon as spring had come. At last he died, but before he did, he told the people:

"I will not be with you much longer. Now I am getting old. I have lived as long as I want to live, but before I die, I want to tell you something. Do not forget what I shall tell you now, and do not forget what I have taught you. When I am dead, I want you to come together often to talk over these things. When you do, always call my name.

"A time is coming when other people will arrive. You will fight them, and you will kill each other. One tribe will want the land of another tribe, and you will always fight over it."

Pointing south, Sweet Medicine continued, "Far away in that direction there is another kind of buffalo. This animal has long hair hanging down from its neck, and its tail drags the ground. It has a round hoof, not split like the buffalo's, and it has teeth both above and below in its mouth. You will be able to ride on the animal.

"The buffalo will disappear, and when they are gone, you will have to eat an animal that is spotted. When you come to this last time, you people will turn gray very young, and you will have to marry those who are related to you. You will reach a point when you will feel shame for nothing, and you will act crazy.

"Soon, there will come to you a people who have hair on their faces and whose skin is white. When this time comes, you will become controlled by them. These white people will spread over the land, and you will disappear."

Sweet Medicine died that summer when he was still a young man. His brother was also alive until then, but when Sweet Medicine died, his brother did not. He stayed middle-aged for many generations, but, at last, he died, too, having lived even longer than Sweet Medicine.

Hero Stories of the Great Plains *(cont.)*

Activities

1. Hero stories show the hero to be stronger, braver, and more physically adept than the average man. Many Indian stories tell of someone with humble beginnings who comes to be such a hero. "Orphan Boy and the Mud Ponies" is a good example of this kind of story, because to the Plains native, none was lower than a person with no family. One of the worst insults that could be thrown at someone was, "You have no family!" The person who could surmount his humble beginnings to become a hero was larger than life.

   • Can you think of any national heroes for whom this was also true? List them.

2. Find a story in the contemporary literature of your culture which shows a hero doing superhuman deeds. Learn the story and tell it to the class. In discussion, explore the possible reasons a person might become a hero to his or her own people.

3. What kinds of qualities might someone from the following categories have in order to be considered a hero in his or her field?

   • contemporary professional football player
   • contemporary movie star
   • current Olympic champion
   • famous president or prime minister
   • soldier
   • Nobel prize-winning peacemaker
   • fire fighter

4. Which of the above categories do you consider to be heroic?

5. Finish this sentence: A hero is someone who . . . .

6. Name two people who you think are heroes. One should be someone you know and the other should be someone you do not know but admire as a hero. Explain why these people are your heroes.

7. What might you do that would make you feel like a hero?

8. What is the most heroic thing you have ever done?

Metaphors for Feelings

Instead of saying, "I feel sad," or "She is old," as an English speaker might do, the Crows paint pictures of things with words. In the Crow language, expression often comes in the forms of metaphors and similes.

Metaphors are created when two different things are compared to one another in a phrase. An example of a metaphor in English is "the evening of life," which suggests that a certain age is the ending part of life just as evening is the ending of day. In this phrase, the time of life is compared to the time of day as though they were the same.

Another kind of term in the Crow language is the *simile*. In a simile, two unlike things are compared to each other by using the words "as" or "like." An example of an English simile is "eyes like stars," in which the eyes are said to have the qualities of stars.

Read the following phrases that describe feelings as they would be said in Crow. Write what you believe to be the meaning of each phrase and determine whether it is a metaphor or a simile. Notice that most of these expressions begin with the word "heart." The term "breath feathers" indicates the very light, downy feathers found on a baby bird or certain underparts of a bird's body.

1. My heart sang. _____

2. Our hearts floated like breath feathers. _____

3. My heart stuck in my throat, and I could hardly speak. _____

4. My heart fell to the ground. _____

5. He was so old, his skin crackled and tore when he moved about. _____

Questions: Why would the Crow use the word "heart" in these sayings? What do we sometimes think of when we talk about the heart? Can you think of any phrases in English containing the word "heart"? Write that phrase, or phrases, on the back.

Buffalo Math

1. The following buffalo require the indicated amount of grassy land to provide them with enough food for one year. What is the average amount of land needed to support one buffalo?

   Buffalo A = 31 acres (12 hectares) _____

   Buffalo B = 26 acres (10 hectares) _____

   Buffalo C = 43 acres (17 hectares) _____

   Buffalo D = 27 acres (11 hectares) _____

   Buffalo E = 35 acres (14 hectares) _____

   Buffalo F = 39 acres (16 hectares) _____

2. If it takes 37 acres (15 hectares) to support one buffalo for one year, how many acres (hectares) would be needed to support 1.5 million buffalo? _____

   Nine million buffalo? _____

   Fifteen million buffalo? _____

3. If one buffalo drinks two gallons (8 liters) of water each day, how many buffalo can survive on 1,754,004 gallons (7,016,016 liters) for one week? _____

4. If it takes 32 acres (12.8 hectares) to support one buffalo, how many buffalo can a rancher raise on his Montana spread if he sets aside 100,000 acres (40,000 hectares) for their use and does not plan to supplement the food of his buffalo with hay or grain? _____

5. If a buffalo cow has one calf each year, and a herd begins with six cows, how long will it take for the herd to grow to 100, assuming that half the calves born are males? **Hint:** Use decimals and round to the nearest .5 each step. _____

6. If the average buffalo naturally lives to the age of seventeen years, how many buffalo will die from natural causes in a herd of 500 each year? _____

7. If one buffalo provides enough food to feed four people for seven days, how many buffalo will be needed to feed 250 people for 28 days? _____

8. If it takes eighteen buffalo hides to cover one tipi, how many hides will it take to cover 346 tipis?

   _____

9. A Plains native village contained 492 people. If six people lived in each tipi, and the tipis averaged 17 hides each, how many buffalo hides would it take to make tipis for these people?

   _____

10. Inside each tipi in problem #9 were robes for the inhabitants to sit on and cover themselves. If each inhabitant used 5 buffalo robes, how many robes were inside each tipi?

    _____

    How many robes were needed for the 492 people? _____

Prairie Math

Solve the following problems which might have been faced by a resident on the Great Plains.

1. A scout leaves camp at 8 AM with instructions to cover as much distance as possible and return at 4 PM. If his pony averages 15 miles (24 kilometers) per hour, and he takes an hour for lunch, how many miles (kilometers) can he ride before starting back? _____

   How many miles (kilometers) will he ride altogether? _____

2. A good archer can shoot an arrow 90 yards (81 meters) at an average speed of 30 yards (27 meters) per second. If he can keep shooting three arrows consecutively so that the three are in the air at once at even intervals and the arrows all land in the exact same place, how many seconds apart will they land? _____

3. If a racing horse can run an average of 27 miles (45 kilometers) per hour, how long will it take it to run 3 miles (5 kilometers)? _____

4. If an Indian pony can drag 155 lbs. (70 kilograms) on a travois, and the average tipi weighs 31 lbs. (14 kilograms), how many ponies and travois will be needed to drag 45 tipis?

   _____

5. A horse can eat 10 lbs. (5 kilograms) of grass in one hour. If it eats 4½ hours per day, how many pounds (kilograms) of grass will it eat in one day? _____

   In one week? _____

   In one year (364 days)? _____

6. If a village can move 1½ miles (2⅖ kilometers) per hour, and it travels ten hours in a day, how far can it travel in one day? _____

   In one week? _____

   In one month (30 days)? _____

7. If a man can swim approximately 2½ miles (4 kilometers) in one hour, and he can swim from 9 AM until 3 PM without losing speed, how far will he swim? _____

8. If it takes a village 250 years to grow from 45 people to 145 people, how many more years will it need to grow to 495 people? _____

9. If the villagers make 20 lbs. (9 kilograms) of pemmican from 5 quarts (5 liters) of berries, how many quarts (liters) of berries will they need to make 175 lbs. (81 kilograms) of pemmican to last the winter? _____

10. If a village of 500 people eats 400 buffalo during a four-month winter stay in camp, how many buffalo will be needed the following year when they camp with an additional 575 people?

    _____

Naming the Months of the Year

Have you ever thought about why the months are named as they are? Not all people call the months by these same names, nor does everyone have the same year. Different cultures often use different methods for dividing time into segments, which is ultimately easier to deal with than infinite time. And time, itself, is thought of differently by different people.

The following list contains the names of the "moons" of the Arapaho which correspond with the months of January to December to some extent. However, there are some major differences between these names and the ones you are probably most familiar with.

- Moon of Snow Blowing Spirits in the Wind *(January)*
- Moon of Frost Shining in the Wind *(February)*
- Moon When the Buffalo Calves Are Born *(March)*
- Moon of Ice Breaking in the River *(April)*
- Moon When the Ponies Shed Their Shaggy Hair *(May)*
- Moon When the Hot Weather Begins *(June)*
- Moon When the Buffalo Bellow *(July)*
- Moon When the Chokecherries Begin to Ripen *(Late July)*
- Moon of Geese Shedding Their Feathers *(August)*
- Moon of the Drying Grass *(September)*
- Moon of the Falling Leaves *(October)*
- Moon When the Rivers Start to Freeze *(November)*
- Moon of Popping Trees *(December)*

What is the first thing you notice about these names? Probably that they are named for moons rather than months. That is because the Indians used lunar months rather than dividing the year into 12 months as many others do. They did not have printed calendars, but they "carried" calendars in their heads.

Activities

1. In small groups, brainstorm the answers to the following questions, and then come together with the class and discuss your opinions and reasons for those opinions.

   a. What is the second thing you notice about the names of the Arapaho moons?

   b. What did they name their moons after?

   c. Why do you think they named their months after the things above?

   d. If the Indians did not have printed calendars, how would they know when one month ended and another began?

   e. Would time mean the same thing to an Indian of long ago as it does to you today?

   f. Would Indians of long ago have kept schedules of any kind? If so, what would they have been like?

   g. In what times of the year do you think the Indians would be more conscious of time passing than in others?

   h. Since the Plains Indians were not farmers, would they have been particularly interested in plants and when they ripened?

2. Rename the months of our year according to what is important to you. Give reasons for your choices.

Measles and the Native American

When the white man came to North America, he brought some dangerous and destructive things with him which were catastrophic for the natives. One such thing was alcohol, a substance the natives had never used and for which they had built up no tolerance. Even more destructive, because it affected everyone including children, were contagious diseases like smallpox and measles. The natives had no natural immunity for these diseases.

Until recent history, measles were one of the "childhood diseases" thought by European Americans to be a relatively harmless illness that every child would have and recover from. Parents would often intentionally expose their children to others who had one of these diseases so that they would have the disease while they were still young rather than get it in adulthood. Now, however, most people are aware that these diseases can leave a child with serious problems including deafness, blindness, or mental retardation. Occasionally, measles is the cause of another serious illness called encephalitis, an inflammation of the brain. Measles can even cause death.

Most childhood diseases start with the same symptoms that signal a cold or flu: runny nose, fever, sore eyes, and a cough. The person feels sick. With measles, after about three or four days a red rash appears on the head and neck and spreads down to the rest of the body. The rash lasts about three days, and then it starts going away. Often the person comes down with ear and chest infections, diarrhea, or vomiting soon after the rash goes away.

Most of the Europeans who came to North America had either natural immunity or acquired immunity to certain diseases like measles and smallpox. These diseases are caused by viruses or bacterias. Natural immunity is the immunity with which one is born so that person has a built-in protection against certain diseases. Acquired immunity develops either when a person has had a viral or bacterial disease or when he or she has been immunized against it. A mother who breast feeds her baby also will pass down some of her own immunities to her child while it is nursing, which helps protect the baby until the child can acquire immunities of his or her own.

The natives of North America had never had diseases like measles, mumps, chickenpox, and smallpox, and when they were exposed to a white person who had one of those illnesses, they had no resistance to it. Consequently, these diseases spread from one person to another very rapidly, and many people died as a result. When the Europeans first came to North America, there were millions of natives living there in over three hundred tribes, but within a short time, contagious diseases brought by the Europeans had killed somewhere between eighty and ninety per cent of the native population. No one knows exactly how many died, but the number was enormous.

Today there are vaccines available for most of these old diseases. The United States, Canada, and all developed countries require that before starting school a child be immunized against diseases like measles, mumps, and polio, and because of this, those diseases have almost been eliminated. After a worldwide immunization program against smallpox by the World Health Organization, the disease was declared extinct in 1980. However, there are still some areas in undeveloped parts of the world which experience epidemics of one or another.

Use the chart on the next page to tally how many people you know who have either had each of these diseases or have been immunized for them, and total your results. Compare your results with those of your classmates.

Measles and the Native American *(cont.)*

IMMUNIZATION CHART				
	Had It	**Immunized**	**Not Had, Not Immunized**	**Total**
Measles				
Chickenpox				
Mumps				
Smallpox				
Polio				
Total				

Respond

1. Did you find anyone who has not had a disease or been immunized? _____

2. How many young people did you find who have had any of these diseases? _____

3. How many people over thirty had these diseases? _____

4. As a result of your survey, what conclusions can you come to regarding these diseases?

_____

_____

_____

_____

_____

Ring and Pin Game

There are many versions of the ring and pin game, at least one for nearly every tribe on the North American continent. This simple version made from hollow pieces of deer bone was a favorite of the Oglala Sioux (the tribe of Crazy Horse) and was played by both women and men.

Several *phalangeal* (longer than wide; hollow inside) bones are strung together on string or sinew 15 inches (37.5 cm) long. At one end of the string is tied a sharp-pointed stick or stiff piece of wire 5 inches (12.5 cm) long. Seven loops of variegated glass beads hang from the end of the string opposite the pointed stick. The beads add weight to the end of the string.

Holding the pointed stick or wire, the player throws the bones upward in a quick motion and then jerks them back again by the cord to which they are attached. He tries to catch the bones with the pointed stick so that the stick goes through one or more of them.

This can be played by one or several players. Each bone caught counts one point, although some tribes counted one point for the first caught, two points for the second, three for the third, and so forth. Sometimes bets were made on the outcome of the game, but at other times it was played simply for amusement.

Activity

You can make your own version of this game with a straight piece of sturdy wire or a pointed stick, cord for the sinew, and large wooden beads, hollowed acorns, or other small, hollow objects for the rings.

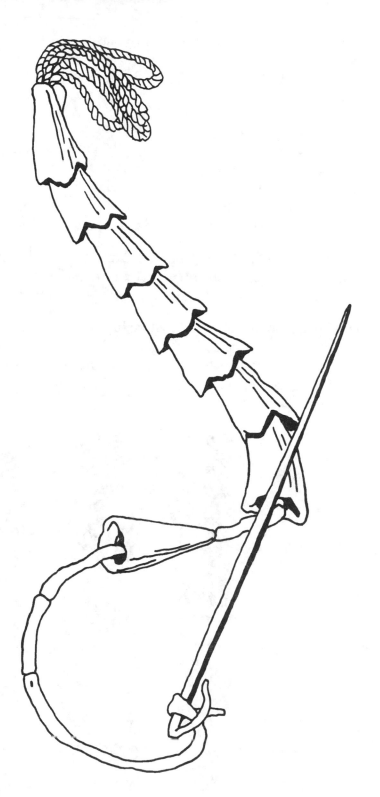

Great Plains Indian Beadwork

The natives of the Great Plains were master artists and craftsmen who loved to decorate almost everything they used or wore. Many exquisite examples of the clothing, moccasins, and utility containers such as parfleches, tobacco and pipe cases, and quivers may be seen in museums featuring Native American exhibits.

Before the white man came to North America, designs were done in materials which were native to the continent. Nothing was wasted. Shells, porcupine quills, natural paints, and even elk teeth were used. The designs used by a tribe were passed down by family members, and the clothing thus trimmed was highly prized. Designs were traditional, and many of them were symbolic. For example, a cross symbolized four winds, and a zigzag line symbolized lightning. Wampum was made from shells which were shaped and polished. Some typical designs are given below.

After the coming of the white man, French traders brought glass beads made in Italy to trade for furs. The large ones called *pony beads* were soon used to make decorations formerly made with porcupine quills. After about 1850, however, *seed beads* from Czechoslovakia became the favorites.

Originally, the thread used for stringing came from sinew, the tough, fibrous, connective tissue of animals. This would be split into strands fine enough to thread through the beads. When cotton thread became available, however, it soon took the place of sinew. Today, nylon thread may also be used, and crochet thread no. 30 is a good choice for loom threads. (Waxing the threads prevents tangling.)

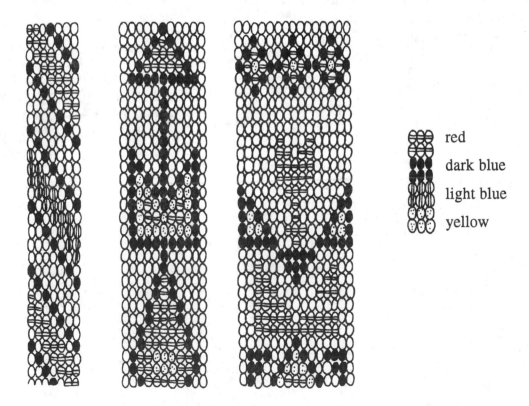

red
dark blue
light blue
yellow

Activity

Make your own design on graph paper. Use fine-tipped markers or colored pencils.

Great Plains Indian Beadwork *(cont.)*

Making a Loom

Materials:

- 1 piece white pine or similar wood ½" (1.25 cm) thick
- 2 piccccs white pine 4" x 6" x ½" (10 cm x 15 cm x 1.25 cm)
- ten 1" (2.5 cm) screws
- 1 curtain spring about ³⁄₈" (1 cm) in diameter (found in variety or hardware stores)
- 2 small, large-headed carpet tacks

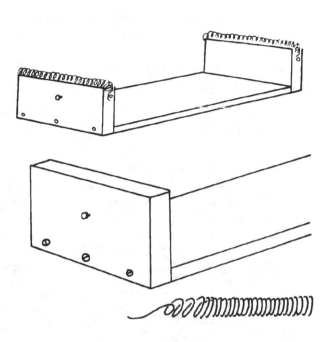

Directions:

Assemble as illustrated.

Beadwork Headband

Materials:

- beads in various colors
- thread (no. 40)
- one package fine bead needles
- one piece beeswax or a candle stub
- graph paper (small size) for planning designs
- colored crayons or pencils

Directions:

1. Tie the thread to the carpet tack at one end.

2. String the thread through the spring and around the carpet tack at the other end. Continue wrapping thread in this way until the width of the rows of thread is the one you wish for your headband.

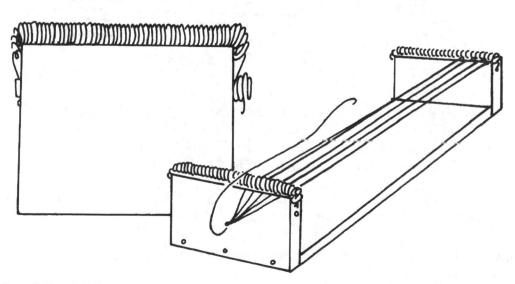

Great Plains Indian Beadwork *(cont.)*

Beadwork Headband *(cont.)*

3. Now that the loom is threaded, the fun begins. Be patient with the first row. It sometimes takes a little effort to get it straight. Once it is complete, however, the rest is easy.

4. Draw a design on graph paper, with one square standing for each bead, and use crayons or pencils to mark the colors.

5. Thread the needle with a long thread. Double it and tie the ends in a knot. Wax the knot and tie it to the outer loom thread nearest you.

6. Pick up the beads needed for the first row, according to your design plan, and thread them on the needle, sliding the beads down to the loom strings. Pass the needle under the loom strings, and with your left index finger move the beads into position with one bead between each pair of strings.

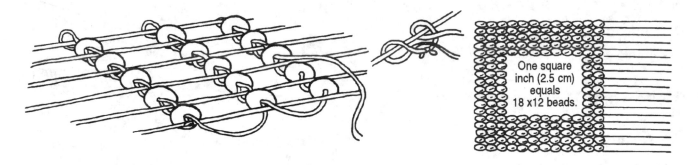

One square inch (2.5 cm) equals 18 x12 beads.

7. Pass the needle back through the loom strings on the opposite side of the first thread. Pull the thread so the beads fit tightly.

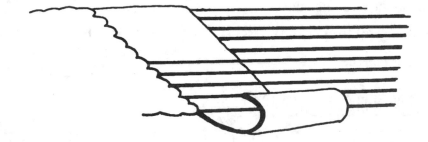

8. Repeat the weaving row by row, following your paper design. When you need to change to a new thread, start your weaving by passing the needle and thread through five or six beads of the last row and then continue. To end a thread without knotting, pass the needle once around the outer loom string and then through four or five beads before cutting.

9. When the beadwork is complete, finish off the ends by placing a piece of gummed paper tape below the loom strings. Cut the loom strings along this tape.

History of the Ceremonial Pipe

Almost every North American child has heard of the pipe used by the Native Americans. These pipes were often called peace pipes because the Natives would always take a pipe into negotiating sessions or when signing treaties with the white man. The pipe and the smoking of tobacco, however, meant much more to the Indians than a symbol of peace. It was the center of a ceremonial rite which had its origin in their mythology and religion.

All of the Plains natives and many other natives, as well, had stories explaining the origin of smoking tobacco and why it was important. The Sioux, for example, believed that in ancient times the Great Spirit stood in the form of a large bird on a wall of rock and called all the tribes to hear him. He broke out a piece of red stone, formed it into a pipe, and smoked it. Wafting the smoke to fan out over the people, he told them that they were made from the smoke, that they must smoke to him through it, and that they must use the red stone only in pipes. The ground where they smoked was holy ground, and they must never carry any weapons onto the ground where the pipe was being smoked. Most of the tribes had similar stories which were regularly told with great reverence. Together, they show how important the smoking of the pipe was to the people.

The raising of tobacco was the only form of agriculture practiced by most of the Plains Indians. Each year they would plant a small plot in a place they would return to several months later for the harvest. The tobacco usually was not smoked alone, but instead other herbs were often placed into the pipe along with it.

The bowls of the pipes themselves were made from a particular soft red stone which could be found only in a few areas of the vast continent. The most important of these areas was near a small town now named Pipestone, Minnesota. Pipes could be found everywhere, however, because of the vast trading system extending over much of North America.

The soft red stone used for the bowls of the pipe is a form of soapstone easily carved with simple tools. Many of the early pipemakers were physically handicapped men who were unable to take part in raids against the enemy. Some of these great pipemakers had names such as One-armed-chief and One-legged-Jim. The ability to carve beautiful pipes was a very specialized craft, highly valued by the Indians, and the carvers were paid by other tribal members for their work.

Many of the early pipes still in existence are exquisitely made, carved into the forms of birds, animals, reptiles, or human beings. They required great patience and skill to make. The tools needed by a pipemaker were saws and scrapers, hammerstones, reamers, gouges, various drill points, and drills. Even an old piece of hoop iron or a broken knife blade could have been used. Only the long stems of the pipe, however, were considered sacred, and these were often very elaborately decorated with carving, beads, dried porcupine quills, feathers, or paint.

The pipe was ceremoniously smoked when preparing for warfare, trading goods and hostages, before ritual dancing, and as part of certain medicine rituals. It sometimes was also a form of hospitality to be shown an important visitor. Many beautiful and artfully decorated accessories were developed around the smoking ceremony. Animal skin pouches for carrying pipe bowls, stems, and tobacco were decorated with porcupine quills, paints, or beads in symbolic designs, and they were often stored with other sacred items in a medicine bundle. Ashes were disposed of in special places, and when a warrior or chief died, his pipe was buried with him.

The Sioux and the Pawnee were considered the master pipemakers, although other tribes also had their own pipemakers. Pipes dating back as far as 2,000 years have been unearthed, but the artistry of pipemaking really got its main developmental impetus after the Europeans arrived during the seventeenth century because they brought with them metal tools. By about 1700, the Dakota Sioux controlled the quarries holding the red stone, and from then on it was distributed only by trade.

History of the Ceremonial Pipe *(cont.)*

White Americans were fascinated by the pipes, and as the westward movement grew, increasing contact with the Indians led to increased trade and also inspired the development of new designs. Some pipes were even decorated with effigies of white politicians and explorers, and they became a source of income for their makers. To ensure that they could continue to control the quarries, the Sioux secured free and unrestricted access to them by an 1858 treaty.

The art of making pipes, or *calumets* as they are sometimes called, is not dead. The quarry near Pipestone, Minnesota, is now a national monument, and thousands of people visit it each year. The monument includes a visitors center and a small museum with an extensive display of beautifully carved and decorated pipes of all sizes. Visitors may take a self-guided tour of the historic and scenic quarry grounds and watch a video of how the pipes are now made. Native craftworkers give regularly scheduled demonstrations of pipemaking, using the stone from the quarry.

Make a Model Pipe

The two parts of the ceremonial pipe are the soapstone bowl and the wooden stem. These were stored separately. Indian pipemakers used a wooden drill to hollow out the bowl. The carver first cut a T-shaped piece from a flat piece of soapstone. He chipped and scraped until he had the piece roughly shaped as he wanted it. After the initial carving was done, the carver used a wooden drill tipped with a sharpened piece of flint to hollow out the bowl. He poured sand and water into the hole to intensify the abrasive action of the drill. Then he left the bowl plain or carved it into the shape he wanted. Finally, he polished and buffed it by rubbing it with sand.

The stem was made from hardwood such as ash. The branch was split lengthwise into two halves to create a narrow shaft running through both halves. The halves were then glued back together with glue made from sap and tied with a strong cord. Sometimes a single piece of wood was hollowed out by running a heated wire through the core to ream it out. The end was sharpened and fit into a hole at the end of the bowl so the smoke could be drawn through the hole now created. Next, the women would decorate the stem with quills, beads, feathers, or painted designs.

Since you do not plan to smoke your pipe, you will not need to bore a hole through it. Make your pipe as simple or as fancy as you wish following these general directions.

Materials:

- 1 large bar of soap (pink or red, if possible)
- 1 piece of wood approximately 1" x ½" x 30" (2.5 cm x 1.25 cm x 75 cm)
- craft knife
- decorative items (optional)

1. Carve the soap into a T-shape.

2. Carve any designs onto the soap you wish.

3. Carve a hole to insert the stem.

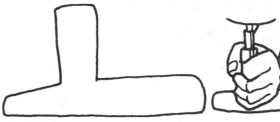

4. Sand and smooth the bowl until it is the way you want it.

5. Sand, smooth, and decorate the stem and then join the two pieces.

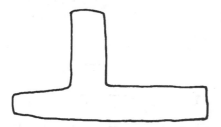

Quiz

1. List three important things you have learned about the natives of the Great Plains. _____

   _____

2. What are some things not known about the Battle of Little Bighorn? _____

   _____

3. Where did Dull Knife go and with whom? _____

   _____

4. How did the Plains natives hunt buffalo before they had horses? _____

   _____

5. Why was the disappearance of the buffalo a great loss for the Plains Indians? _____

   _____

6. Who was Sweet Medicine? _____

   _____

7. What are some phrases used by the Crow Indians, and what do they mean? _____

   _____

   _____

8. Explain the effect of the white man's "childhood diseases" on the Indians. _____

   _____

   _____

9. List the important differences between the use of tobacco by the Indians and people today. _____

   _____

   _____

10. On the back of this paper, describe what you believe to be the worst and the best results of the white man's coming to North America.

Fishermen of the Northwest Coast

The people who lived along the Northwest Coast of North America were surrounded by an intricate environment of mountains, forests, and water. The coast was rocky with many deep, fjord-like indentations and scattered offshore islands. The inland valleys were steep-sided, heavily glaciated, and covered with dense forests of cedar and Douglas fir. The sea abounded with many kinds of fish, seals, and sea birds, and the forests teemed with many kinds of game animals. The wild plant food which grew there included berries, seeds, fruits, and mushrooms.

As far as is known, the Japanese and Russians were among the earliest visitors to this area. When they arrived, they found the natives living the same way their ancestors had for centuries, maybe even thousands of years. They used stone tools and practiced no agriculture. With such an abundance of natural foods, they had no need to farm. Although the practice of agriculture is often thought to be a mark of civilization, without it the people of the Northwest lived quite a comfortable and advanced life when compared to people in other areas.

The people of the Northwest made remarkable watercraft for fishing. Dugout canoes as long as 50 feet (15 meters) and capable of holding forty men were their main form of transport. They built their villages near the mouths of mountain rivers, utilizing the shelter afforded by the steep bluffs and cliffs which sided the rivers. Their houses were also remarkable and built to withstand heavy storms, although they were constructed without nails or other metals.

Most of the people were warlike. As with the natives of the Great Plains, winning military victories over their neighbors was the favorite way to gain prestige. The main tribal groups were the Kwakiutl of the north and the Tlingit and Haida of the south, as well as the natives of the Queen Charlotte Islands.

Villages consisted of clustered groups of houses, each of which were inhabited by a different family group including the extended family of grandparents, aunts, uncles, and cousins. The houses were made of heavy timber framing with elaborately carved corner posts of the family totems and entry posts, as well. Some villages contained as many as a thousand people, although most had several hundred.

Social organizations centered around fishing expeditions, hunting, and war parties. Important families were divided into groups similar to clans who traced their heritage to family totems. Whether one belonged to the Killer Whale people, Cannibal Spirit people, or the Beaver people, one gave one's allegiance to that group. This did not mean that they "worshipped" the animal of the totem or that they thought themselves to be descended from it. It meant simply that an ancestor had a special relationship with that totem, and it had almost the same meaning as a family crest would have meant in Europe. When someone visited another village, he only had to look at the totem poles to see where his kinsmen lived so that he would know where he could stay while he was there.

Fishermen of the Northwest Coast *(cont.)*

Much of the structure of life depended on the ability to cut down big trees and make them into magnificent houses and boats. The people developed serviceable stone axes and adzes out of hard, polished stone. Very often these tools were beautifully decorated with carving and sculpturing. The blades of these tools were lashed by leather thongs to wooden handles, and although they were slower than metal tools, they were remarkably efficient. The people did not weave, but they were able to make a kind of textile out of cedar bark which they then fashioned into cloaks, aprons, and fringed skirts. They also made beautifully designed hats and baskets from the bark.

The immense shoals of salmon were another part of their surroundings which the people were able to use well. The flesh of the fish was both eaten fresh and dried for later use. Huge quantities of oil were extracted from the fish, as well, and this oil was stored in wooden bowls.

When the people were not hunting or fishing, they turned their energies to their favorite pastime—war. Mainly this consisted of raiding other villages which were not so close that they needed to be friends during the fishing season. War was a very dangerous, no-holds-barred game for them. Slavery was practiced, but although captured enemies were treated fairly kindly, they were not adopted into the tribe and treated as equals in the way the Plains Indians treated captives.

The potlatch festival was without doubt the most important social activity. This was a means of giving away wealth to gain social prestige, but it also served as a means of exchange. The group which was the recipient of a potlatch was bound in honor to later give a potlatch itself, and this meant that they would give back goods at least as valuable as the ones they had received. Because of this, there was a constant transfer of carved chests, blankets, jewelry, and all the goods manufactured by them, although the people did not practice trade as we think of it. Most villages, however, were self-sufficient, and they subsisted on the foods which they gathered or hunted as well as their own manufactured goods. What they got from others outside the group was extra.

Ceremonial life was rich, particularly during the months of winter when the long nights became a time of storytelling and dancing. The carved animal masks and paint used during the ritual dances and gatherings were frightening, but as children repeatedly saw the recitals and learned the legends, they became less so. There was no written language, yet some of the objects made for daily use were almost history books in themselves because of the legends and stories with which they were associated. Even houses were associated with stories.

The historical was, in a way, linked to the religious. The gods all came from the world of nature. In heroic tales the totems acted like humans but were able to change into animal form at will. There also were individual spirits who were sometimes seen in visions, but these were not worshipped. There were no religious ceremonies of the kind that Europeans had. It was believed that there was an underworld to which one could go to contact one's ancestors, but if one went there, he had better not eat while there, or he would have to stay.

Some of the mythological characters were part human, part animal, and part spirit like the Thunderbird, the seadragons, and the heroes. As with most native peoples, the stories were told mainly during the winter, and storytelling was as much acting as telling with masks and robes for props. The powers of nature were personified, and those powers were shown to retaliate when man injured a fellow creature of nature. For example, the salmon spirits expected man to use some of their members for food, but if the people caught more than they needed, or if they threw away and otherwise wasted or tortured the salmon, the natural world would demand retribution, possibly in the form of a volcanic eruption.

Many stories were told of heroes who could overcome the natural world with spiritual power. All the myths were influenced by the dominating features of their lives, and therefore, salmon and bears occur again and again in the stories. Often the spirits of these animals must be placated. Other creatures, the ones which could be dangerous to man, were feared for their supernatural powers as well as their physical powers. Almost all the stories emphasize the importance of force and cunning.

Fishermen of the Northwest Coast *(cont.)*

Activities

1. Research the effect of geography on the development of another native North American culture. In writing, compare the ways in which geography influenced the lifestyle of those people with the ways geography influenced the lifestyle of the people of the Northwest Coast. For example, long ago the people of the Great Plains practiced agriculture, but between two and three centuries ago they became settled into a hunting culture which, except for the ritual planting of tobacco, did not grow crops. Why was this true? What was there about the surroundings which led them to live the kind of lives they did?

2. Research salmon fishing and canning. Describe or draw the process from beginning to end.

3. Make a poster illustrating one of the following:

   • life cycle of the salmon

   • oxygen cycle of plants, animals, and air

   • possible effects of ozone deterioration on the people and animals of the Great Northwest.

Longhouses, Canoes, and Totem Poles

What the buffalo was to the Indians of the Great Plains, the cedar tree was to the Indians of the Northwest Coast, except as a source of food. The Northwesterners were masters of wood working, and the cedar tree was used for houses, canoes, clothing, and dishes, and it was done without metal tools or nails. Their totem poles are a cause of wonder all over the world, but the way in which they built their houses, canoes, and even wooden dishes is no less incredible.

The cedar longhouses were massive, plank-covered buildings which could withstand heavy storms. In order to get the planks from the giant cedar tree, the carver first girdled the tree by stripping off the bark all around at the height at which he wanted to cut it. This killed the tree and allowed it to dry out while it still stood. A cut was then made into the tree, and a wedge was inserted and hit with stone hammers until a slab came away cleanly. The planks were then trimmed to the right size and smoothed with adzes. Huge supporting posts and beams were erected, and the planks were then placed against them to form the sides of the house.

To make the roof, heavy planks were anchored with heavy poles and stones and then covered with bark. Inside, the supporting beams were elaborately carved and decorated. There were no windows and only one door at one end of the house. A firepit was in the center of the house, and a smoke hole opened in the roof to allow smoke to escape. The interior was tiered and covered with planks to provide sleeping room for as many as twenty to forty people, all related to each other. Each house was named, and the family's totem carved into a large pole at the front of the house.

GROUND PLAN

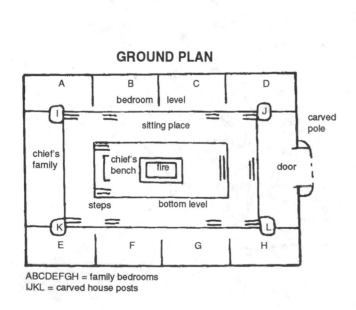

ABCDEFGH = family bedrooms
IJKL = carved house posts

INTERIOR PLAN FROM THE SIDE

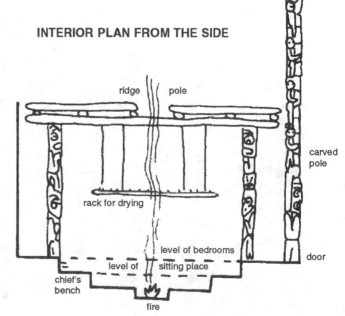

Longhouses, Canoes, and Totem Poles *(cont.)*

The Indians of the northwest have long been excellent fishermen and sailors. The boats which they have traditionally built vary from small, one-man crafts to boats large enough to carry fifty to sixty passengers.

Different styles of boats were made for different purposes: hunting, fishing, trading, or warring. Some of them had beautifully decorated bows rising up out of the water, and after the natives had contact with Europeans, the boats sometimes included sails. Whatever the style or size of a boat, it was made in one piece from the cedar tree.

First a straight-grained tree, free of knots, was found, usually deep in the forest but close to a river so it could be floated back to the village. To determine whether or not a tree was suitable, test holes were driven into the interior to make sure it had no rot in its core.

The tree was then felled and roughly shaped before it was floated back to the village. The wood was kept wet to prevent it from splitting.

The tree was hollowed out with stone adzes. Fire was used as well because charred wood was easier to scrape out than fresh wood. The side walls were made thin, but the bottom was thicker because it often had to be dragged over rocky shores.

Next, the hull was filled with water and hot rocks which had been heated in fires. The rocks soon caused the water to begin boiling and steaming. This allowed the boat builders to insert cross pieces to stretch the sides until the desired width was reached.

Finally, the canoe was smoothed and sanded with the aid of shark's skin, and it was carved and decorated with the images of animals or birds made into crests. Each image had a special meaning, just as the images on a totem pole did.

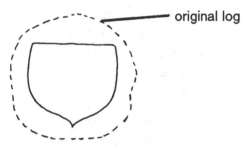

original log

Shaping the Outside

bottom thick because of rocky shores

side walls thin

Shaping the Inside

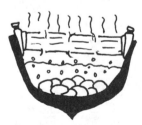

Steaming and Spreading

seat

Finished Shape

Longhouses, Canoes, and Totem Poles *(cont.)*

The art of carving totem poles is alive and well. Woodcarvers use traditional designs but modern metal chisels and adzes instead of the old stone ones. It is fascinating to watch a carver at work when in front of one's eyes an elaborate design of two to five figures of animals and symbolic crests slowly emerges from the large, round log. The crests on a totem pole are family crests which are passed down from one generation to the next, in much the same way a European coat of arms would be passed down.

There are four basic types of totem poles. *Frontal poles* were built at the front of a longhouse with a large opening at the bottom which formed the entrance to the house. *House posts* supported the main beams of the house. *Memorial poles* were carved and raised in honor of someone who died. The heirs raised the poles and gave a memorial potlatch in order to gain their rights as heirs. *Mortuary poles* had a hollowed-out box at the top to contain the body of the deceased. A carved plaque covered the box.

The totem pole served several purposes. Commissioned from the woodcarver for specific occasions, a pole signified a person's upward move in rank, commemorated a highly significant event, and indicated the rank and status of the villagers to strangers. A totem pole also told others to which clan the residents belonged so that when people from other villages came to visit, they would know in which house they could stay.

A famous woodcarver would claim a high fee for a pole he carved. The poles were always raised at a potlatch to ensure there were public witnesses. When a pole was raised, stories were told about the crests on it. Each of the figures represented some element of the family history.

Just as a poem suggests more than it blatantly tells, the totem pole hints at more than is there. The figures carved on it represent sky, river, forest, sea, and mountain beings from the mythology of the family, and they tell family legends of how ancestors had taken these beings as their family crests. The poles last up to a hundred years, even in the humid, rainy climate of the sea. When an old totem pole falls, it is allowed to rest where it has fallen and a new pole is carved.

FRONTAL POLE   **HOUSE POST**   **MEMORIAL POLE**   **MORTUARY POLE**

Longhouses, Canoes, and Totem Poles *(cont.)*

Another ingenious way the Indians of the Northwest Coast used cedar was for bentwood boxes. This is how they did it.

1. A plank is cut from a tree.

   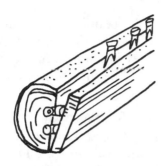

2. The plank is planed and polished to the correct thickness. Grooves are cut to form corners. Then, it is soaked in hot water or steamed.

   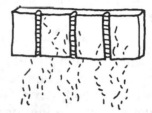

3. The softened wood is bent at three corners to form the sides of the box.

4. The ends are fastened tightly together. The box is wrapped with bark rope to keep its shape while drying.

   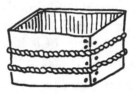

5. The box is set into the tightly fitting, grooved slab. The lid is made to fit.

6. The box is carved or painted on all sides.

Activities

1. Make a "bentwood box" of your own using heavy pasteboard or cardboard instead of wood. Draw and paint designs of your "family totem" on the sides.

2. Make a model longhouse with your choice of materials using the illustrations as a guide.

3. Design your own totem and write an explanation of the meaning of each animal or crest on your totem. Share your design with the class, telling what each symbol represents.

Folktales of the Northwest

It has been said that you can tell much about a people by the stories they tell. What can you tell about these natives of the Northwest from their stories?

Beaver Steals the Fire
(Kalispel)

The Kalispel who live along the Columbia River say that long ago when the people and the animals spoke the same language, the only fire was in the world which was far above the sky. The people had only raw food to eat, and they were very cold in the winter, so one day they had a meeting to make plans for stealing some fire. They decided that the one to get the fire would be the one who had the best war song, so they had a contest to see who was best.

Muskrat sang first, but his song was not good. Others sang as well. Then, from a small knoll nearby, they heard the sound of someone whistling. They went over to see who it was, and they discovered Coyote and his friend, Wren. Wren was carrying a little bundle of arrows. The two were invited to join the council and to sing for it. Coyote sang first. His war song was so good everyone else began to dance, so Coyote was made the chief of the party of fire stealers.

There was a big problem involved in getting the fire, however. Because the upper world was far above the sky, they needed to find a way to get up there. Wren volunteered to shoot an arrow into the sky to pierce it. Then he would shoot another into the end of the first arrow and continue shooting arrows, one into the other, until there was a long line of them from the sky down to the ground. In that way, they would have a kind of ladder to climb.

Everyone thought this was a grand idea, so Wren began to shoot. Wren was also lightest, so when he had made the arrow ladder, he took a long piece of bark rope and began to climb up through the sky until he reached the upper world. When he at last arrived there, he let down the rope, so all the others could climb after him.

The last one up was Bear, who was a very greedy fellow. He took two big baskets of food up with him, but they were so heavy that when he got halfway up the ladder, the rope broke, and he fell back down to earth. Of course, he was very fat as well as greedy, so he was not hurt.

In the upper world it was discovered that Curlew was keeper of the fire, and he was also keeper of the fish weir. Frog and Bullsnake were sent as scouts to find out in which house the fire was kept, so they crept up very close to the village and stopped to listen. Frog led the party. Bullsnake became hungry, and he began to lick Frog's feet. Suddenly, he took one big gulp and swallowed Frog. He turned around to the others and told them that Frog had been eaten, but he did not tell them he was the one to do it.

Coyote, who was still chief, told Beaver to go into the village and steal the fire. Beaver made a plan with Eagle. He went to the nearby river and floated down it, pretending to be dead. Curlew was keeping watch along the river, and when he saw Beaver floating down, he wanted his soft fur, so he reached into the river and pulled him out.

He threw Beaver into a corner inside his house. Just then, Eagle flew to Curlew's house and alighted on the roof, pretending to be wounded. Everyone inside the house ran out to try to catch Eagle because they wanted his beautiful feathers, and when they did this, Beaver suddenly jumped up and grabbed the fire, running away as quickly as he could.

Just as Beaver got to the river, the upper world people saw him and started chasing after him, He dived into the water, carrying the fire in his little claws in such a way that it did not get wet. In the meantime, Curlew sent Spider down the river in order to spread his net to catch Beaver, but Beaver swam too quickly, and he reached the rope safely. He climbed down the rope with everyone else following, and that is how we first got fire.

Folktales of the Northwest *(cont.)*

The Image That Came to Life

(Tlingit)

There was once a young chief who married, and soon after his wedding the lovely woman who was his bride fell ill. The chief was distraught. He sent to one shaman after another to come and help his loved one, but none of them could help, and after a long illness she died.

The young chief was despondent. He went from one place to another trying to find a woodcarver who could carve a likeness of the dead woman, but no one dared try. Finally, a woodcarver who lived in his own village said to the young chief, "I have often seen your wife walking with you before her illness, and if you would like me to try, I will attempt to capture her image in wood."

The young chief was overjoyed. At last, a good carver was willing to try his skill at carving the dead wife's image!

The woodcarver obtained a flawless piece of cedar wood and began to work. When he finished, he went to the young chief and said, "Come and see what I have carved."

When the young chief went to the woodcarver's house and looked inside at the image, it was as though he saw his dead wife before him. He asked the woodcarver, "What do I owe you?"

The woodcarver, who was unable to place a value on his work, said, "Do as you please about it. I carved this likeness because I felt so badly for you, so do not pay me too much."

The young chief was delighted, however, and paid the carver well. He took the image to his home and dressed her in the dresses and robes of his dead wife. He felt as though his wife had returned to him, and he treated the image as though it, indeed, was his wife.

One day as he sat near the image, still in mourning, it seemed to him as though it had moved. At first he thought it was only his imagination, but he continued to watch it carefully, waiting for it to come to life. He kept it near him whatever he did inside his house.

Then one day, he heard a sound coming from the chest of the image. It sounded like cracking wood. He had someone move the image away from the place where it had been sitting, and what should they find in that place but a small cedar tree growing right on top of the flooring. They left it where it was, and it became very large and beautiful. It is because of this that the cedar trees on the Queen Charlotte Islands are so good. Now when people look for cedars and find a good one, they say, "This looks just like the baby of the chief's wife."

With each day that passed, the image of the young wife became more like a human, and the people in villages from far away came to marvel at the image. The image did not move around, and it did not talk, but at night the young chief would dream about his wife and hear her talk to him in his dreams. This way, he knew all that she wanted to tell him.

Folktales of the Northwest *(cont.)*

The Wolf Clan and the Salmon
(Nass River)

In a canyon near the mouth of a river lived a very fortunate people. They had everything they needed to live. There were plentiful deer in the forests, many large cedar trees, wild berries, and the river teemed with salmon, more even than they could eat. The villagers who lived in this place had so much they were able to trade with other villages. They were widely respected.

As time went by, however, the young men of the village began to grow careless. They began to kill small animals which they did not need for food, just for the fun of killing them. The carcasses of these animals were left by the young men to rot. The village elders warned the young men that this would surely bring disaster on them, but the young men simply laughed in disbelief.

One day, these same young men devised a new amusement for themselves. They caught salmon from the river which they did not intend to eat. They cut slits into the backs of the salmon while they still lived and put pitch into the slits. They then set the pitch afire and set the salmon into the water to swim around in pain with fires in their backs. The young men thought it was exciting to watch the salmon thus, whirling and twirling in the water, making a light show for them.

Again the elders protested, saying dire consequences would soon befall the entire village because of the carelessness and cruelty of the young men. When the village people prepared for their winter ceremonies, a sound like that of a beating medicine drum came from the nearby mountain. The young men began to laugh and dance around, saying, "Aha! The ghosts are waking up! They wish to have a ceremony, too. They are going to eat you up!"

The elders complained among themselves, certain that trouble was coming, but after a time the pounding went away. Within several days, however, it began again, this time louder than before. The elders noticed that now the young men were also afraid. They said again that if some terrible fate befell the village, it would be the fault of the young men.

Suddenly, a loud noise like the crash of thunder was heard. The mountain opened up, and a river of fire gushed out from its side. It seemed as though the whole world was on fire. Fire poured down the river, and the forests burned. Very few of the villagers were able to escape the fire, and after it was all over, the shamans said it was because of the anger of the spirits at the torture of the salmon that the mountain opened up causing the deaths of many. This is the way the powers of nature repay people when they do not regard nature with respect.

Folktales of the Northwest *(cont.)*

Raven and the Moon
(Snoqualmie)

One day, Raven, who was a trickster, heard that an old fisherman and his daughter kept a beautiful white ball of light called the moon in their house. He was a greedy fellow and wanted this moon for himself, so he changed himself into a leaf hanging from a berry bush. Later that day, the fisherman's daughter came walking by looking for berries. She pulled at the twig on which the leaf hung, and it fell down and entered her body.

Nine months later, the daughter gave birth to a boy. This boy did not look as one would have expected a child of the young woman to look. He was very dark in color and had a large nose, almost like a beak. The child grew rapidly, and one day he began to cry loudly.

"What does your son want?" the old man asked his daughter.

"He says that he wants to play with the moon," she replied.

"Well, then," the old man said, "give it to him so we can have some peace and quiet in here."

The daughter did as her father told her, and for some days the child was content, rolling and tossing the moon around inside the house. On another day, however, he began crying just as before.

"What does your child want now?" the old man asked his daughter.

She listened carefully to the child, then told her father, "He wishes to see the stars through the smoke hole in the roof, but it is closed."

"Well, then," the old man said, "open it so we can have some peace and quiet in here."

The daughter did as she was told, and no sooner had she opened the smoke hole than Raven changed back into his real self, and holding the moon in his claws, flew up through the hole. He landed on a mountain top, then threw the moon up into the sky where it hangs to this day.

Activities

1. In small groups, brainstorm the answers to these questions. Then come together as a class to share what you have decided.

   a. What can you tell about how the natives of the Northwest Coast saw their world? What was important to them? How can you tell?

   b. Many groups of people have stories about tricksters. What other trickster have you encountered in your study of the natives of North America? Why would a people have seen the powers in the world as being just as apt to trick you as to support and nourish you?

   c. Have you read another Native American story which warns against wasting nature's gifts? Can you name any examples in your world today which warn that nature must be protected?

   d. What does "The Image That Came to Life" tell you about the way the Northwest peoples saw the cedar tree?

2. It is sometimes said that as people have come to live in industrialized urban areas, so they have grown away from the land, and they no longer see themselves as being part of a larger whole. That was not true of earlier societies.

   Divide a paper in half. On one side draw a picture of an example of how a native child a century ago would have regarded an animal. On the other side, draw a picture of a city child today as that child regards an animal.

The Power of Words

European Americans are often fascinated by Native American names. Many centuries have passed since their own names originated, and they usually have no idea how those names began. Pretty-shield, a Crow Indian woman, once said about this subject, "Words are powerful, but names are the most powerful words of all."

What did she mean by this?

First, stop and think about words. How could something we take for granted and use every day be powerful? The meaning of a word depends on the context in which it is used. A word may have one meaning when it is used by a certain person in a certain place and another when used by another person elsewhere.

An example of this can be found with the word *fire*. *Fire* is not powerful in and of itself. It gains in meaning, however, when it is used in a sentence, like this: "At camp, John lit the fire, and we sat around it singing songs." Through this sentence, a picture probably comes into the head of the reader of a cozy, friendly, happy time spent with friends around a campfire. A very pleasant feeling comes along with this picture of fire.

Now, take the word *fire* used in another time and place. Imagine yourself sitting in a crowded theater watching an engrossing movie. Suddenly, someone calls out, "Fire!" What picture do you get in this situation? It is not the same one you had in the first example, is it?

The word *fire* has power in both these examples. Its power in the first one is the ability to cause one to feel happy and cozy because that person knows that time spent around a campfire in the past has been happy and cozy. On the other hand, the word *fire* has the power to throw fear into a person if it is used as it is in the second example because the person knows that a fire inside a crowded theater could injure or kill.

Some words might be called *taboo* words because in certain times and places one probably would not dare to use them. For example, you might use certain words when talking to a friend that he or she would not use in a job interview. Or that person might use them when laughing with people at a party but not say them aloud in church. Words naming body parts and certain slang phrases might be included in a list of taboo words.

Words have the power to make people feel wonderful or to destroy their self-confidence, to encourage or to devastate, to free or to enslave. When laws are written, they must be written very carefully if they are to have the end result for which they are intended. When a writer writes, he or she must choose words carefully to convey the meaning he or she wishes to convey.

The Power of Words *(cont.)*

Names are the most powerful words of all. Unlike a word which takes much of its meaning from the context in which it is used, a name all by itself has the power to elicit certain feelings or reactions. It does not have to be used in any certain way in order for it to have a special meaning.

Completing the following activity might help you to understand better the power which names can have.

Activity

Interview as many people as possible, asking them the questions given below pertaining to the names on the chart on the next page. Include both young people and older people in your survey. Note the expressions which come to their faces when they answer.

Tell the people you interview that you are going to say some names to them, and you want them to answer some questions about each name. If the person does not recognize a name, tally "no" and go on to the next name without asking further questions about that name.

Tally up the responses you get. Then bring your results back to class and compare them with those of your classmates. Can you come to any conclusions about the meaning of the results you got?

1. Do you recognize this name? (yes or no)

2. Does the name make you feel good or bad? (good or bad)

3. Would you like to meet this person, have this thing, or be in this place? (yes or no)

4. Has this person, place, or thing ever been important to you? (yes or no)

The Power of Words *(cont.)*

Name	Question 1		Question 2		Question 3		Question 4	
	Yes	No	Good	Bad	Yes	No	Yes	No
Sitting Bull								
Jane Goodall								
Disneyland								
John F. Kennedy								
Geronimo								
General Custer								
Crazy Horse								
Abraham Lincoln								
Auschwitz								
Mother Theresa								
Chocolate								
Hawaii								
Queen Elizabeth II								
TOTALS								

Potlatch Math

You are planning a potlatch and will invite everyone in the nearby village. You want to be certain you have enough to go around. It would be highly embarrassing if you did not give your guests at least as much as you were given as their guest. Solve these problems.

1. There are a total of 340 villagers who will come to your potlatch. Thirty-five percent of them are women, thirty percent are men, and the remainder are children. How many are there of each? Round off your answers to the next number.

    Women =

    Men =

    Children =

2. You plan to give each woman a large wooden dish and a large basket, each child a blanket and a small basket, and each man a ceremonial shield and knife. You also plan to give your cousin a bear robe. Make a list of how many you need of each item.

    Large wooden dishes =

    Large baskets =

    Blankets =

    Small baskets =

    Ceremonial shields =

    Ceremonial knives =

    Bear robes =

3. You plan to serve grilled salmon, fresh berries, baked bear meat, and bread made from ground roots. You will need an average of $\frac{1}{2}$ lb. (240 g) salmon, 2 cups (500 mL) berries, $\frac{1}{3}$ lb. (160 g) bear meat, and bread made with flour from two roots for each man, woman, and child who will attend. How much of each food will you need to prepare for your guests?

    Salmon =

    Berries =

    Bear meat =

    Roots =

4. You will send boats to bring your guests. Each of your boats will hold twenty people. You have only two boats. How many trips will each of your boats have to make?

    Boat A =

    Boat B =

5. There are six adults and five children in your family. Using the figures in the third problem, how much additional food will you need to prepare for your own family?

    Salmon =

    Berries =

    Bear meat =

    Roots =

6. If you had to buy food in the amounts given in the third problem, how much would it cost you, given the following prices?

    Salmon: $5.98 per pound (480 g)

    Berries: $2.49 per cup (250 mL)

    Bear meat: $8.99 per pound (480 g)

    Roots: $1.50 for 10

    Total cost =

Fishy Math Problems

1. a. If a female salmon lays 10,000 eggs and 40% of them hatch, how many hatchlings will there be? _____

    b. If 30% of the hatchlings make it to the ocean, how many will make it there? _____

    c. If 30% of those that get to the ocean make it back to the mouth of the river on their way to the spawning grounds, how many will start up the river? _____

    d. If 50% of the salmon starting upstream actually get to the spawning grounds, and 50% of those are female, how many eggs will be laid? _____

2. Given the following assumptions, answer the questions. The average salmon caught weighs 14 lbs. (6 kilograms). A fishing boat can carry 4200 lbs. (1800 kilograms).

    a. How many fish can be caught and stored in the hold of the boat? _____

    b. If the fisherman gets $1.39 per pound ($3.24 per kilogram), how much money can he sell all the fish for? _____

    c. If the captains's expenses for the fishing trip include the following, what will be his profit for the trip?

    Pay for helpers: 2 men x 3 days x $100 each per day = how much? _____

    Fuel for boat: $150 per day x 3 days = how much? _____

    Boat rental: $750 per day x 3 days = how much? _____

    Profit = amount left over = how much? _____

3. If the boat must travel 96 miles (150 kilometers) to the fishing grounds, and the boat's average speed is 16 miles per hour (25 kilometers per hour), how long will it take to get there? _____

4. If the average fish after cleaning and readying for canning weighs 7.5 lbs. (3 kilograms), how many cans containing ¼ lb. (.1 kilogram) will one fish fill? _____

5. The cannery used the fish waste to make cat food. Based on the above problems, answer the following questions:

    a. How much waste is there per fish? _____

    b. How many ¼ lb. (.1 kilogram) cans of cat food can be made per fish? _____

    c. If the cannery gets $.25 per can of cat food, how much do they make per fish? _____

6. a. If the grocery store sells the cat food for $.50 per can, and your cat eats one can each day, how much will you spend for cat food per week? _____

    b. How much will you spend per thirty-day month? _____

7. If your part time job after school pays you $3.00 per hour, how many hours per month will you have to work to pay for cat food each month? _____

The Magnificent Salmon

According to Squamish legend, in the days when people and animals still spoke the same language, four brothers went to the village of the Salmon People. They persuaded the chief to let some of his people come to where the Squamish people lived because they were starving and needed the food. The Salmon chief agreed to do so, but only on one condition: that all of the bones left after the salmon were eaten would be thrown back into the water. In this way, the salmon would come back to life and be available for food another time.

This story is an example of those told by the first peoples of the Northwest to encourage an early kind of recycling. Waste not, want not, it seems to say. The salmon is, in and of itself, a kind of naturally recycling phenomenon, and its life story is one of the most interesting of all Earth's creatures.

The young salmon begin their life cycle as tiny eggs which are deposited by a female between the stones high up the mountain in a freshwater stream. The eggs, which may number 10,000 from each female, are then fertilized by a male with a milky substance called *milt*. After about two-and-a-half months, the young burst from the eggs as small creatures called *alevins*. Each carries with it a huge yolk sac which nourishes it for several weeks as it hides among the rocks to gain size and strength. After several months, the young ones, now called *fry* and recognizable as small fish, begin their hazardous journey down to the sea.

The vigorous young fish are about five inches (13 cm) long by now and able to prey on even smaller fish. They start downstream, and as they go, they must encounter and escape from many larger fish who lie in wait along the banks of the river. They also must cope with all the wastes and pollution which have been leaked or put into the river. At long last, a small portion of the original 10,000 alevins actually reach the ocean. Once they are there, however, they find plenty of food, mostly in the form of *pink feed*, a kind of tiny shrimp which the salmon eat in vast amounts.

For a number of years the salmon swim in the ocean, sometimes ranging hundreds, or even thousands, of miles (kilometers) from the river mouth from which they emerged into the ocean. They prey on smaller fish even as they are preyed upon by larger animals such as seals, sea lions, sharks, lampreys, sea bass, and sea birds. But there comes a time in each salmon's life when an irresistible instinct within it says, "You must go home again."

The salmon take their time, maybe as long as several months, to work their way back to the exact river mouth from whence they had swum some years before. The way back is not easy, and once the salmon reaches the mouth of the river, the struggle begins. In the run up the river, the salmon leap through rapids and up waterfalls, sometimes as high as ten feet (3 m) or more. They cover ten to twenty miles (16-32 km) per day, fighting against tremendous odds. Not only is the river strewn with rocky hazards, but the salmon must also face the dangers of fishermen and birds. The ones uncaught continue up the river until they reach the spawning grounds where their lives started.

The Magnificent Salmon *(cont.)*

By the time the salmon reach the spawning grounds, they are weary, bruised, and starved. The rocks over which they have swum have taken their toll on the bodies of the fish, and they have very little energy left. What energy there is left is dedicated to the process of spawning. Just as their parents had done several years before, the salmon put their last, best energy into recreating themselves. When the last egg has been laid, and the last drop of milt has been spread, the salmon head back down the river to die.

Industrialization has been hard on the salmon. Many of their rivers have been dammed up in the process of cultivating land and producing hydro-electric power. Because of this, some areas have been targeted for protection of the salmon. Artificial waterfalls called *fish ladders* have been made in some places for them. Many of the salmon headed for the spawning grounds are caught alive before they reach them, and the eggs and milt are milked out so that fertilization can be done by hand. In this way, the small salmon can be raised in protected hatcheries and then set free when they are of the right size.

There are five kinds of salmon. The largest is the *chinook* salmon, which is sometimes called *king salmon*. The chinook has an average weight of 25 pounds (11 kg), but sometimes it reaches one hundred pounds (45 kg) or more, and it usually lives about two or three years. This fish is often canned, salted and refrigerated, or lightly smoked. It is popular in the fish market and highly prized by fishermen.

Sockeye salmon live in the Pacific waters off the Northwest Coast of North America. They usually live from two to six years and often spend one or two winters in an inland lake before migrating to the sea. The average weight of the sockeye is five pounds (2.25 kg), and its deep red flesh is often canned. It is the most important commercial salmon. Most sockeye are produced along the coasts of Alaska.

Coho salmon is a silver-sided fish weighing 25 pounds (11 kg) or more. It is commercially important, and it is canned, frozen, salted, smoked, and sold fresh. Its range is California to Alaska.

Other kinds of salmon are the *pink* salmon and the *chum* salmon. These salmons run from late summer into fall. Pink salmon is the second most important salmon used for canning. Chum salmon is sometimes called *dog* salmon because it has dog-like teeth on its upper jaw.

Activities

1. Write a fable using salmon as the subject. What lesson will your fable teach?

2. Make a poster illustrating the life cycle of the salmon.

3. Use the diagram on the next page to build a model salmon ladder.

The Magnificent Salmon *(cont.)*

Salmon Ladder

Follow the diagram to construct a model salmon ladder similar to one used in a salmon hatchery.

Materials:

- shoebox lid
- cardboard
- balsa wood

- wood block
- sand
- scissors

- craft saw
- craft glue or heavy tape

Directions:

1. Turn the shoebox lid upside down.

2. Cut five partitions from balsa wood to fit in the lid.

3. Fill the lid ³/₄ to ⁷/₈ full with sand. The sand will represent water.

4. Place the partitions in the sand at angles, as shown.

5. Tilt the lid as illustrated. Prop it up with the wood block.

6. Cut out cardboard salmon and place them appropriately on the ladder.

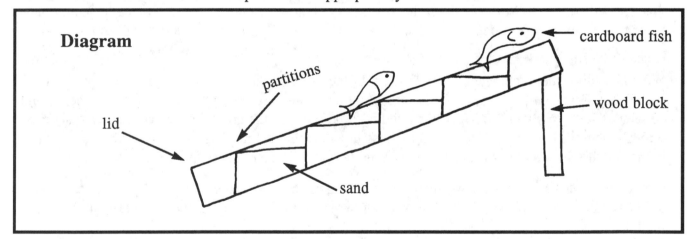

Diagram

partitions

lid

sand

cardboard fish

wood block

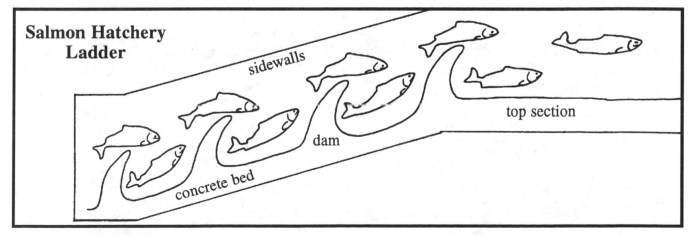

Salmon Hatchery Ladder

sidewalls

top section

dam

concrete bed

Moon Illusion

Most early peoples of the world told stories and legends about the moon and stars. Some of these stories showed sun, moon, and stars personified as people who in the early days had interacted with man just as the animals had. The Chippewa told a story about a beautiful maiden who did not want to marry, so she went up to the moon who kept her and loved her forever.

In stories from other cultures, two girls married stars and one of them later had a star boy-child. Some thought that Sun and Moon were brother and sister, while others thought they were husband and wife who never seemed to be able to get to the same place in the sky world at the same time. The Snoqualmie said that Raven stole the moon from an old man and his daughter who were hiding it in a box, and Raven put it into the air. Why all these legends about the moon?

On a clear night, a full moon can be an awesome sight. Its beautiful glow lights up the night sky in a way which seems almost magical, especially to someone who does not know what it is or where it is. One thing about the moon which seems magical is the way in which it seems to shrink in size as it climbs the sky. Why does the moon grow smaller the higher it is in the sky?

The answer is, of course, that it does not. It just seems this way because of an optical illusion. You can prove this for yourself.

Activity

Wait until there is a full moon. When it first rises, look at it through a hole in a piece of binder paper. Later that evening, when the moon is "higher," look at it again, holding the paper the same distance from your face as before. You will see that the moon is the same size both times.

What has happened to change your perception of the moon is that with the hole in the paper as a reference, instead of your physical surroundings, you block out the other forms around you so the moon can be seen as it is. Without the paper, the buildings and trees on the ground cause your eyes to subconsciously compare the size of the moon to those things when the moon is low. When the moon is high in the sky, it seems smaller because there are no large forms there to compare it with.

Now compare the two stars below to each other. Which one looks bigger? Actually, the two are exactly the same size, but the picture fools your eyes and your brain into thinking one is larger than the other.

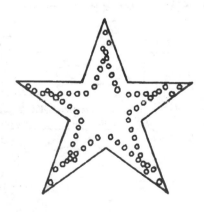 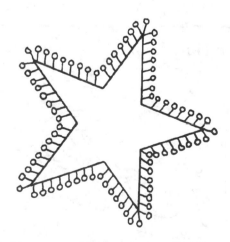

String Games

Have you ever played Cat's Cradle? Many people who have played this game do not know that it was a favorite of many Native American young people, particularly in the Northwest. The Inuit people used either sinew or leather to make the strings for their games, while others of the Northwest used string made from the inside of cedar bark. In some places even human hair or horse hair was used, but you do not need to pull out your hair or cut a tree to get string.

You can use any line of string for this game, but the best string to use is nylon cord because it can be joined without having to tie a knot. Ask an adult to help you melt the two ends of a piece about two yards or meters long and join them so they fuse together. Then, you are ready to begin.

Cat's Cradle (Opening Position)

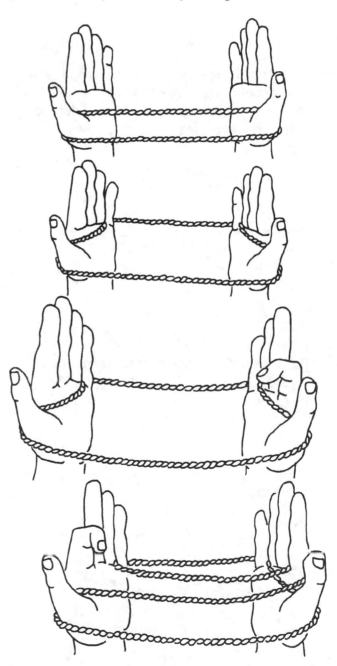

1. Hang the string on your hands as shown. Stretch your hands apart to make the string loop tight.

2. Pick up the string with your little fingers. The string now crossing the palm of your hand is the *palmar string*.

3. Pick up the palmar string of your left hand with the index finger of your right hand. Tighten the string.

4. Pick up the palmar string of your right hand with the index finger of your left hand, and tighten the string as shown. This is the *opening position*, also called Cat's Cradle.

5. Two string formations follow on the next three pages.

String Games *(cont.)*

Cat's Whiskers

1. Follow the previous steps one through four.

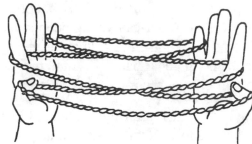

2. Drop the thumb loops.

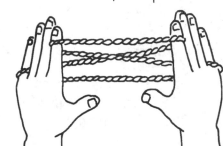

3. Turn your hands away from you. With your thumbs, pick up from below the far little string on the bottom and bring it under the strings on your index fingers.

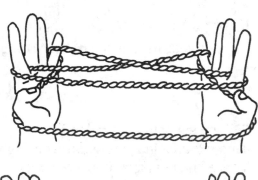

4. Reach your thumbs over the near index string, pick up the far index string, and bring them back.

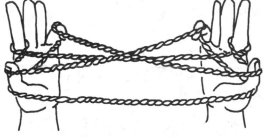

5. Put your little fingers over near the index strings; get the far thumb strings, and bring them back.

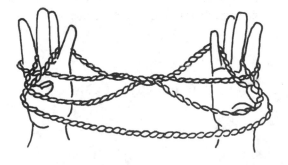

6. Drop the thumb loops. Now you have Cat's Whiskers.

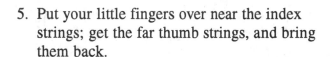
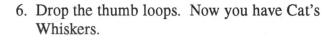
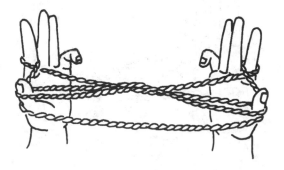

String Games *(cont.)*

Bananas

1. Hang the string around the back of the first two fingers of your left hand.

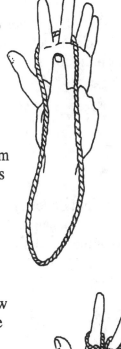

2. With your right index finger, take the string from behind through the two fingers and pull it out as far as it will go.

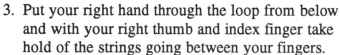

3. Put your right hand through the loop from below and with your right thumb and index finger take hold of the strings going between your fingers.

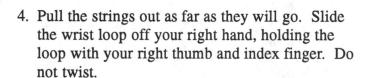

4. Pull the strings out as far as they will go. Slide the wrist loop off your right hand, holding the loop with your right thumb and index finger. Do not twist.

5. With your left thumb and little finger, take from below one of the bottom strings. Drop the strings from your right hand.

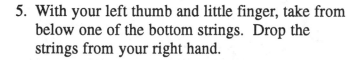

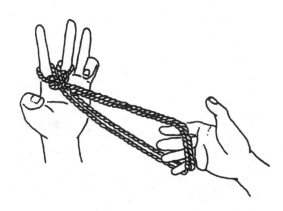

String Games *(cont.)*

Bananas *(cont.)*

6. With your right thumb and index finger, pull out the small loop that goes around your left index and middle fingers. Do not pull too hard.

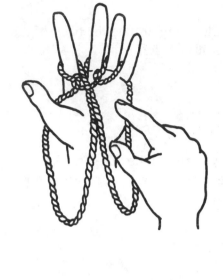

7. Take the fingers of your left hand out of their loops. You now have a bunch of bananas. Can you pick one of them without the bunch falling apart?

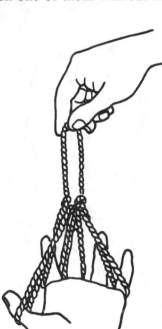

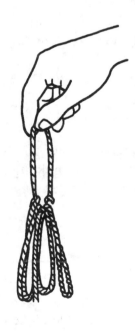

Make a Button Blanket

One craft unique to the natives of the Northwest Coast is the making of blankets decorated with white mother-of-pearl buttons. Originally these blankets were made using shells, but with the coming of the white man, buttons made of a substance resembling mother-of-pearl became available, and these buttons are generally used today. Designs are comprised of either geometric shapes or animals, and the colors of the blankets are red and black, contrasting nicely with the gleaming white of the buttons.

A particularly attractive blanket may be made by either piecing together red and black fabric or sewing red and black fabric together and "cutting out" a design. This is more complicated but can lead to dramatic designs.

To make your own version of a button blanket, follow the directions given below. Of course, you do not need to make an entire blanket. You can make a wall hanging of almost any size by using the same technique.

Materials:

- red and black felt of any desired size
- quantity of white or mother-of-pearl buttons
- sewing needle and thread or glue
- scissors
- sewing chalk

Directions:

1. Plan your design and draw it on the fabric with sewing chalk.

2. Using either needle and thread or glue, sew your buttons onto your design.

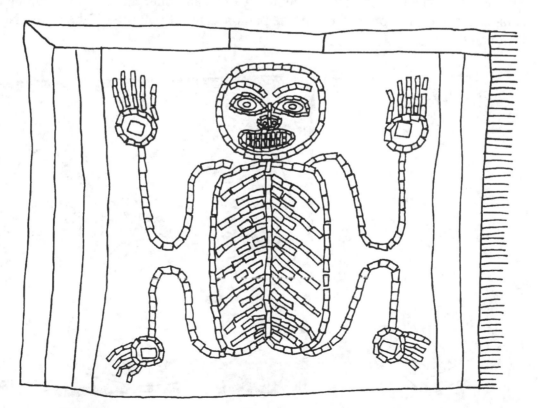

Make a Sand Painting

Natives of both the Northwest and the Southwest often made sand paintings. When medicine men made them, they used natural earth paints. They sang and chanted as they painted.

You can make sand paintings using your own design. Follow these directions.

Materials:

- a flat pan
- wet sand
- flat block of wood smaller than pan
- watercolors

- plaster of Paris
- small piece of looped wirc for a hanger
- brush

Directions:

1. Partly fill the pan with wet sand. Tamp it down solid with the block of wood, leaving a border of sand 1" (2.5 cm) higher than the center.

2. Make a pouring dent just outside the flat area. Pour a wet solution of plaster of Paris into the dent so it flows into the flat area about 1" (2.5 cm) thick.

3. Place the ends of the looped wire into the plaster and let it dry until set.

4. When dry and solid, remove the plaster from the pan and brush off the loose sand with a stiff brush. (The surface will still be sandy.) Carve off the pouring dent.

5. Plan your design. When the plaster is completely dry, paint onto the sand by dripping thinned watercolors. Do not rub it on or brush in the paint because it will rub off the sand. Now you have your sand painting.

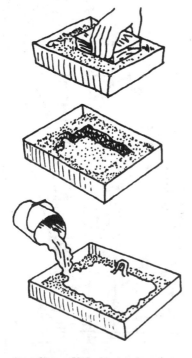 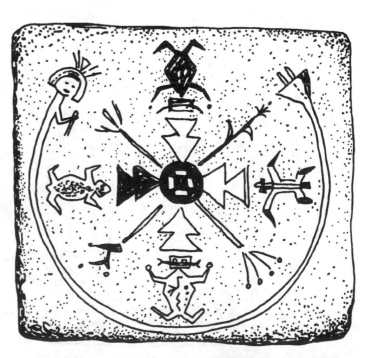

Make a "Wooden" Mask

The natives of the Northwest Coast are master wood-carvers. Everything is carved from the wood of the cedar tree with extremely fine craftsmanship. Some of the most interesting pieces of wood carvings are the masks which were used in ceremonial dancing and, of course, the totem poles. In the masks and totem poles the effigies of animals are used.

One of the most popular designs is the highly stylized face of a beaver. Use the pattern below to make a beaver mask for yourself. Use colored construction paper. Enlarge the pattern if you need to. To make layers of different colors, trace the patterns of individual parts such as the teeth, eyes, or nose, and transfer them onto construction paper of contrasting colors. Cut them out and glue them into place on the mask.

Quiz

1. List three important things you have learned about the natives of the Northwest Coast. _____

   _____

2. Why did the natives of the Northwest Coast not practice agriculture? _____

   _____

3. Describe the religion of the Northwest Coast Indians. _____

   _____

4. How were the homes of these natives different from those of the Plains Indians? _____

   _____

   _____

5. What did the Northwest Coast natives do with the cedar tree? _____

   _____

6. How would someone prepare to give a potlatch? _____

   _____

   _____

7. Describe the life cycle of the salmon. _____

   _____

   _____

8. Why would the Indians have been awed by the sun, moon, and stars? _____

   _____

9. What are some differences between ordinary words and specific names? _____

   _____

10. On the back of this paper, retell one of the folktales which came from the natives of the Northwest Coast.

The Anasazi

Fourteen hundred years ago, when the Europeans were deep in the midst of the Dark Ages, a highly developed group of people lived in the area now called Four Corners. This is where the corners of four states, Colorado, Utah, Arizona, and New Mexico, come together. We do not know what these people called themselves because they left no written language. We can assume from what we know of other ancient people, however, that the word they used for themselves was one which meant "The People." We now call them Anasazi from the Navajo word meaning "The Ancient Ones."

About one century ago at a place now called Mesa Verde, some cowboys found the first of a remarkable group of cliff dwellings in which people had lived for about one hundred years and then left, probably to join with the ancestors of the people now called the Pueblo Indians. There are cliff dwellings all over the Southwest, but those at Mesa Verde are some of the most spectacular. These ruins have fascinated everyone who has seen them, and while their builders left no written language, we have been able to learn a great deal about them. We now know that for centuries before the people built their cliff dwellings, they lived on top of the tabletop mountain.

The first Anasazi settled in Mesa Verde about 550 AD. They had been a nomadic people, but they chose this place to settle when they decided to practice farming rather than hunting and gathering as they had done before. They lived in *pit houses* which they usually built into the top of the mesa, although a few of them were built into cliff recesses. These pit houses were probably the forerunners of the *kivas* built later. Here the people learned to make pottery and acquired the bow and arrow.

This was a prosperous time for the people, and they grew in population. They began to build houses above ground which had upright walls of poles and mud. These houses were built adjacent to each other in long, curving rows, and since that time the people have been called Pueblos, which means *village dwellers* in Spanish. By 1000 AD, the Anasazi were able to build houses of stone. The thick, double walls often rose two or three stories high and were joined together in units. During this time, the Anasazi also began decorating their pottery in lovely geometric designs of black and white.

The Anasazi *(cont.)*

The population between 1100 AD and 1300 AD may have numbered in the thousands. Round towers began to appear as part of the dwellings, and all the crafts of pottery, stonework, weaving, jewelry making, and tool making grew in sophistication and artistry. The stone walls of the large pueblos built then are made of carefully shaped stones laid in straight courses. For an unknown reason, the Anasazi began to move into the caves and recesses where their ancient ancestors had lived long before them. It may have been that they moved into the cliff dwellings for defense or because they offered better protection from the elements. The reasons could even have been religious. Whatever the case, this era saw the beginning of the beautiful cliff dwellings which we can now visit and wonder at.

There are many ruins on top of Mesa Verde, but it is the sight of the cliff dwellings which most excites the visitor. The ruins at Mesa Verde are eloquently beautiful. The builders were skillful, and their workmanship suggests a society which was both artistic and practical. They left behind not only their lovely and intricately fitted stonework buildings but evidence of an advanced skill in farming as well. The Anasazi themselves had obviously been the heirs of a vigorous group of ancestors who had used the centuries to learn and pass down many skills and traditions.

Most of the cliff dwellings at Mesa Verde were built during the mid-1200s. In size, they range from houses with only one room to villages which contained over 200 rooms and no standard floor plan. The walls were single courses of stone, and some buildings were made of better quality than others.

The Anasazi took advantage of what nature had given them by building their homes under overhanging cliffs because the overhangs protected them from the weather. They certainly were easier to defend than villages built on flat land would have been. The homes were made of sandstone which the builders shaped into rectangular blocks about the size of a loaf of bread. They were then mortared together with a mixture of mud and water. The rooms averaged about six by eight feet (1.8 x 2.4 m), although some rooms obviously intended for communal use were much larger. Separated rooms in the rear of a structure were used for storing food.

Much of the daily life of the people took place outside in the open courtyards in front of the buildings. We can tell by the artifacts that it was there the women made pottery while the men made knives, axes, awls, and scrapers from stone and bone. Smoke-darkened walls and ceilings still stand, blackened by the fires needed to cook at all times of the year and needed for heat in the cold months of winter. Some of the walls were decorated, although most of the decoration has worn away over the seven hundred years since the Anasazi lived there. Here and there can be seen original plaster, some of it covered with paintings.

Clothing was basic and followed the seasons. Adults wore loincloths and sandals in the summer, and in winter they wrapped themselves in animal hides and blankets made of turkey feathers. Rabbit skins were used for clothing and winter footwear. The native yucca plant was useful for making sandals, and after the turkey was eaten, its bones were used for making tools. The people were quite self-sufficient, and at times they had enough extra to exchange with other groups for goods they wanted: seashells from the coast and turquoise, pottery, and cotton from the south. An extensive network of trails found their way to many different, far away places, and traders carried goods from one place to another.

One of the most important methods the archaeologist uses to learn about an ancient people is by studying the garbage sites. Here one can find scraps of food, broken pottery and tools, and anything else that was no longer wanted and thrown down the slope in front of the dwellings. These refuse heaps were also where the people buried their dead, probably because the ground was easier to dig than it was elsewhere.

The Anasazi almost certainly lived with several generations in the same household. Each family occupied a set of rooms, and when the family grew out of the rooms they had, they added on new rooms to the ones they already had. Several families constituted a clan, and because many of the old families were matrilineal, the Mesa Verde clans probably were as well. Each clan would have its own kiva and rights to its own gardening plots on top of the mesa.

The Anasazi *(cont.)*

The Anasazi lived in the cliff houses for less than a hundred years, and by 1300 Mesa Verde was deserted. Scientists now know that the twenty-five years or so at the end of the century was a time of drought and crop failures. It could be that the people had to leave because the soil had been depleted due to extensive farming. Also, the wooded areas had been denuded for use in building and for firewood. It is believed that when the Anasazi left, they traveled south into what is now New Mexico and Arizona, possibly to join and meld with other groups.

The illustration below shows the floor plan of a Mesa Verde cliff dwelling now named Cliff Palace. This village was built into a huge cave on the side of a cliff which faces toward the east where the sun rises. The individual buildings are from one to four stories high, and on visiting many of these ancient dwellings, one is amazed at how the people were able to adapt their living patterns to the natural environment. For example, some of the buildings have a kind of natural air-conditioning system with vents for air circulation. The round structures were the kivas, and these were probably central rooms for a family or clan.

Follow the directions on the next page to make your own model kiva.

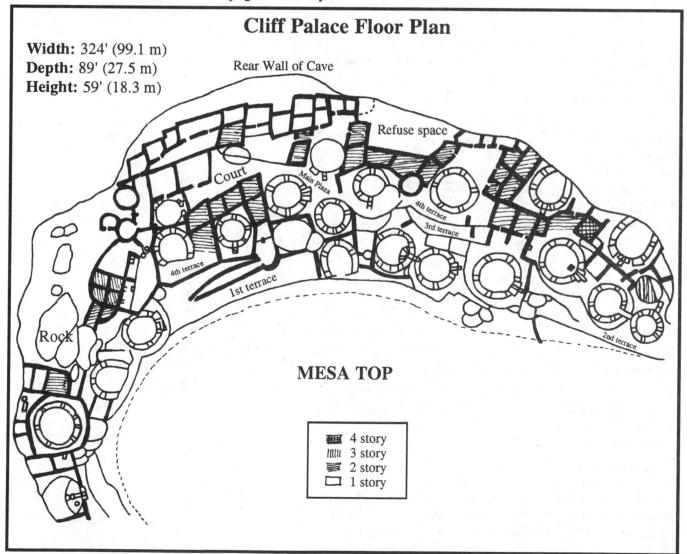

Cliff Palace Floor Plan

Width: 324' (99.1 m)
Depth: 89' (27.5 m)
Height: 59' (18.3 m)

Rear Wall of Cave

Refuse space

Court

Main Plaza

4th terrace

3rd terrace

4th terrace

1st terrace

2nd terrace

Rock

MESA TOP

4 story
3 story
2 story
1 story

Make a Kiva

A kiva is a large, sunken, circular form found in many ancient ruins of the Anasazi. Kivas are also built and used by the Hopis today. The word *kiva* means *ceremonial room*. It was, and is, used for ceremonies, as a workroom, and as a social gathering place.

Each old kiva generally contained six pillars on the inside wall to support the roof structure, and the roof was built of thick timbers, smaller poles, and a mud mixture strong enough to be used as a courtyard. Inside the kiva was a bench-like shelf which went around most of the inner wall, providing storage space for pottery and other objects. In the center of the roof was a hole which served a dual purpose as entry and as a hole to allow smoke to escape from the firepit which was directly under it. A ladder extended down from the hole to allow entry. When a fire was burning, the smoke rising through the smoke hole caused a partial vacuum, pulling fresh air through the ventilator shaft into the room.

One very interesting feature of most kivas is a small hole in the floor between the firepit and the wall called a *sipapu*. Hopi mythology says this hole, which is sometimes called the spirit hole, represents the hole through which the Hopi ancestors emerged from several previous underworlds.

Activity

Using the illustration below of a kiva, make a model of it with clay, bricks you make yourself from clay, or another building material. You may wish to leave your kiva roofless so it is possible to see the interior.

Kiva Model

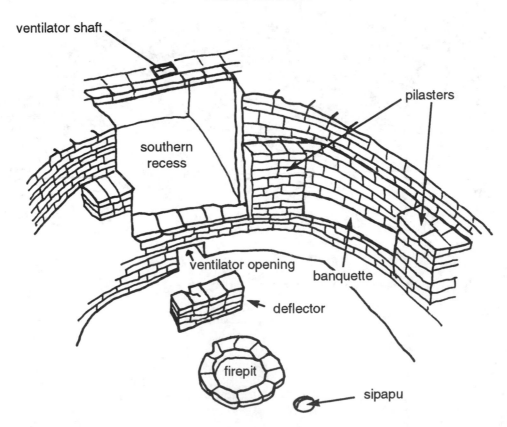

The Long Walk

At one time, the Navajo made treaties with the Americans, and their leaders, including Manuelito, tried to keep the promises of the treaties. However, a few young Navajo did something the Americans did not like, so the Americans came to Navajo country and burned the hogans and killed the livestock. The Americans also said that though the Mexicans who lived in Santa Fe were now Americans because New Mexico now belonged to the United States, the Indians were not Americans for the simple reason that they were Indian. Therefore, when Navajo animals strayed near the American forts, the soldiers shot them. Manuelito grew confused and angry.

Manuelito and his followers raided some American horses and supply trains to replace what had been taken from them, so the soldiers began attacking the Navajo. The Navajo did not have the powerful weapons of the soldiers. When the Navajo joined together to remove Fort Defiance, they did so to protect their country and their families, but the soldiers thought they were challenging the flag which flew over the fort.

After a long meeting between the Navajo and the soldiers, there seemed to be friendship at last. For several months, that peaceful period lasted. The Americans built another fort, and the new friendship grew to the point where the Navajo began having horse races at times with the American soldiers at the new fort named Wingate. On the days of the races, the Navajo dressed in their best clothes and rode their best ponies. Many bets were made, both by Navajo and by soldiers, until a lot of money and goods depended on the outcomes of the races.

One day in 1861, there was a special race between Pistol Bullet, the name the soldiers called Manuelito, and a lieutenant on a quarter horse. More was bet on this race than on any other that had taken place, but within a few seconds after the race had begun, Manuelito was obviously in trouble. His horse went out of control and ran off the track.

Everyone looked at the pony's reins, and it could be plainly seen that the reins had been cut with a knife. The Navajo told the judges, but the judges were all soldiers and they refused to allow the race to be rerun. "Too bad," they said. The soldiers formed a victory parade and lined up to collect their bets. When the Navajo tried to go into the fort after them, the gates were shut against them and one of their men was shot dead by a soldier. The Navajo scattered in all directions as the soldiers chased them with guns and bayonets. Women and children were killed along with men, and after that, the Navajo stayed away from the white soldiers.

The Long Walk *(cont.)*

In 1862, a new commander came to Fort Wingate. His name was General James Carleton, and he was called Star Chief because he wore stars on his shoulders. Star Chief called Navajo country "a princely realm" because of its beauty and wealth of gold. He said there was a place about three hundred miles away which would be a much better place for the Indians, both the Navajo and Mescalero Apaches, and that they had to move there.

The Navajo and Apaches did not want to move. They liked it where they were. But Star Chief said there would be no discussion about the matter, and they would have to go. There were not many Mescaleros, even less than a thousand, so he began with them. He told them the only way they could have peace was to move to Bosque Redondo, the reservation he had set aside for them, and they all either gave in to him or fled to Mexico.

Then, Star Chief ordered Kit Carson, whom the Navajo called Rope Thrower, to help get the Navajo out of Navajo country. He said they had until July, 1863, to come in peacefully, and after that they would be treated as hostiles. No Navajo came in voluntarily, so Star Chief ordered Kit Carson to prepare for war against the Navajo. Kit Carson liked Indians and did not want to do this, but he gave in, too. He headed for the Navajo stronghold, the beautiful Canyon de Chelly ("dashay").

Canyon de Chelly had at one time been a home to the Anasazi, and many cliff dwellings lined its steeply rising, red canyon walls. There the Navajo had for many generations raised their sheep and goats and cultivated their corn, wheat, fruit, and melons. The things they liked most, along with their sheep, were their peach orchards, which they attended carefully. Water was abundant in the canyon, and cottonwood and box elder trees lined the streams, giving them plenty of firewood and wood to build their hogans. The Navajo did not want to leave their lovely canyon, but Star Chief said they could not stay. They must go to Bosque Redondo.

Kit Carson sent Major Cummings to round up the Navajo's animals and to burn all their crops. The Navajo were furious. They shot and killed the major, but they could not stop the tide of Star Chief's determination to take Canyon de Chelly from them. Star Chief offered to pay twenty dollars for each Navajo horse or mule brought to him by a soldier, and one dollar for each sheep. The soldiers only made twenty dollars a month, so they jumped at the chance to make extra money. Anyway, who cared what happened to a bunch of Indians? Then, the soldiers started scalping the Navajo themselves.

Meanwhile, Kit Carson systematically destroyed the grain fields and the bean and pumpkin patches. In September, Star Chief ordered that any Navajo seen was to be shot on sight unless he surrendered. He asked for another regiment of cavalry to "protect the (American) people going to the gold mines." By autumn, most of the herds and fields had been destroyed by Carson, and the Navajo, beaten, began to trail in by the hundreds to the fort. Their clothing and food had been destroyed. They could not survive the winter. The first ones who surrendered were taken to Bosque Redondo, and Star Chief had them treated well. He wanted them to tell their people what a good place they were going to. However, some Navajo did not surrender.

One Navajo leader, Barboncito, raided an army mule herd and chased the mules he got into the canyon to use for a winter food supply. Star Chief was angry. He ordered that there would be no further delay. The Navajo were to be forced out, even though it was winter, and marched on their way to Bosque Redondo. The half-starved Indians tried to defend themselves with stones and pieces of wood, but it was impossible to stop the soldiers. Their hogans and scanty food caches were destroyed, and the soldiers captured everyone they found. But the worst thing the soldiers did to the Navajo was to destroy the beautiful peach orchards, the ones they had had for generations, since the time of the Spaniards. The Navajo lost heart, but they never forgave what was done to the peach trees.

The Long Walk *(cont.)*

By March, three thousand Navajo had surrendered at the fort, and they began what has come to be known ever since as The Long Walk to Bosque Redondo. Many died on the way. What the ones who lived found when they got to the reservation Star Chief had prepared for them was a desolate place without good water or firewood. For shelter, they had to dig holes in the sandy ground and line the holes with mats of woven grass. When they tried to plant wheat and corn, the floods, droughts, and insects killed everything. Disease began to kill the weaker people, and the stronger ones began to sneak away whenever they could to run back to their beloved canyon. Star Chief ordered that any Navajo found off the reservation without a pass should be killed.

In 1865, the crops failed, so the army gave the people corn meal, flour, and bacon which had been condemned by the army. The people began to die again. Star Chief continued to hunt down and kill anyone who escaped. Then suddenly, Star Chief was taken away, and a new chief, A.B. Norton, came to take his place. Norton did not hate Indians. He looked around him at Bosque Redondo and said the place was unfit for people to live. The water was black, the earth too alkaline to grow crops, and the only wood for building fires was twelve miles away. How could a human being live in this place?

The people in Washington talked about it. They sent inspectors to Bosque Redondo, and they talked about it some more. In came the great white warrior, General Sherman, and he asked the Navajo if they would obey the laws of the United States if he let them go back to their home. They agreed. They promised four times, and the Great Warrior said, "My children, I will send you back to your homes."

They had to sign another treaty first, and when they left in 1868, they could not get home quickly enough. They whipped the mules to move faster, and when they got there, they kissed the ground. They had come home. The Americans took a lot of the land they had previously lived upon, but they did not take Canyon de Chelly. The Navajo replanted their fields and their orchards. They rebuilt their hogans and restarted their sheep herds. By 1935, the Navajo had grown to 35,000 members.

No one can go into Canyon de Chelly without a Navajo guide. It is a very special place to the people, their home, and it is also a national monument. The Navajo lost many people trying to save it, and they want to keep it safe. The Navajo now call themselves the Navajo Nation, and they also call themselves the *Dineh*, which means the *People*. They have retained their individuality as a tribe, and they do not feel they have ever been a conquered nation because they kept their dignity and their soul. Despite all the changes around them, their culture has remained alive.

The Long Walk *(cont.)*

Activities

1. Work in groups or separately to complete a research project on one of the following topics or on a topic of your own which you can then share with the rest of your class. You may choose a diorama, written report, oral report, demonstration, or any format approved by your teacher.

   - Canyon de Chelly
   - the Navajo
   - the Apache
   - Kit Carson
   - Utes
   - Los Hermanos Penitentes
   - Zuni
   - Hopi
   - Fort Sumner
   - Fort Defiance
   - hogans
   - adobe
   - Gadsden Treaty
   - Mexican War

   - sheepherding
   - Southwest Indian art
   - Southwest Indian jewelry
   - Southwest Indian pottery
   - the Anasazi
   - Southwest Indian blankets
   - The Indian Removal Act
   - Mesa Verde
   - Chaco Canyon
   - weaving
   - Southwest Indian folktales and legends
   - Spanish occupation of the Southwest
   - Mexican occupation of the Southwest

2. Review a television show, video, or movie about Native Americans, and write a critical review of it to share with your classmates. When doing your review, ask yourself the following questions.

   a. Is this presentation biased in favor of the white civilization?

   b. Is this presentation biased in favor of the Native American groups portrayed?

   c. Does this presentation have many Native American stereotypes, portraying them as always good or always bad?

   d. Does this presentation try to appear fair to all involved?

   e. Is this presentation historically correct within the limits of your own knowledge?

   f. Does this presentation preserve the dignity of the people it concerns?

3. Compare an old western movie or television show and one made within the last two or three years. Ask the above questions about both of the presentations. How are they alike? How are they different? Do you see a change in the ways in which the Native Americans are portrayed today when compared with the way they were portrayed years ago?

From Nomadism to Farming

At some distant time in history, all people were food gatherers and hunters. Because there was not a constant supply of foods at any one place, this meant that people had to "follow" the food supply. How did the peoples of the North American continent advance from being dependent on wild foods growing naturally to being able to grow plants intentionally? Scientists, historians, and anthropologists have pooled their knowledge, so we now have a good idea of when such progress in human development in the Americas came about, although we do not know exactly how.

Long ago in Middle America, there were small, wandering groups of hunters who were equipped with flaked knives, pebble tools, and choppers. Half or more of their food they got from hunting and the rest was from wild vegetable sources which included species that would later become domesticated plants such as gourds, pumpkins, peppers, and runner beans. Shortly after 6500 BC, some inhabitants began to cultivate cotton, chili peppers, and a type of squash. The people became dependent on these plants, and as they did, they began to adjust their hunting patterns to seasonal changes. This encouraged two or three families to settle down together each year in order to cooperatively harvest these vegetable foods.

Sometime between 5000 and 3500 BC, the people started eating the early ancestor of corn, which in its wild form was only about one inch (2.5 cm) long, and they began planting the corn. Mutations occurred in the corn gradually, until by the end of this period it was very much as we now know it to be. As these mutations in plants took place, the people began to depend on the vegetable sources they found where they lived or which they cultivated.

The earliest plant foods developed in the Americas were squash and gourds which were in regular diets before 2500 BC. By this time, these foods were finding their way north as far as what is now Tennessee. Beans appeared after 3500 BC, and from that time on, ten percent of the foods eaten by the people in Middle America were the beans, squash, and maize (corn) they cultivated. The likely date of their first cultivation was somewhere between 5000 and 3000 BC. It is not known how these people first began to cultivate these plants, but the varieties which developed at that time had to have been done by someone who figured out how to crossbreed and hybridize. The results most likely could not have developed naturally.

The people still were basically hunters and fisherman, but by 2300 BC, the people living in what is now known as Kentucky and Tennessee were cultivating gourds, sunflowers, and grasses. By 2200 to 1800 BC, agriculture was furnishing as much as twenty percent of the food. Along with pottery, which was being developed by this time, scraps of wattle and daub (a way of building in which mud is smeared over a framework of sticks or reeds) have been found, indicating that permanent homes were being built by some of the people. They were no longer spending all their time following herds and wild foods.

From Nomadism to Farming *(cont.)*

By 2000 BC, small villages were appearing throughout the midsection of the continent. The people had made the transition from being nomads to being farmers, at least part of the time. The knowledge of how to cultivate plants spread northward, and before long a whole set of mythologies to explain the growth of plants began to develop. Most groups had stories to explain how corn, squash, or other plants came to be.

It is almost certain that one of the first things to happen in the beginning of farming was that someone noticed certain plants growing in certain places at certain times of the year, and over time they made connections between seeds or parts of plants falling on the ground and in some way being covered up and new plants later growing in that same spot. It could have been that in religious ceremonies seeds were "sacrificed" by being buried in the dirt. When new plants later appeared, someone got the idea of what was happening.

Farming in those early days was in many ways very different from the huge modern agribusinesses which are now common in the United States, particularly in California. For one thing, there was no irrigation, and the farmer was dependent on rainfall for moisture to germinate the seeds. In some areas, such as in the eastern parts of North America where there is sufficient rainfall, this would not have been a problem. In southwestern North America, however, it would have been a big problem. The annual rainfall was scarce and unpredictable. Many long months go by without any rainfall at all, and then sometimes huge downfalls occur causing destructive flash flooding.

The farmer needed to develop inventive ways to ensure a good crop if he was to allow himself to become dependent on farming. He had to become very aware of when the rains were likely to come and how to give the young plants the best chance of sprouting and growing to maturity. He had to determine which soils would be the most productive. He needed to become even closer to nature than he had been when he was simply a hunter-gatherer, because now, instead of watching for wild plants to mature, he had to be able to predict with some degree of certainty just where and when to plant in order to take advantage of natural weather patterns.

The new farmer, who had no *Farmer's Almanac* or gardening guide to follow, learned to observe when rains would be coming and when the weather was warm. He learned to plant his seeds deeply to give them the best chance of thriving because by planting deeply, the roots of the plant are cooler, closer to any moisture in the ground, and the new plants have greater stability in case of high winds or floods.

These early farmers became more settled than they had previously been, but every so often each group migrated from one place to another. The maps of migration patterns over the centuries tell a fascinating tale of people moving in more or less continuous cycles. It is not known exactly why these migrations repeatedly occurred. Sometimes a group may have moved for defensive purposes or periodic droughts might have led a group to move on. It also could have been that the soils had been depleted where the group was, and it became necessary to go to a new, unfarmed area.

From Nomadism to Farming *(cont.)*

Corn and cotton, which were two of the few staple crops grown by the early farmers, are very greedy plants. They quickly use up the nutrients in the soil without putting anything back into it. These plants were two of the culprits accounting for the "dust bowl" which occurred during the last century. And, of course, these early peoples would not have known about fertilizers as farmers do now.

One interesting thing done fairly early by some people which would have helped, or at least delayed, soil exhaustion from repeatedly planting corn and cotton, was to plant beans with the corn. The bean plant is part of the legume family. This family of plants is very interesting in that the roots of the plants hold what are called "nitrogen-fixing bacteria." These nitrogen-fixing bacteria replace nitrogen in the soil. You could say that, in regards to soil, legumes are "givers" and corn and cotton are "takers." Other legumes include alfalfa, clover, and peanuts.

Moving from a worn-out farming area to another area which had not been farmed would have allowed the old area to "rest." Modern farmers often leave a certain percentage of their fields to go fallow each year in order to allow them to recuperate from the repeated farming of greedy plants.

In any event, we are the inheritors of thousands of years of plant cultivation on most of the North American continent. Farming gave the early people a better chance of survival because they were not totally dependent on one source of food. One of the main reasons the Indians of the Great Plains were so devastated by the decline of the buffalo was that they had become dependent on one food source. This made them much more vulnerable than they would have been had they cultivated plants as well.

Activities

Here are several activities to help you get a better idea of some major principles of farming.

1. Grow an avocado plant from a pit. Instead of throwing away the large seed inside, peel off the brown skin, stick three toothpicks into its sides, and suspend it over a glass of water, big end down. Keep water just on the bottom end, and watch the roots grow first and then the leaves.

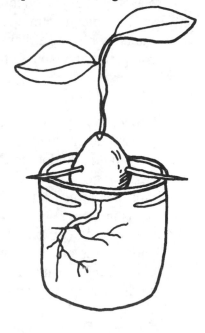

2. Grow a sweet potato plant. Stick three toothpicks into the sides of a sweet potato and submerge one end into a glass or jar of water. You will see tiny leaves growing from the tuber.

From Nomadism to Farming *(cont.)*

3. Grow a plant from a cutting. Cut a healthy three or four-inch (8–10 cm) piece with a slanted cut just below a node (the place where a leaf comes out). Strip the lower leaves from the stem and insert it about halfway into a pot containing sand or vermiculite. Cover the cutting with a plastic bag or jar and keep the cutting damp. You might notice that it wilts down for a few days, but this is just part of the process. Soon it will perk up, and you will have a small plant. Plants which "slip" easily this way include geraniums, fibrous begonias, daisies, and chrysanthemums.

4. Make a cold frame. A cold frame is a slanting box with a lid that will protect delicate plants such as tomatoes. The air inside a cold frame is warmer than that around it, and the lid will protect the plant from frost to allow it to grow outside earlier than it could otherwise. A small one can be made by using a heavy cardboard box from which you have cut the top and bottom. Sink the sides of the box into the dirt and bank it up with dirt to hold it. Cover the box with heavy plastic which you anchor with stones. You can see how much warmer the air is inside a cold frame by putting a thermometer inside and then comparing the temperature to the air outside.

5. Grow some sprouts to eat. Many people like to put sprouts in salads or sandwiches. They are easy to grow indoors. Obtain seeds from a health food store. Alfalfa and mung bean are the most common. Put a tablespoon (15 mL) of seeds in a wide-mouthed jar. Cover the seeds with an inch (2.5 cm) of water and cover the jar with a piece of clean gauze which you hold down with a rubber band. In the morning, drain the seeds without removing the cover and rinse with clean water. Empty the water when you are finished. Do this each day, and in about five to seven days you will have a crop of sprouts for your salad.

Folktales of the Southwest

Creation of the Sun and Moon

(Hopi)

In the beginning there was endless nothing, and soon after the world was made the boy warrior gods, Pokangahoya and Polongahoya, said, "We need light in this place," for there was only grayness.

Spider Grandmother agreed with them, saying, "Let us do something to bring light and warmth to the world."

She called together all the chiefs and medicine men, and they brought out many things they had taken with them when they left the Lower World. They cut a piece of buckskin into the shape of a disk and fastened it over a ring. Then they painted it with white clay and speckled it with black. They next lay the buckskin disk on a kwatskiavu cloth and began to sing. Next, four strong chiefs took the cloth at the four corners and, lifting it quickly, sent the disk soaring into the sky. They sang, and their songs were so strong they kept the disk moving upward until it disappeared. Soon after, however, the disk reappeared in the eastern sky, and it slowly moved high overhead.

The people now could see better than they had been able to, but it still was not light enough and the earth was too cool for them to grow corn. Spider Grandmother said, "We must try again." They made another disk much like the first one but larger. They painted it with egg yolks and sprinkled it with golden pollen. Then, they painted a face on the disk in red and black. Around its edges they fastened corn silk, and on its forehead they attached an abalone shell. Then they were through. They put this disk on a kwatskiavu cloth, and just as they had done before, the four chiefs grasped the four corners and, lifting quickly, sent the disk sailing into the air.

This time a bright glow appeared on the horizon in the east, and soon the disk appeared, shining brightly and lighting up the whole land. Now the people could see around them, and they could see all the wonderful things the boy warrior gods had created. This disk also cast warmth on the earth. The people were happy, because now they had a sun and a moon.

The sun traveled across the sky from east to west, throwing its rays of light and warmth all over the land. When it went down below the horizon in the west, the moon soon came to take its place. The people rested now for they were tired, but they forgot to put away the things they had used to send up the sun and moon.

While all of the people slept, Coyote came prowling around. He looked at the things and turned them over, but he could not find anything which he could eat, and in anger he threw some of them up into the sky. That is how Coyote made the stars. He also picked up some paint pots the people had used when making the sun and moon and threw them in all directions. The paint spattered all around, and that is how our buttes and rocks became so colorful—because of Coyote.

Folktales of the Southwest *(cont.)*

Corn Smut Girl

(Hopi)

A handsome young man named Rainbow Youth lived in one of the Hopi villages. Each day before the Sun rose he practiced running, and he often made offerings to the Sun and the gods so they would help him become strong and swift. But during the day he stayed inside the house.

One day he said he wanted to marry, but he did not want just any girl. He wanted one who could make cornmeal so fine it would stick to the large shell he had hanging on the wall in his house. The girls in the village thought Rainbow Youth was a fine young man, and they all wanted to marry him. Each young maiden in turn would grind cornmeal, making it just as fine as possible, and each in turn went to the house of Rainbow Youth to present him with her best cornmeal. But it was all to no avail, and one after another the disappointed maidens sadly left Rainbow Youth's house after her cornmeal failed to pass his test.

Now, in this village there lived another young maiden. She was named Corn Smut Girl because she was ugly and dirty. Her brothers often teased her, saying, "Why do you not marry Rainbow Youth?" But privately they laughed and said among themselves, "He would not keep his promise to marry her, even if she made the finest corn meal."

Corn Smut Girl did not let her brothers' laughter stand in her way, however, and when she had made her cornmeal, which was exceptionally fine, she put it in a basket and took it to the house of Rainbow Youth. He was very kind to her, and he invited her into the house. "Why have you come?" he asked her.

"I have come for you," Corn Smut Girl replied.

"Very well," Rainbow Youth said, and he dipped his hand into her basket, taking a handful of cornmeal. He threw the meal against the shell, and it stuck fast.

"Good!" he exclaimed. "I have given my word. I said I would marry the maiden whose meal would stick to my shell, and your meal has done so. I will go with you."

The two of them went to Corn Smut Girl's house, because when a Hopi man and woman marry, he goes to live with her family. The mother and brothers of Corn Smut Girl were very surprised that this handsome young man had married the girl, but they welcomed him warmly.

When evening drew near, and it was time to eat the evening meal, Corn Smut Girl went into the next room. Within minutes, a lovely young woman came in and sat down with the others to eat. Rainbow Youth wondered where his wife was and who this young woman was, but he said nothing.

When bedtime came, his new brothers-in-law told him that the beautiful woman was his wife, Corn Smut Girl. Her ugly face was only a mask which she wore during the day, but every night she removed the mask, and her true self showed in the midst of her family. She was, in truth, a goddess!

The other girls in the village, who did not know Corn Smut Girl's true identity, were angry and jealous that Rainbow Youth had married someone as ugly as Corn Smut Girl, but Rainbow Youth did not listen to their insults and jibes as he walked through the village with his wife. He knew that his wife was really more beautiful than any of the other young women.

After several years, Corn Smut Girl told Rainbow Youth it was not right for her to live with mortals, so with her entire family, including her husband, she disappeared into the ground. At the place where she and her family went into the ground, the Hopi now pray to Corn Smut Girl as a goddess, begging her to send them good crops of corn.

Folktales of the Southwest *(cont.)*

Coyote Steals the Sun

(Zuni)

It is true that Coyote is a trickster, but he is not a very good one because he always gets things wrong. He also is a bad hunter. One day he was watching Eagle hunt rabbits. Eagle was so good he caught one after the other.

"I think I'll join up with Eagle," he thought to himself. "He's a good hunter, and if I team up with him, I'll always have meat to eat."

"Friend Eagle," Coyote said to Eagle when he finally caught up with him. "We should hunt together. Two is always better than one."

"You may be right," Eagle replied, so Eagle and Coyote started off together.

It was not long, however, before Eagle noticed that while he had caught many rabbits to eat, Coyote, who was a bad hunter, had caught only a few little bugs. Now at this time there was no sun and moon, so the world was dark all the time.

"Friend Eagle," Coyote said one day, "it is no wonder I can not catch anything. I can not see. Do you know where we can get some light?"

"Yes, Friend Coyote, we should have some light," Eagle said. "I think I know where there is some in the west. Let's go see about it."

So the two went off to look for the sun and moon. They came to a big river. Eagle flew over it, and Coyote swam across. He swallowed so much water he almost drowned. When he climbed out of the water, Eagle said, "Why don't you fly like I do?"

"I don't have any feathers," Coyote said. "I have only hair. It takes feathers to fly."

Eagle just shook his head and they went on.

After awhile they came to a pueblo where the Kachinas were dancing. The people were hospitable and invited the two to eat with them while they watched the sacred dances. Eagle saw that the Kachinas had great power, and he said, "I think these are the people who have the light."

Coyote became excited and looked around him. He noticed a little distance from where they were sitting two boxes, one large and one small. Every time someone wanted light, he would go over to one of the boxes and slightly raise the lid. If he wanted more light, he would completely open the box. The light in the smaller box was dim and shone with a silvery color, but when the large box was opened, a great yellow light that lit up the whole place came from it, and they knew it was the sun.

Coyote nudged Eagle. "Friend Eagle, do you see what I see? They have the light we are looking for. Why don't we steal it?"

Eagle frowned and said, "You always want to steal things. Why don't we just borrow it?"

"I don't think they will lend it to us," Coyote said.

"You're probably right," Eagle said after he thought a minute. "Wait until the dancing is over, and we'll steal it!"

When the Kachinas went to sleep, Eagle swooped down and picked up the large box with his claws and flew off. Coyote ran after him. After awhile his tongue started to hang out and he was panting, so he called up to Eagle, "Wait a minute, Friend Eagle! Let me carry the box awhile."

Folktales of the Southwest *(cont.)*

Coyote Steals the Sun *(cont.)*

"I don't think so," Eagle said. "You never do anything right. You'd probably drop it!" and he flew on with Coyote running after him as fast as he could.

"Friend Eagle," Coyote tried again, "You're my chief, and it's not right for you to be carrying the box. People will think I am lazy. Please let me carry it."

"No way!" Eagle said. "You always mess everything up," and he continued on with the box.

This kept up for quite awhile with Eagle flying and carrying, and Coyote panting along behind.

"Friend Eagle," Coyote began again, "please let me carry the box." And it went on as before, Eagle flying and carrying, and Coyote panting slower and slower behind.

At last, Coyote called out again, "Friend Eagle! I am asking you for the fourth time! You must let me carry the box." And this time, Eagle knew he must relinquish the box to Coyote because when anyone asks you something four times, you must do it.

"All right, but only on one condition," Eagle said. "You must not open it!"

"I promise," said Coyote. But do you think he could keep a promise? The two continued on their way, but now that Coyote had the box, he lingered behind, and soon Eagle was far ahead. "I don't think there would be anything wrong if I just took a little peek," he said to himself. "Eagle just wants to keep it for himself."

He opened the lid, and as soon as he did, the sun flew out of the box and into the sky. Whoops! Suddenly all the plants began to shrivel up and die, and the leaves fell off the trees. It was winter, just that fast! Coyote tried to catch the sun, but as fast as he could run, and that was not very fast, the sun flew on ahead of him. It flew far away, and all the fruits on the trees and the squashes and melons began to shrivel up and die.

Eagle flew back to where Coyote was standing helplessly watching the sun fly away. "You fool!" he said. "You let it get away. I knew I shouldn't trust you!"

And as he said that, it began to snow. "This is all your fault," Eagle said to Coyote. "You are the one who brought cold into the world."

And, for sure, if Coyote had not been so curious and full of mischief, we would not have winter at all. It would be summer all the time!

Activities

1. "The Corn Smut Girl" is in many ways like the European-American story of Cinderella. To compare the two, divide a piece of paper down the middle. On the left side of the paper put the heading "Alike," and on the right side of the paper put the heading, "Different." List alike or different characteristics under each heading.

2. Remember the saying that you can tell what is important to a people if you know their stories? What do you think the people who first told the story of Cinderella considered to be important? What do you think the people who first told the story of Corn Smut Girl considered to be important?

3. Find a story in the mythology of another culture that tells about the sun or the coming of winter and summer. Do you know of a Greek story which told about how evil came into the world? How is it like "Coyote Steals the Sun"?

Vitamin Math

The natives of the Southwest grew large quantities of corn, beans, melons, and squash, and these foods provided much of their diets. They are very nutritious foods containing many of the vitamins and minerals needed every day for good health. Today, much is written about whether the foods we eat provide sufficient vitamins and minerals for us. Work the following problems to get a better idea about just how many nutrients are in these foods.

1. The minimum daily requirement of vitamin C to prevent scurvy is about 30 milligrams (mg), but some authorities believe we need 1,000 mg.
   a. If a serving of cantaloupe contains 50 mg of vitamin C, how many servings will you need to get 30 mg of vitamin C?
   b. How many servings will you need to eat to get 1,000 mg?

2. The recommended daily amount (RDA) of beta-carotene, which contains vitamin A, is 150 International Units (IU). One serving of spinach has 75 IU.
   a. How many servings of spinach would you need to eat to get 150 IU?
   b. How many servings of spinach would you need to eat to get the amount of beta-carotene in one beta-carotene supplement containing 25,000 IU?

3. If one orange contains 75 mg of vitamin C, but you have a cold and think you should take extra in the amount of 400 mg, how many oranges will you need to eat?

4. You do not want to eat the number of oranges suggested in the problem above, so you decide to eat one orange and get the rest of your vitamin C from cantaloupes. One serving of cantaloupe contains 50 mg of vitamin C. With the one orange, how many servings of cantaloupe will you eat in order to get your desired 400 mg?

5. Baked squash is an excellent source of beta-carotene. If one serving of squash provides 200 IU of beta-carotene and you eat one serving of squash each day for one year (364 days), how many units of beta-carotene will you obtain from squash in one year?

6. Dried beans are a good source of niacin. If one serving of dried beans contains 20 mg niacin, and the RDA is 100 mg per day, how many servings of beans per day will you need to eat if you eat nothing else containing niacin?

7. If a capsule of beta-carotene contains 25,000 IU of beta-carotene, and one serving of corn contains 20 IU beta-carotene, how many servings of corn will you need to eat to get the amount of beta-carotene in the capsule?

8. A serving of melon contains 50 mg vitamin C, and a village of 437 people each eat two servings of melon per day.
   a. How many mg of vitamin C does the village consume in one day?
   b. In one week?
   c. In one year (364 days)?

9. Green peppers are an excellent source of vitamin C, as well as iron and beta-carotene. A serving of one pepper contains 60 mg of vitamin C, and each person in a village of 365 eats three servings per day.
   a. How many mg of vitamin C does the village eat in one day?
   b. In one week?
   c. In one year (364 days)?

10. On the back, write a problem involving vitamins which you can ask your classmates to solve. Include sufficient data for them to do the problem and work the problem yourself before you ask them to do so.

Hoop and Pole Games

One of the most universally played games in North American was the hoop and pole game. Every native group played at least one version of this game which requires a hoop or target of some kind and two darts. Some versions also require especially made counting sticks for keeping score. The game can be played by several players; however, usually it involves only two.

A common form of hoop is twined with sinew or cord to resemble a spider web. Scores are made when the dart or pole is accurately thrown through the center. The hoop itself can be made from a piece of green sapling which bends easily. The ends are secured together to the size desired, and they are then lashed with rawhide. Other groups use hoops carved from stone. Some groups trim their hoops with beads, feathers, or cornhusks, while others leave them plain.

There are also variations among groups as to how the darts or poles are made. Arrows or plain, long, wooden poles are sometimes used. The Hopi used feather darts and a netted hoop. The Apache used long, jointed poles, and the Navajo used jointed poles with a thong attached.

There is much ceremony surrounding the playing of the game. Some groups play it only at certain times of the year. The Zuni, for example, see the hoop as having stood for the shield of their twin war gods, Ahaiyuta and Matsailema, and they say this shield was actually used in warfare in ancient times. Others see the hoop as representing Grandmother Spider and her magical web. Zuni ceremonials sometimes use miniature hoops with tiny bows and arrows, and they sometimes sacrifice feather darts on the altar of the war god.

Many Indians saw the hoop as representing the sacred circle of day and night or the zodiac. The colors customarily used to paint the hoop include yellow, red, blue, and black, each of which represents a quarter of the globe or the places of the four winds. In this case, if the hoop was laid on the ground, it would be laid with the juncture of the yellow and red to the north, giving each of the four winds its proper color: north to east is yellow, east to south is black, south to west is blue, and west to north is red. Each pole or dart belongs to the wind represented by its color.

One version of the game is described on the next page. In a variation, the Indians threw sticks, arrows, or poles at a rolling hoop. Sometimes the hoop was laced or was solid in the center. The object of this form of the game was to send the dart through the center of the rolling hoop.

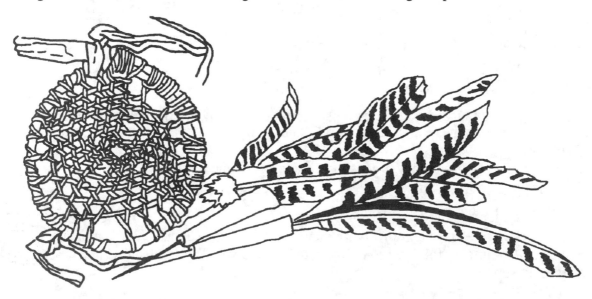

Corn Darts Game

You can make a corn darts game similar to those played by Southwestern Indian groups.

Materials:

- several corn cobs 3" (8 cm) long
- clay
- trimmed feathers
- sharpened pencil
- reed or rope for hoop
- dried cornhusks or raffia
- red, blue, yellow, and black paints (optional)

Directions:

1. Make a circle about 5" (13 cm) in diameter with the reed or rope, and tie the ends together. Wrap your hoop with cornhusks or raffia, trim it with beads and feathers, or paint it.

2. Hollow out the centers of the corn cobs. Fill the hollows with clay, and while the clay is still soft, stick the blunt end of the pencil into the clay with the point sticking out. Make sure it is in straight and firmly in place. Stick the feathers in the opposite end to the pencil. Let the clay dry completely.

3. To play, place the hoop on the ground outdoors at a marked distance from the players. Toss your dart toward the hoop, trying to make the dart stand up inside. The winner is the one who gets the largest number of darts to stick inside the hoop.

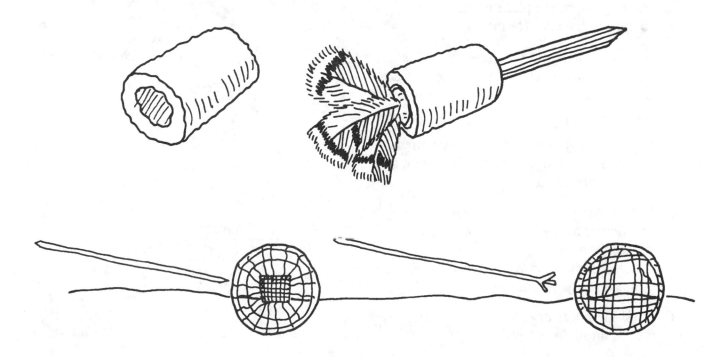

Make a Coiled Pot

The Anasazi made pottery which remains beautiful today. The early designs were almost entirely in black and white, although later pieces were painted with many different colors made from natural clays. These early people made vessels of all kinds: pots, bowls, canteens, ladles, jars, and mugs. Many of the pieces were used for cookware and storage, but the more elaborately decorated ones were probably used for ceremonial purposes. Women were the ones who made the pottery, and the designs were passed down from mother to daughter. Today, archaeologists can use the designs on the pottery to track who the ancient peoples were and where they lived.

Most of the early pottery was made by a process called coiling. This kind of pottery making involves molding ceramic clay into long coils and spiraling them together in such a way as to build up the vessels.

You can make pottery in this way.

Materials:

- ceramic clay
- water
- a clean, smooth work surface
- ceramic paint (or another kind that will adhere to pottery)

1.

2.

Directions:

1. Roll the clay into a long, round rope, making sure it is about the same diameter throughout its length.

2. Form a flat, round piece of clay about 2" (5 cm) in diameter for the base.

3. Start spiraling your clay rope from this base and continue building up the coiled clay until it is the shape you wish to make it.

   3.

4. Wet your fingers or use a pottery knife to blend the coils together until they form a smooth surface.

   4.

5. When your piece looks like you want it to, allow it to dry thoroughly. You can put it in a warm oven to dry, or if you are lucky enough to have a kiln available, you can fire your pot in that.

   6.

6. After the pot is dry, you can paint a design on it.

Make a God's Eye

God's eyes (or *ojos de Dios* in Spanish) are a traditional craft among Indians of the Southwest, including the Navajo. Usually they are used as good luck charms or symbols; however, they are sometimes used by the Navajo to subdue unruly children. Would you misbehave if you were made aware that God was watching every move?

God's eyes are fun and easy to make. Here is how it is done.

Materials:

- two sticks 12" (30 cm) long
- yarn in 3 to 6 different colors
- scissors
- saw or chisel for notching wood
- needle with large eye for yarn
- white glue

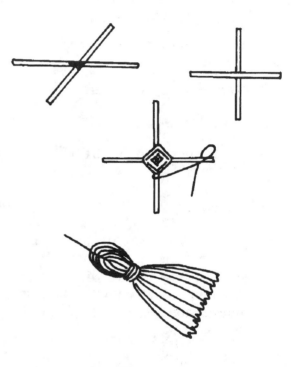

Directions:

1. Notch the exact center point of each stick. Glue and press the sticks together and let them dry before starting to make your God's eye.

2. Loop yarn around one stick near where the sticks cross. As you work, cover the tail end of the yarn.

3. Working counter-clockwise, loop the yarn around first one stick and then the next. Change colors as you wish, but keep one color dominant.

4. When the sticks have been totally covered, attach tassels to the bottom and side points. Attach a yarn loop at the top for hanging your God's eye,

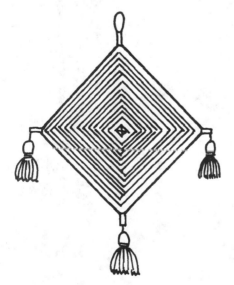

Tassel Directions:

1. Wrap yarn approximately 25 times around a piece of cardboard or 2–3 of your fingers.

2. Slip a strand of yarn under one fold of the yarn and tie it tightly.

3. Cut the other end and then wind another strand of yarn to make a topknot.

4. Trim the ends to any desired length.

Unweave Burlap

You have probably been introduced to the craft of weaving, but have you ever learned to unweave? If you enjoy needlecrafts, you will enjoy unweaving. You do not need to now how to sew to do it. This is an enjoyable activity in which you pull strands from a coarse fabric like burlap and, using colors and designs of your own, replace the strands in patterns with different colored yarns to make interesting and beautiful wall hangings. Follow these directions.

Materials:

- piece of burlap in any color and size desired
- yarn (variety of colors)
- tapestry needle
- scissors
- wooden beads (optional)

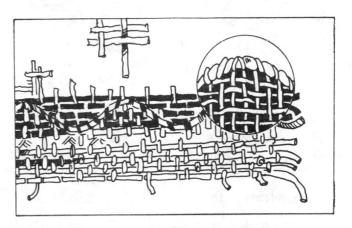

Directions:

1. Cut the burlap to the size and shape you wish.

2. Gently pull out threads in the direction you wish the designs to go. With the needle, weave yarns in and out and up and down through the now empty spaces in any way you like. Yarns and designs can go both ways. Do not be afraid to experiment. If you do not like the way it looks, you can pull it out and do it another way.

3. You can finish your hanging in different ways. One way is to fringe the bottom of the hanging by pulling out crosswise threads and letting the vertical ones hang. You can string wooden beads on the threads, or if you know how to crochet, you can make a crocheted fringe at the bottom and loop a hanger at the top.

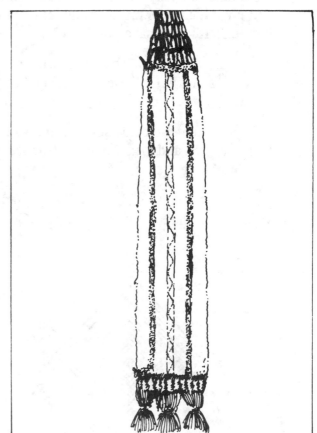

Indian Symbols and Meanings

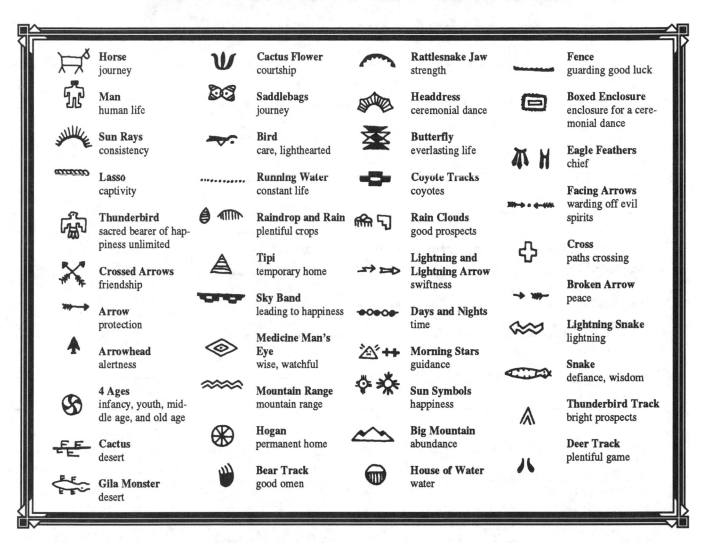

Horse journey	**Cactus Flower** courtship	**Rattlesnake Jaw** strength	**Fence** guarding good luck
Man human life	**Saddlebags** journey	**Headdress** ceremonial dance	**Boxed Enclosure** enclosure for a ceremonial dance
Sun Rays consistency	**Bird** care, lighthearted	**Butterfly** everlasting life	**Eagle Feathers** chief
Lasso captivity	**Running Water** constant life	**Coyote Tracks** coyotes	**Facing Arrows** warding off evil spirits
Thunderbird sacred bearer of happiness unlimited	**Raindrop and Rain** plentiful crops	**Rain Clouds** good prospects	**Cross** paths crossing
Crossed Arrows friendship	**Tipi** temporary home	**Lightning and Lightning Arrow** swiftness	**Broken Arrow** peace
Arrow protection	**Sky Band** leading to happiness	**Days and Nights** time	**Lightning Snake** lightning
Arrowhead alertness	**Medicine Man's Eye** wise, watchful	**Morning Stars** guidance	**Snake** defiance, wisdom
4 Ages infancy, youth, middle age, and old age	**Mountain Range** mountain range	**Sun Symbols** happiness	**Thunderbird Track** bright prospects
Cactus desert	**Hogan** permanent home	**Big Mountain** abundance	**Deer Track** plentiful game
Gila Monster desert	**Bear Track** good omen	**House of Water** water	

The above chart shows some of the symbols natives of the Southwest might have used when leaving a message for a friend or when writing on the canyon walls. Write a message to your teacher using these symbols and any others you create.

_____

_____

_____

_____

_____

_____

Quiz

1. List three important things you have learned about the natives of the Southwest. _____

   _____

2. What is the common name used for the forced march taken by the Navajo in 1864?_____

   _____

3. Describe a kiva and tell its purpose. _____

   _____

4. Why might some of the ancient peoples of North America have moved from one place to another
   at times?_____

   _____

   _____

5. How do we know things about ancient peoples? _____

   _____

6. What part did games traditionally play in Native American life? _____

   _____

7. How did ancient peoples go from being hunters-gatherers to being farmers?_____

   _____

   _____

8. According to the legend, how did the rocks and buttes become colorful?_____

   _____

9. When Coyote wanted to carry the box containing the sun, what was Eagles' response?

   _____

10. On the back of this paper, compare and contrast the stories of "Cinderella" and "Corn Smut Girl."

Ishi in Two Worlds

In August, 1911, the sheriff of Oroville, California, received an excited phone call from the butchers of a local slaughterhouse. At daybreak that morning, they had found an Indian crouching in the corral outside and dressed in nothing but a ragged poncho-like garment. When the sheriff arrived, he found a thin, emaciated Indian man who was obviously exhausted and terrified. The sheriff was not sure what to do with the man, and discovering that his new prisoner  knew not one word of English, the sheriff handcuffed him and took him to jail. The Indian was Ishi.

Ishi did not resist arrest. Close to starvation, he later said that the cell for the insane into which he was first put was in a fine house, but in his extreme fatigue and fear, he ate not a bite nor slept a wink his first day of captivity. He fully expected to be put to death, because the only white men he had ever seen had killed his people. Local Indians tried to talk to him in Maidu, Wintu, and Spanish, but he understood not one word they said. The language with which he replied was not understood by anyone.

The story of Ishi's capture made the newspapers quickly and soon came to the attention of two anthropologists at the University of California, Professors Kroeber and Waterman. They knew that three years earlier some surveyors had surprised and chased away a small band of Indians near where Ishi was found, and at that time, they had spent several weeks trying to find them. Kroeber and Waterman wired Sheriff Weaver to hold Ishi. They said they would come and get him and take responsibility for him. They correctly guessed that Ishi was a Yana, and because of this, they were able to develop a beginning communication with him using words from a related language. Time soon showed Ishi to be the last living member of his tribe, but through him, the anthropologists were able to learn much about his people.

The Yana had lived in the foothills of Mount Lassen along the streams flowing westward toward the Pacific Ocean. They were not very many, but they were feared by their Maidu and Wintu neighbors as swift and courageous people. The foothills where they lived were covered with fir, oak, chaparral, and pine, and the heavy rains which frequently occur during the winter had cut deep gorges. Salmon climbed the streams at spawning time, and the Yana knew every stream, but living in this particular part of a bountiful state was not easy. The winters were cold and the summers hot. Not many foods were available, so even the acorn, which takes so long to prepare before it is edible, was a staple in the diet.

When the first whites came to the Lassen foothills, they were surprised. They expected to find tall, handsome, and arrogant warriors like the ones they knew of on the Great Plains. But here, the Indians were smaller and rounder, and they did not go about on horses. When they fought, they used bows and arrows, spears, and knives, and they did not scalp their enemies. Instead of living in buffalo-hide tipis, these people built conical shaped houses from poles and bark, banked with dirt up to four feet (1.25 m) high to conserve heat. The inside measurement was ten feet (3 m) high at the most with a diameter of eighteen to twenty feet (5.5 to 6 m). Inside was a circular pit about three to four feet (1–1.25 m) deep, within which were the firepit and cooking utensils. This was where the family cooked, ate, and slept during cold weather. The walls were lined with tule mats, and blankets, baskets, and hunting gear hung there. In this place, a man, a woman, their children, and maybe one or two grandparents lived together.

Ishi in Two Worlds *(cont.)*

A man who was a good hunter and provider might have two wives, and if he did, they all lived together as a family. As with some of the Great Plains Indians, the wives were often sisters. Sometimes two or more families lived in a large house, and when this was true, there might be a men's house which served as a club house and got the men out of the way while the women worked in the home. Families were not large, and every child was wanted and loved.

Never with the Yana or with any other California Indian group was there ever a conception of the woman as a slave-like squaw. The division of labor was fair and reasonable, and everyone worked hard by necessity.

Time was marked by day and night, the moons, and the seasons. The Yana ate clover early in the springtime when it was tender, but later there were tender bulbs to dig up and eat. Deer meat was a favorite food all through the year. It was cooked in a strong broth of meat and greens. Springtime was the time to repair the coverings of the houses. Immune to the poison oak which was everywhere, the people had no need for clothing in the hot months of summer and several times a day would go for long swims in the streams. After the early morning hours, it was too hot to work. The time was better used by swimming and drinking the cool, nourishing drink the women made from manzanita berries.

Sometimes the people would go for a time up the cool, tree-covered slopes of Mount Lassen, and the men would go off for several hours to hunt for deer. As they brought the deer back, the women would cut it and dry it, and when they returned home, their baskets would be loaded with deer to feed them during the stormy days of winter. In autumn, acorns would be shelled and dried and then stored along with the nuts of the buckeye, pine, and hazel. The salmon would be caught and dried as well. Autumn was when families and communities socialized out in the open together. Then it was winter again, the time to spend inside one's own house where it was warm. This was the time to repair ropes and nooses, bows, quivers, and arrow points. It was the time for making baskets and telling the stories of how the world began and how men and animals were made.

Just as the discovery of gold had marked the end of other native cultures in North America, so, too, the discovery of gold in California ended life as it had been for many centuries for Ishi's people and other native Californians. Ten years before Ishi's birth, between two and three thousand of his people had occupied over 2,000 square miles (5,200 square kilometers) of land. Twenty-two years later, in 1872, only twenty or thirty individuals still lived in scattered small groups. As many as a hundred thousand whites a year came into the area. The newcomers were racist in outlook, unencumbered by wives or families in many cases, and since there were no controls on their behavior and they believed anyone non-white to be inferior, the native populations were usually wiped out in a very short time. No more care was given to killing an Indian, or Indians, than would have been given to killing an insect or a coyote. Thousands of Indian children were kidnapped and sold as slaves or kept for cheap help. As if that were not enough, the whites brought with them all their diseases which ran rapidly through the populations that had no immunity to them. At least sixty percent of the natives died from the diseases within ten years of their introduction.

The few Yana that were left learned quickly to distrust and fear the white man. They could not use their traditional means of obtaining food for fear of being captured or killed, and food gathering became raiding, getting it when and where one could, because one might not get another chance. The white man called the Indians "wild," and said, "You can't tell one Indian from another," and "The only good Indian is a dead Indian." There were a few instances in which the Yana and its sub-group, the Yahi (Ishi's own group), took revenge on the white man and killed them, but by the time Ishi had outgrown his childhood, the Yana were a desperate people. That was the way Ishi spent his life until the day he was found, cowering and starving in the corral in Oroville.

Ishi in Two Worlds *(cont.)*

While Ishi awaited the anthropologists, the good people of the town tried to help. The women made dishes to tempt his appetite, and others donated clothing for him to wear to San Francisco. He could not wear the shoes, however. No matter how he tried, feet which had always had contact with the earth could not learn to wear the stiff, unnecessary objects. They marred his balance, so the shoes were returned.

When Professor Waterman arrived, he walked with Ishi from the jail to the railroad station. People watched but kept their distance. Perhaps a little afraid or ashamed, they kept silent. Ishi had become somewhat of a myth and a mystery to them by now. He approached the big, black train with some of his own fears. He had heard it every day he could remember, and his mother had told him it was a demon who followed white men wherever they went. He had never been near it, and now he was going to ride in it.

He was quiet during his trip but also excited. The view of the passing scenery and the curious strangers on the train who watched him caused him to lower his eyes so as not to look directly at them. Time passed, and soon he had crossed the bay on the ferry and arrived at his new home. In the museum was where he would spend the less than five years he had remaining in his life, demonstrating how to make arrows and bows and how his people lived.

The museum had a small room where Indians from other tribes had sometimes stayed as they helped the professors learn about their people and their languages. It was into this room that Ishi moved in 1911, and there he met Professor Kreober.

Kreober was impressed with Ishi's gentleness and timidity. Constantly barraged by new and unfamiliar noises, he started at any sudden sound like a cannon in the distance or the voice of a stranger coming into the room. His shyness was acute. The first time he spoke to Kreober, he blushed as though he had done something wrong. But more than anything else, Ishi knew that he was alone. There were no more of his own people, so in his own, quiet, bashful way, he adopted these strange new beings with whom he now lived. He liked to be with people, and he liked to smile. He was interested and amused by everyone he met. He learned some of the white man's ways, like how to use a fork and knife and how to greet and say goodbye. Yet he always remained himself. He slowly learned a little English; however, he was forever Yahi.

Ishi in Two Worlds *(cont.)*

Ishi was not his real name, of course. He never revealed what his real name was, because a California Indian seldom spoke his own, private name aloud and used it only with someone who already knew it. When Ishi was asked what his name was, he replied politely that he had been alone so long he had had no one to give him a name. Kreober, knowing of the Indian's reluctance to name himself, gave him the name Ishi, which means *man* in Yana. But once the new name was given to him, he never said the word aloud again.

His name was now Ishi, and his address was the museum. From the time he arrived in San Francisco, the impresarios and exploiters swarmed around, wanting to package him and sell him to waiting audiences around the world. The reporters descended on the museum with their cameras, and the public clamored to see him. They wanted him put on display. Barkers wanted to show him to lonely drifters and sailors next to the nude women and freaks. The professors were so careful to prevent this from happening that no one was allowed even to photograph him except museum personnel. Unfortunately, the only moving film ever taken of Ishi was discovered some years later to have dissolved into a glutinous mess, so only still photos now exist.

Finally, Kreober and Ishi "received" the public on Sunday afternoons in a large upstairs room of the museum, where Ishi would demonstrate how to chip an arrowhead or string a bow. He was allowed to come and go freely in the museum when he was not working with Waterman and Kreober, and more and more he came to see the museum as his home. He grew able to distinguish non-Indians. He was most impressed by a mounted policeman, because he thought that with such a horse and such a uniform, the policeman had to be an important chief. He practiced saying "policeman" until he could do it to his satisfaction.

Ishi went many places with others. He often went to Waterman's home in Berkeley for dinner. The first time he did, he closely watched Mrs. Waterman use her napkin, choose a fork, and how much she put on her plate, and he copied her movements. He went for automobile rides through Golden Gate Park and to the beach. He had heard of the ocean and looked forward to seeing it, but when he got there, he was more impressed by the thousands of people covering the beach than he was with the beach itself. He said over and over, "Many white people! Many white people!" He had not known so many people existed. He was not impressed by the sight of the tall buildings because they were small when compared with the canyon walls and mountains he knew. When Ishi attended vaudeville, his reaction was much like the one at the beach: he spent the first two acts looking at the audience.

In December, 1914, Ishi developed a hacking cough. The doctors tested him at the university with what were at the time the only known tests for tuberculosis, but he seemed to recover so they assumed he had had a mild infection of some kind. The following spring, however, he became sick again, and this time he tested positive for the disease. Again, the doctors said he had recovered, and he went to live with the Watermans in Berkeley. He seemed happy with them, and he worked several hours each day with Edward Sapir, the famous linguist, helping him to record material about his native language.

In late August, however, Waterman noticed that Ishi was tiring easily and had little appetite, so he took him back to the museum where he could be under the watchful eye of the doctor. He soon was put back into the hospital with acute symptoms. It became apparent that he would not live much longer, and knowing that the Indian always wanted to be at home when he died, Ishi was brought back to the museum. He was put into the sunniest room with a wide view overlooking Sutro Forest in the park. He never complained, and he remained interested in all around him until his death March 25, 1916. He was cremated, as was the custom of the Yahi, and his ashes placed into a small black pueblo jar which was inscribed, "Ishi, the last Yana Indian, 1916."

Ishi in Two Worlds *(cont.)*

Activity

Ishi spent the last years of his life living in a museum. Today the idea of someone living in a museum while being studied by social scientists seems strange, and yet, for Ishi, it seemed to have been a happier situation for him than continuing to live alone in fear and without the basic necessities of life. The people around him truly loved and appreciated him, and there seems to be no suggestion that he was ever treated by them with anything other than respect and affection.

In a box, make a miniature model museum showing what you think the room used by Ishi to greet his "guests" looked like. In your museum room, place replicas of the bows, arrows, spears, and other artifacts which you believe Ishi would have had about him. Label each of these artifacts and write a glossary explaining the use, manufacturing, and purpose of each.

Keeping in Balance

Ishi soon grew accustomed to many of the white man's customs, including his clothing. However, there was one thing he never became accustomed to, and that was the wearing of shoes. Shoes felt hard and heavy to this man who had never worn them. In fact, they almost crippled him.

From the time he first learned to walk, Ishi had been barefoot, and he learned to feel the earth on the bottom of his foot and use his big toe for balance. With his foot encased in a stiff shoe, he could not feel the earth or use his toe.

What is balance? To understand what balance is, set a book on the edge of a table. Gradually ease it over the edge. As long as you push it only so far, the book will remain on the table, but as soon as you push it too far, you will upset the balance of the book, and it will fall. The point at which this happens, the balancing point, is called the *center of gravity*.

Try the following experiment to help you understand the concept of the center of gravity and balance. You will be making a balancing acrobat.

Materials:

- heavy paper or cardboard
- pencil
- crayons or markers
- scissors
- tape
- glue
- string
- two small coins

Directions:

1. Fold the cardboard or paper in half and trace the acrobat pattern onto it. Cut the two acrobats out so there is a front a back side which match.

2. Draw and color clothes on your acrobat.

3. With tape, affix one coin behind each hand of the front half of the acrobat. Then, glue the two halves of the acrobat together.

4. Stretch the string taut and affix it on two props to make a tightrope. After the glue on the acrobat dries, try balancing the acrobat on the tightrope. (You can also balance it on the edge of a glass or on your finger.)

5. Discuss what has happened. Why is the acrobat able to balance? (Teacher note: See the answer key.)

Captain Jack and the Modoc War

The Indians of California were gentle and peaceful. When the Spaniards first went into California to build their missions, there was no resistance from these docile people.

Until the 1850s when prospectors poured into the territory, the Modocs of Northern California had seen very few whites, but when the white settlers began to come, they came in droves. It was then the Modocs tried to fight to keep their land, so the whites set out to exterminate them.

Kintpuash was a young Modoc who wanted peace with the whites. After his father, the chief, died, Kintpuash found many things changing for his people. A lesser one of these changes came in the form of the white men giving new names to the Indians. This did not upset the Indians because they found it amusing. Kintpuash's new white name was Captain Jack. However, a more serious change came with the dismantling of the peace the Modocs had always known.

Kintpuash / Captain Jack

The year was 1872. The white settlers did not like the Modoc's taking their cattle for food or using the land they now considered theirs, so they asked white treaty commissioners to come in and make a treaty with the Indians and then move them out. The treaty commissioners told Captain Jack that there was a reservation north in Klamath and that they could go there. The Modocs wanted to stay in Tule Lake and the lava beds there, but the commissioners said they had to go to the Klamath Reservation.

They went to the Klamath Reservation, but the Klamath Indians did not want them because the Klamath Reservation had been promised to them. The Great Council in Washington did not send any supplies for the Modocs, so Captain Jack moved his people back to their home, warning them to stay away from the whites. The Indian Bureau told Captain Jack that the Modocs had to move back to Klamath. Captain Jack refused, so the army, under Major Jackson, said they would move the Indians back.

Because Captain Jack did not want war, he agreed to go. However, he no longer trusted the white man and told him so. Major Jackson said he did not want to make trouble. He asked Captain Jack to gather all his men in front of the soldiers. Captain Jack did this. Then the major told them to lay down all their guns. Captain Jack asked why. The major explained it was to avoid trouble, so finally Captain Jack laid down his gun and motioned for his men to do the same. Everyone did except Scarfaced Charley who kept his pistol. The major told him to put it down, but Charley refused. The major yelled at him, and Charley told him not to. Then, the major told a lieutenant to take Charley's gun, and the lieutenant and Charley both fired. The Modocs grabbed back their rifles. The soldiers started firing, and the Indians ran away, leaving one man dead and seven wounded.

Captain Jack and the Modoc War *(cont.)*

The Modoc women and children fled in their dugout canoes, and the men followed on land, hiding in the reeds. They headed for the California lava beds. They hunkered down in them, knowing the soldiers would not be able to get to them with their big guns because of the good cover the lava beds provided. What Captain Jack hoped was that the soldiers would now leave them alone, but the soldiers did not.

When all this was happening, a small group of Modocs with their leader, Hooker Jim, was camped on the side of Lost River. Some settlers came into their camp and started shooting. One white man shot a baby out of its mother's arms and killed an old woman. Hooker Jim and the people he had left fled to the lava beds, but on their way they decided to get revenge. They shot twelve settlers in isolated houses. Captain Jack was very unhappy about this because some of the murdered people had been his friends. Also, he now knew the whites would come after them.

Two hundred and twenty-five soldiers and one hundred and four volunteers joined together to go after the Modocs. Captain Jack wanted to surrender, but all but fourteen of the other warriors wanted to stay and fight. They were well hidden, and the first day of fighting the Modocs killed some soldiers and captured their guns and ammunition. The soldiers stayed away for awhile. Captain Jack thought that perhaps the soldiers would not come back, but the major requested more troops.

A Modoc woman who was married to a white man tried to arrange a peace council between the Modocs and the soldiers. The Modocs asked what would happen to Hooker Jim. The peace commissioners who came said they would all be taken to a reservation in Arizona or to Indian Territory. So Captain Jack said he would meet with the commissioners.

General Canby came. He did not put Hooker Jim and his men under arrest, so they wandered out to look at the soldier camp. A soldier saw them and told them he was going to have them arrested and hanged, so Hooker Jim and his men got on their horses and rode back to the lava beds as fast as they could. General Canby withdrew the offer of amnesty.

Captain Jack wrote a letter to the commissioners. He said that if everything was wiped out and no more blood was spilled, he would give up. However, he could not give up his men to be hanged. Messages went back and forth many times, and then General Canby moved his men in to surround the lava beds. Captain Jack asked why they did this, and General Canby said it was merely because he had just moved his headquarters closer in. But Captain Jack did not believe him. He asked about Hooker Jim, and he said they would not talk about surrender unless Hooker Jim and his men were treated like the other Modocs.

The general set up a council tent on a sagebrush flat in full view of the soldier camp. Captain Jack went to meet some other white men, including one named Meacham, because he did not trust the general. He asked that his people be given a reservation on Lost River so that he and his people could take care of themselves. "Let us have the same chance other men have," he said. Meacham said that in Oregon, he would be tried for murder. So Captain Jack asked to be given the lava beds.

Meacham agreed under the condition that Captain Jack give up the men who did the killing on Lost River. Jack asked who would try the men. "White men, of course," Meacham said. So Captain Jack wanted to know if Meacham would turn over the white men who had killed Modoc women and children on Lost River to be tried by the Modocs. Of course, Meacham would not agree. He said that Indian law was dead and only white law mattered. Captain Jack also did not agree, for he knew that the white man's law was only good for the white man and not for the Indian. He refused to give up the young men without a fight.

The Modocs became very angry at the soldiers. They dared Captain Jack to kill the general. He promised he would, but then he changed his mind. Hooker Jim reminded him of his promise.

Captain Jack and the Modoc War *(cont.)*

On Good Friday, 1873, Captain Jack, Hooker Jim, and a few of the Modocs met with commissioners in the council tent. The general brought cigars, and they all had a smoke. Then, he said if they went with him he would take them to a good country where they could live like white people. Captain Jack refused to go. His people wanted to stay where they were. He also said the Modocs wanted the soldiers to go away so they could live in peace. Another Modoc got angry and told the commissioners to take away the soldiers and give the Modocs back their land. He said they did not want to talk any more. Captain Jack drew his pistol and fired at the general, but the gun did not fire. He pulled the trigger again, and this time it fired and the general fell dead. Scarfaced Charley shot another man.

The Modocs slipped away and hid. The soldiers kept chasing and shooting, and the Modocs kept running and shooting when they could. They scattered, and they ate their horses for food. Hooker Jim and his followers left Captain Jack with thirty-seven men to fight a thousand soldiers. Hooker Jim surrendered to the soldiers and led them to Captain Jack. After several days, Captain Jack finally came out to surrender. He only had three men left with him. " I am ready to die," he said.

The War Department said he must have a trial. Captain Jack was not given a lawyer, and while the trial was going on a gallows was being built outside the stockade in view of the courtroom. Hooker Jim testified against Captain Jack. Captain Jack was asked what he had to say. He said, "You white people did not conquer me. My own men did."

He was hanged October 3, 1873. The next night, someone took his body, embalmed it, and then took it back east. It was exhibited in eastern carnivals. They charged ten cents to see it.

The 153 Modocs who had survived were taken to Indian Territory, and by 1909 all but fifty-one of them were dead. The ones who were still alive were taken to a reservation in Oregon.

Captain Jack and the Modoc War (cont.)

Activity

Imagine that the Supreme Court has ruled that Captain Jack was not given a fair trial and that he must have a new one *in absentia.* You are going to give him his trial. Do the following.

1. Read everything you can find about California Indians, in general, and the Modocs, in particular, and carefully read the *Constitution of the United States*, paying especial attention to the *Bill of Rights*. Learn as much as you can before the day of the trial.

2. Choose the following people to take part in the trial.

   - a judge

   - a prosecuting attorney to try the case for the government

   - at least one defense attorney to try the case for the defendant

   - Captain Jack

   - witnesses for the defense

   - witnesses for the prosecution

   - twelve honest peers to serve as a jury

   - a bailiff to swear in the witnesses and jurors

3. Any students not filling one of the above positions in the trial will serve as members of the media. They will need to write truthfully about what happens in the courtroom, but they can also make it as exciting as possible so they will have a large audience.

4. Set the trial date and prepare for the trial. Do whatever you can within the law to present a good case for whichever position you have. Remember, in a court of law you must swear "to tell the truth, the whole truth, and nothing but the truth, so help you, God."

5. When the trial is over, discuss the results and decide if a better job can be done in another way. How does this trial compare with the one Captain Jack actually had?

Killing with Words

For centuries, many Americans have freely allowed themselves to stereotype people by color, race, religion, or any category which defined a person simply by group affiliation. This was the main reason the American Indians were collectively seen as less than human and, therefore, unworthy of respect or compassion.

Americans are not the only people to stereotype others. Stereotyping was and is done by many of the world's people. While stereotyping may once have served a function—as an aid to survival whereby groups formed for mutual protection—in today's ever-shrinking world it is just plain wrong.

When reading or listening to others, whoever they may be, it is important to recognize and avoid stereotypes about people or groups of people because stereotypes prevent us from truly learning about or understanding each other. They get in the way of really knowing another person for whom and what that person is because they encourage fitting others into conceptual boxes.

What is a stereotype? The dictionary defines stereotype as "a conventional and simplified conception or belief, one considered typical of the kind and without individuality." How does stereotyping occur? It happens anytime generalizations are made about someone without respect to that person's individuality. Usually, these generalizations are negative. That is, they put a whole group of people into a category that is, in some way, bad. Some of the generalizations which have been made about the Indian include the following.

- Indians are lazy and dirty.
- Indians only want to gamble.
- Indians are savages.

Believing such things about the Indians gave certain people the idea that the Indians were very bad so it was all right to kill them and their families. It was all right to refuse to give them citizenship, because they were "just Indians." It was all right to refuse them the same freedom of religion which white people had, and it was all right to deny them the protection guaranteed to the citizens. In other words, it was all right to take from them their property, their life, their freedom, their home, and their dignity, simply because they were Indians and therefore not worthy of respect. "All men are created equal with certain inalienable rights, among which are life, liberty, and the pursuit of happiness" did not apply to the Indian. Moreover, it did not apply to almost anyone else who was non-white, non-Christian, and non-European.

Activity

In groups of four or five, brainstorm a list of ways that people are often grouped. Using the form on the next page, make a heading of each of the groups on your list. (You may need several copies of the form. One member of each group can be the recorder.) Under each heading, list all the sayings or beliefs you can think of that stereotype the people who belong to that group.

Once your chart is complete, make a list of all the ways you can think of to keep yourself from stereotyping others.

As an extension, discuss the following question as a class. Can you also stereotype by making one group or another always good?

Killing with Words *(cont.)*

160

Celebrating Differences

Everyone who lives on the continent of North America is descended from immigrants. Even the ancestors of the people we often call Native Americans at some far point back in history migrated to North America. One characteristic of the people of much of North America is that they are mixtures of almost every different national or ethnic background to be found in the world, and they have learned some very hard lessons about the results of racial and ethnic discrimination.

One hundred years ago, most Americans could probably have told you what their national or ethnic background was. "I'm English and Danish," or "I'm Cherokee and Irish," they might have said. Today, however, many young people who have been born in this country say, "I'm a native American," and they do not realize that they, too, are descended from immigrants to North America.

Everyone likes to know about himself or herself. We all want to know what our roots are. Making an ancestor quilt will help you learn more about who your ancestors are and how they came to this country. You may find some surprises in your own personal background. Ask your parents and grandparents the following questions.

From which countries did you come, or have you always lived in the United States?

What nationalities did my ancestors have?

What races did my ancestors belong to?

When did my ancestors come to this country?

What is there about my ancestor's heritage that is special?

When you know the answers to these questions, you will be ready to make an ancestor quilt. Follow these directions.

Materials:

- old white sheets
- colored permanent markers
- paper
- pencils
- needle and thread
- scissors

Directions:

1. Cut sheets into enough 12" (30 cm) squares so that each student can have one. Be sure to cut the lines straight and even.

2. After the students have learned about their individual ancestral backgrounds, have each child plan his or her quilt square on paper first, illustrating something special about the child's ancestor or where they came from.

3. Lightly copy the illustration onto the square in pencil, and then color it in with markers.

4. After all the squares are completed, sew them together into a quilt representing the ancestral background of the class. A volunteer parent or teacher can help to sew the squares together.

Note: If the quilt is backed and finished, it can be used for a fund-raising project.

Folktales and Legends of the California Indians

Read the following folktales and legends from the natives of California to discover some things and ideas that were important to them.

The Beginning of the World
(Maidu)

In the beginning, the earth was covered with water and there was no light. There was no sun, no moon, no stars. One day, a raft appeared on the water. In it was Turtle. A rope of feathers came down from the sky and dangled over the bow of the raft, and a being who shone with light as bright as the sun came down. He was Earth Initiate, and when he reached the end of the rope, he tied it to the raft and stepped into it.

The face of Earth Initiate was covered, and Turtle could not see it. Neither has anyone else. Earth Initiate sat in the raft for a long time, saying nothing.

"Where do you come from?" Turtle asked him at last.

"I come from above," the being replied.

"Do you have the power to make me some earth, so I can come out of the water sometimes?" Turtle asked him.

Earth Initiate did not answer at first, so Turtle asked, "Will there be people in the world?"

Earth Initiate thought for a time and then said, "Yes."

"How long will it be before you make them?" Turtle asked.

"I do not know yet," Earth Initiate answered. "You want dry land. How will I find any earth to make it with?"

"Tie a stone to my left arm, and I will dive into the water to get some," Turtle said.

Earth Initiate did as Turtle asked him to do, and reaching around he took a rope from out of the air and tied it to Turtle.

"If the rope is not long enough, I will tug it once. If I do this, pull me up. If it is long enough, I will tug the rope two times, and you must pull me up quickly, because I will have the earth you need."

Turtle was gone for six years. When he came back, he was covered with green slime, because he had been gone so long in the water. When he returned, he had only a very small amount of earth under his toenails, because all the rest had washed away.

Folktales and Legends of the California Indians
(cont.)

The Beginning of the World *(cont.)*

Earth Initiate scraped all the earth out from Turtle's toenails. He put it into the palm of his hand and rolled it into a little ball about the size of a pebble. He laid the ball on the raft, and then he went away and left it. Three times he came back to look at it and saw that it was growing. Then he returned a fourth time, and he saw that it had grown as big as the world. The raft was now on the ground, and all around it were mountains.

Turtle saw that the raft was now on the ground, and he said, "I cannot stay in the dark all the time. Will you make me some light, so I can see?"

"Let's get into the raft, and I'll see what we can do," Earth Initiate said. They traveled, and when they got out of the raft, Earth Initiate said, "Look away to the east. I will call my sister to come."

As the sister of Earth Initiate rose from below the earth, it began to grow light and the day began. The sun had risen. "Which way will the sun travel?" Turtle asked.

"I will tell her to go across like this, and to go down over there," Earth Initiate said, and when the sun went down, it became very dark.

"I will now tell my brother to come up," Earth Initiate said, and he made a movement and the moon rose.

"How do you like that?" Earth Initiate asked Turtle.

"I like it very much," Turtle replied. "Will you do anything else for us?"

"Yes, I still have things to do," Earth Initiate said, and he called out the stars by name.

Next he made a tree with twelve different kinds of acorns growing from it. For two days, Turtle and Earth Initiate sat under the tree. Then they set off together to see the world which Earth Initiate had made. As they went along, however, Turtle had trouble keeping up with Earth Initiate. He could see nothing except a ball of fire flashing under the ground and the water. When they returned from going around the earth, Earth Initiate called the birds from the air and made the trees and the animals.

Then he said, "I will now make people."

He took some dark red earth and mixed it with water, forming a clay. He made two figures from the clay, one man and one woman. Then he lay down with the man on his right side and the woman on his left. They lay there together all day and all night, and in the morning the woman began to tickle him in the side. Earth Initiate kept very still and tried not to laugh, but it was hard. When Earth Initiate got up, he put a piece of wood into the ground and it began to burn.

The people which Earth Initiate made were very white. They had pink eyes and black hair. They had very white teeth which shone brightly, and they were very good looking. The man was named Kuksu and the woman was named Morning Star Woman.

Coyote tried to make some people like Earth Initiate had done. "That isn't hard to do," he thought. He did just as Earth Initiate said to do, but when the woman tickled him in the ribs, as she had Earth Initiate, Coyote could not help laughing. Because of this, the people he made had glass eyes. He said that he had not laughed, which was a lie. It was the first lie ever told.

Folktales and Legends of the California Indians

(cont.)

Thunder

(Nisenan)

There once was a man who did not eat the food of this world. He could eat only the food of the sky. When he was hungry, he would speak in the spirit language, and acorn bread would come from the sky.

Now this man had two grandsons who were orphans, and he took care of these boys. They often wondered how their grandfather stayed alive because he never ate the food which he gave to them, so one day they followed him as he left the house so that they could see how he ate. They saw how the bread came from the sky, and they watched their grandfather quickly eat his bread. As soon as he ate one piece, another appeared without end. They went to their grandfather and asked him for some of the food. He gave them a little but would give them no more.

"This is the best bread we have ever eaten," they told him.

"You have plenty of other food. Take no more of this," he said to them.

But as they left him to play with their hoop, they said to themselves, "When he is gone, we will get some more."

They played with their hoop for a long time, and when they got home, the old man was not there. Right away, they went to the bread and got some for themselves. This time, however, it did not replenish itself as it had for their grandfather, and when he came home there was very little for him. He knew what they had done and set out to punish them.

He called them to him and gave them some arrows. He told them to shoot a flicker. When they brought it in, he divided the feathers, those of the right wing to the older boy and those of the left wing to the younger one. He split the tail into two groups of six feathers each and put them on headbands which he made for the boys. Then he tightened their belts and sent them out to play with their hoop. They did not know it, but he had given orders to the hoop to lead them to a good place to live.

When the boys threw the hoop, it rolled away. They ran after it but could not catch it. When they ran, it rolled just ahead of them, and when they walked, it also rolled just ahead of them, but slowly this time. It stayed always just out of reach, and it led them far away and high up a tall mountain, and there it stopped.

The younger boy understood what was happening and called to his brother, "Brother, it is taking us away!"

The boys took off their belts and made them into slings. They used the slings to throw a stone into the air, breaking the sky wide open. The hoop started to roll up in the air, and the boys were carried up into the sky. At home the old man heard them, sounding like thunder in the high mountains.

"Now they are in a good place where they will not get into trouble," the old man said, "and they will have better food where they are now."

And when we hear the thunder, we know it is the boys rolling their hoops.

Folktales and Legends of the California Indians
(cont.)

How the Earth Was Made
(Yuki)

In the beginning was nothing but water, and on this water, floating in a tiny fleck of foam, was a down feather. The feather floated down, down in a circle, and from it came a voice which was singing. It was the creator, Taikomol, coming to make the world. He called himself He-who-goes-alone. He-who-goes-alone carried with him the God Coyote.

As time went on, He-who-goes-alone came to look like a man, and while this was happening, he sang. Then he made a basket from parts of his own body, and from his basket he made the earth. He fastened it and strengthened it with pine pitch, and he traveled all over the world with Coyote still hanging onto his body. He fashioned the four corners of the earth and the sky from the skins of four whales. Then he made people. He lay some sticks of wood in a house for a night, and in the morning the sticks had become people.

He-who-goes-alone wanted people to live forever, and after Coyote's son died and was buried, he offered to bring him back to life. But Coyote said it was better for the dead to remain dead, and that is why people stay dead after they die.

Activities

1. You have now read many folktales and legends told by many different peoples on the North American continent. This is the time for you to try your own hand at writing a story or legend explaining something in your world. Write a story using one of the following topics or an idea of your own.

   - How the earth was made
   - How the sun, moon, and stars came to be
   - The first people
   - Why we have thunder (or wind or storms)
   - The origin of death
   - Why chickens have feathers
   - Why flowers bloom in the spring

2. Many native people left stories written on the walls of caves and canyons. However, most of these stories remain untold because there is no one alive who knows how to read them. This is because they were written in *pictographs* (picture writing) and *petroglyphs* (stone writing), and their meanings went with the people who left them.

   Invent a set of your own pictographic symbols and use them to write a message to your classmates. Ask them to decipher your message.

   If you wanted to leave a message to people who would be coming centuries after you, what message would you leave, and what symbols would you use to write? Remember, these people will probably not read the same language you do because a living language such as English changes over the centuries, even in pronunciation.

Making Math in Your Head

Except for the Cherokees after Sequoyah invented his syllabary, the American Indians had no written language, yet they often had need for solutions to certain kinds of problems which depend on mathematical concepts. What did they do? Sometimes they used counting sticks such as the ones in the hand game, but at other times they probably relied on doing the problems they needed to do "in their heads." You can learn to do this, too.

Doing math in your head means learning how to simplify. There are a number of ways to do this, including:

- reordering numbers
- breaking up numbers
- using equivalents
- approximating and rounding off

1. **Reordering Numbers**

   a. You are in the grocery store and you want to figure out quickly whether you have enough money to buy three items. You need to know how much 14, 38, and 6 are when totaled. Do the following. Reorder the numbers first into (14 + 6) + 38. Fourteen plus six is easy: it is 20. Now add 38 to twenty, which is also easy: 20 + 38 = 58.

   b. You want to multiply 25 x 33 x 8. First, multiply 25 x 8. That is simple! It is 200. Then, multiply 200 x 33 by multiplying 33 x 2 = 66 and then 66 x 100 = 6600.

   c. You need to multiply a fraction by a whole number (for example, ³/₄ x 48). First, divide 48 by 4. The answer is 12. Then multiply 12 by 3. The answer is 36.

2. **Breaking Up Numbers**

   You want to multiply 12 x 19. First, break the numbers up into multiples of 10, so you now have (10 + 2) x 19, which is (10 x 19) + (2 x 19), and that in turn is 190 + 38. The answer is 228.

3. **Using Equivalents**

   Fractions can be very useful numbers. For example, if you want to multiply 50 by any number, simply multiply it first by 100 and then divide it by 2. Fifty is half of 100. Remember that ¹/₄ is the same as .25; therefore, ¹/₈ is one half of ¹/₄, or .125, and ¹/₃ is .333, and ²/₃ is .67, and so forth. Using these may not give you an exact answer, but it can give you one which is approximate.

4. **Round Off and Approximate**

   To round off a number, drop the unwanted digits on the right. If the first digit dropped is 5 or greater, increase the preceding digit by 1. If the first digit dropped is less than 5, leave the preceding digit unchanged. For example:

   - ¹/₃ rounded off to three places is .333
   - ¹/₃ rounded off to two places is .33
   - ¹/₃ rounded off to one place is .3
   - ²/₃ rounded off to three places is .667
   - ²/₃ rounded off to two places is .67
   - ²/₃ rounded off to one place is .7

Making Math in Your Head *(cont.)*

Try doing the following problems in your head.

1. **Additions**

   a. $23 + $64 = _____

   b. $34 + $159 = _____

   c. $18 + $139 = _____

   d. $57 + $166 = _____

2. **Subtractions**

   a. You paid $64 for a coat and your friend paid $47. How much more did you pay?
   _____

   b. You paid $83 for insurance and your friend paid $69. How much more did you pay?
   _____

   c. You pay $221 for rent and your friend paid $176. How much more did you pay? _____

3. **Making change**

   a. You bought items for a total of $3.80 and handed the clerk $5. How much change did you get?
   _____

   b. You paid $16.25 for a shirt and handed the clerk $20.00. How much change did you get?
   _____

   c. You bought canned goods for $3.54 and produce for $4.89. What is your total change from
   $10.00? _____

4. **Approximating**

   a. You want to buy items costing $11.98, $15.95, and $7.96. How much are they all together?
   _____

   b. You want to buy items costing $3.99, $24.88, and $5.95. How much are they all together?
   _____

   c. You want to buy items costing $8.88, $56.75, and $12.90. How much are they all together?
   _____

   d. A pair of shoes regularly $44.99, is on sale for $26. How much will you save?
   _____

   e. A jacket regularly $69, is on sale for $44.95. How much will you save?
   _____

   f. A shirt, regularly $22 is on sale for $17.99. How much will you save? _____

5. Now go into small groups and make up some problems from each category for one another to solve.

A Puzzling World

Thousands of years ago, North America was connected to Alaska by a narrow piece of land called the Bering Land Bridge because it crossed over a strip of water called the Bering Strait. This strip of land is where some of the ancestors of the earliest North Americans are believed to have crossed from Asia to North America.

Sometimes we have to a tendency to think that the earth has always been just the way it is now, because it is the only way we have known it to be, but the earth as it is today is very different than it once was.

Have you ever noticed that the outlines of the different continents look as though they might fit together? If you have, you were observing the aftermath of something that happened long ago. At one time, far back into prehistory, the major land masses of the earth fit together. Africa, Eurasia, South America, North America, Antarctica, Greenland, and Australia were all one piece of land. No one knows exactly why it broke apart, but we do know how it did. To get an idea of this process, do the activity on the next page.

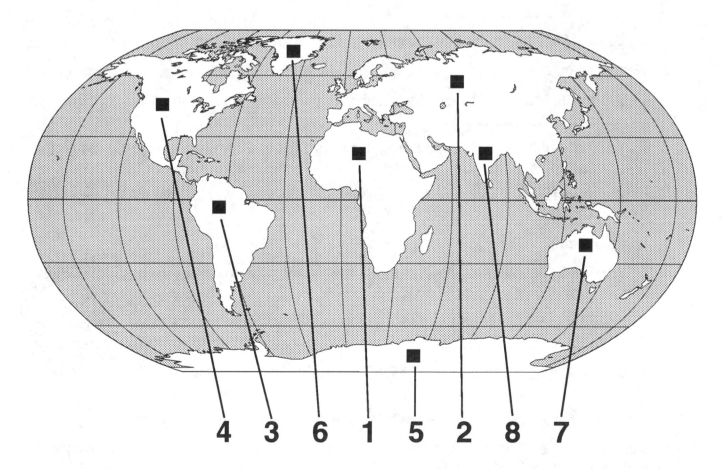

1. Africa	**2. Eurasia**
3. South America	**4. North America**
5. Antarctica	**6. Greenland**
7. Australia	**8. India**

A Puzzling World *(cont.)*

Materials:

- 1 baking potato
- 1 self-sealing plastic bag
- knife
- permanent marker
- ½ lemon
- bowl of water
- ½ cup (250 ml) salt
- spoon

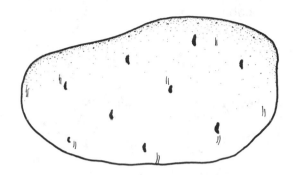

Directions:

1. Cut the potato in half lengthwise. Do not peel it. Set one half aside.

2. Cut the other potato half to look like the pieces in the illustration. Number the pieces from one to eight, as shown.

3. Put the pieces in the plastic bag with the juice from the lemon. This will keep them from turning brown.

4. Take the pieces out of the bag and reassemble them into a potato half.

5. Dissolve as much of the salt in the water as possible. Stir until no more salt will dissolve.

6. Carefully set the reassembled potato onto the surface of the salt water, and observe how it breaks apart. Which pieces went to the "north" of the water? Which pieces went to the "south?"

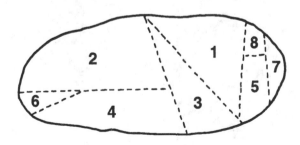

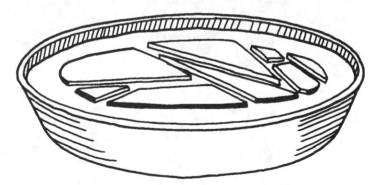

This is exactly the way in which the land masses of the earth broke apart. The even numbered pieces went to the northern part of the planet, and the odd numbered pieces went to the southern part. The complete half of the potato is what the Earth's land looked like 240 million years ago just before the dinosaurs lived, all in one piece surrounded by ocean. This one huge continent is now called *Pangaea*. It is believed that the heat inside the earth caused it to break up into separate continents.

The Hand Game

Many American Indians, including those of California, played a simple game usually called "the hand game." It relied on chance to win. There are many different versions of this game. Each tribe had its own playing pieces and counters for keeping score. The game described in this activity is similar to that played by the Pomo and Miwok Indians.

Materials:

- 2 playing pieces (one of which is marked)
- 8 counting sticks

Directions:

1. One person holds a playing piece in each hand, and the counting sticks remain to the side.

2. Singing a song such as the following one, the person crosses hands back and forth, then behind his back, sometimes changing the pieces from one hand to the other.

> *Tee way yo ho lay,*
> *Tee way yo ho lay,*
> *Hoki hoki la*
> *Hoki hoki la,*
> *Tee way yo ho lay.*

3. The person holding the playing pieces sings the song a number of times, and when the song stops, the other player guesses which hand the marked piece is in. At this point, the person holding the playing pieces keeps his or her hands in full sight so as not to suggest that he changes the pieces after the guess is made. If the player guesses correctly, he or she "wins" a counting stick. If the player does not guess correctly, the person holding the playing pieces wins. The game continues until either person has all the counting sticks.

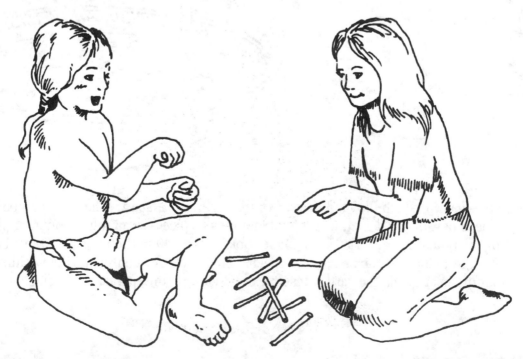

Make the Desert Come Alive!

We often think of a desert as being a place where nothing grows and everything is dead. That is sometimes true, but the desert of the Southwestern United States is a beautiful, growing area filled with spectacular plants which shelter many kinds of animals. You can make a small, easy-to-care-for desert garden of your own with small plants you buy in a nursery or department store. Desert plants have very shallow root systems so they need little water and little care.

Materials:

- 1 low potting dish, with or without drainage holes
- 3 or 4 kinds of small cactus plants
- gravel
- potting soil
- thick gloves or folded newspaper

Directions:

1. Put a layer of gravel on the bottom of your dish and cover it to near the top of the dish with potting soil.

2. Arrange the plants together in a manner which seems right to you. You might add a small stone or two for variety and cover the top of your potting soil with colored gravel, if you wish.

3. To care for your desert garden, set the dish on top of rocks which can be kept wet, and you will probably have all the moisture they will need without watering them. Be careful not to water them too much!

Make a Corn Necklace

During the fall months you can find Indian corn of every possible color in your supermarket or in a florist or garden center. The corn is a very popular decoration to use at Thanksgiving, and your parents may have used it in your home. Besides being good for a decoration, Indian corn is good for other things, too. One way to use it is to make an attractive necklace. It is so easy to make!

Begin by choosing ears of Indian corn in the colors you especially like. Then, follow these directions.

Materials:

- Indian corn
- blunt-tipped tapestry needle
- strong thread
- 6" x ³⁄₈" (15 cm x 1 cm) leather or suede (optional)

Directions:

1. Break off the kernels from the cobs.

2. Place the kernels into water to soak for a day or so until they are soft enough to pull the needle through.

3. String the kernels one at a time onto strong thread. When the string of corn is as long as you want it to be (so it will slip over your head easily), tie the two ends of the thread into a strong knot and you will have your necklace.

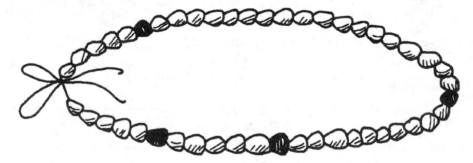

4. Another way to finish off your necklace like the Indians sometimes did is to make the string of corn several inches (centimeters) shorter than you would in the above direction. Then, take the strip of leather or suede and slit the strip in half lengthwise from one end to about ³⁄₈" (1 cm) from the other end. Knot each end of your strung corn to one of the halved ends of the leather. This will give you a necklace which is part leather and very professional looking.

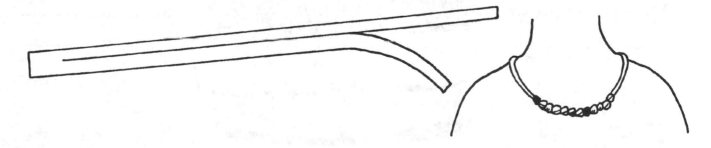

172

Quiz

1. List three things you have learned about the natives of California. _____

   _____

2. Describe some of the major differences between the homes of the natives of California and the natives of the Great Plains. _____

   _____

   _____

3. In what condition was Ishi when he was first discovered by the sheriff of Oroville? _____

   _____

   _____

4. Why did Ishi have trouble wearing shoes? _____

   _____

5. How was Captain Jack's trial unfair? _____

   _____

6. List three stereotypes often applied to Native Americans. _____

   _____

   _____

7. In what ways can it be said that all Americans are descended from immigrants?_____

   _____

8. What do the Nisenan say causes thunder? _____

   _____

9. Describe what the continents of the earth looked like millions of years ago. _____

   _____

10. On the back of this paper, answer the following question. If you could live as a Native American one hundred years ago, which group would you want to live with and why?

Native American Poetry

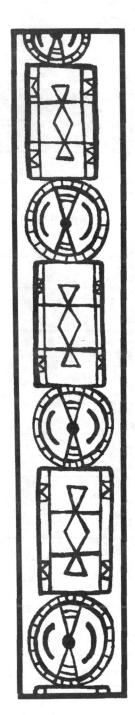

Prayer Sung to the Young Cedar*
(Kwakiutl)

Look at me, friend!
I come to ask for your dress,
For you have come to take pity on us;
For there is nothing for which you cannot be used, . .
For you are really willing to give us your dress,
I come to beg you for this,
Long-Life maker,
For I am going to make a basket for lily roots
        out of you.
I pray you, friend, not to feel angry
On account of what I am going to do to you;
And I beg you, friend, to tell our friends about
        what I ask of you.
Take care, friend!
Keep sickness away from me,
So that I may not be killed by sickness or in war,
O friend!

Song of the Sky Loom**
(Twea Pueblo)

O our Mother the Earth, O our Father the Sky,
Your children are we, and with tired backs
We bring you the gifts you love.
Then weave for us a garment of brightness;
May the warp be the white light of morning,
May the weft be the red light of evening,
May the fringes be the falling rain,
May the border be the standing rainbow.
Thus weave for us a garment of brightness,
That we may walk fittingly where birds sing,
That we may walk fittingly where grass is green,
O our Mother the Earth, O our Father the Sky.

*This song is sung when taking the bark of the cedar tree to use.
**The sky loom refers to the small desert rain in which the rain showers hang lightly from the sky.

Native American Poetry *(cont.)*

Plaint Against the Fog
(Nootka)

Don't you ever,
You up in the sky,
Don't you ever get tired
Of having the clouds between you and us?

Song to Bring Fair Weather
(Nootka)

You, whose day it is, make it beautiful.
Get out your rainbow colors,
So it will be beautiful.

The Heavens Are Speaking
(Pawnee)

I stood there, I stood there,
The clouds are speaking.
I say, "You are the ruling power,
I do not understand, I only know what I am told,
You are the ruling power, you are now speaking,
The power is yours, O heavens."

It is there that our hearts are set,
In the expanse of the heavens.

Native American Poetry *(cont.)*

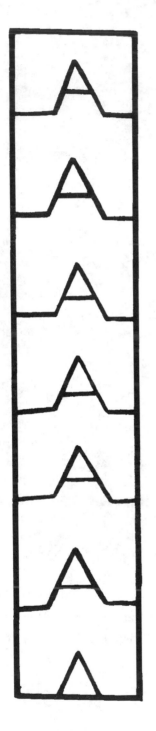

A Prayer
(Havasupai)

Sun, my relative
Be good coming out
Do something good for us.

Make me work,
So I can do anything in the garden
I hoe, I plant corn, I irrigate.

You, sun, be good going down at sunset
When we lay down to sleep I want to feel good.

While I sleep you come up.
Go on your course many times.
Make good things for us men.

Make me always the same as I am now.

Two Rain Songs
(Papago)

Close to the west the great ocean is singing.
The waves are rolling toward me, covered with
      many clouds.
Even here I catch the sound.
The earth is shaking beneath me and I hear the
      deep rumbling.

A cloud on top of Evergreen Mountain is singing,
A cloud on top of Evergreen Mountain is
      standing still,
It is raining and thundering up there,
It is raining here,
Under the mountain the corn tassels are shaking,
Under the mountain the horns of the child corn
      arc glistening.

Native American Oratory

The Surrender Speech of Heinmot Tooyalaket (Chief Joseph)
(Nez Percé)

I am tired of fighting. Our chiefs are killed. Looking Glass is dead. Toohullhulsote is dead. The old men are all dead. It is the young men who say no and yes. He who led the young men is dead. It is cold and we have no blankets. The little children are freezing to death. My people, some of them, have run away to the hills and have no blankets, no food. No one knows where they are—perhaps they are freezing to death. I want to have time to look for my children and see how many of them I can find. Maybe I shall find them among the dead. Hear me, my chiefs, I am tired. My heart is sad and sick. From where the sun now stands I will fight no more forever.

Chief Red Jacket's Address to a Missionary Council
(Seneca)

Brother, listen to what we say. There was a time when our forefathers owned the great island. Their seats extended from the rising to the setting sun. The Great Spirit had made it for the use of the Indians. He had created the buffalo, the deer, and other animals for food. He made the bear and the beaver, and their skins served us for clothing. He had scattered them over the country, and taught us how to take them. He had caused the earth to produce corn for bread. All this he had done for his red children because he loved them. If we had any disputes about hunting grounds, they were generally settled without the shedding of blood. But an evil day came upon us. Your forefathers crossed the great waters and landed on the island. Their numbers were small. They were small. They found

friends, not enemies. They told us they had fled from their own country for fear of wicked men and had come here to enjoy their religion. They asked for a small seat. We took pity on them, granted their request, and they sat down among us. We gave them corn and meat. They gave us poison in return. The white people had now found our country, tidings were carried back, and more came among us. Yet we did not fear them. We took them to be friends. They called us brothers. We believed them and gave them a large seat. At length their number had greatly increased. They wanted more land; they wanted our country. Our eyes were opened, and our minds became uneasy. Wars took place. Indians were hired to fight against Indians, and many of our people were destroyed. They also brought strong liquors among us. It was strong and powerful, and has slain thousands.

Chief Red Jacket's Address to a Missionary Council *(cont.)*

Brother, our seats were once large, and yours were very small. You have now become a great people, and we have scarcely left a place to spread our blankets. You have got our country, but are not satisfied. You want to force your religion on us.

Brother, continue to listen. You say that you are sent to instruct us how to worship the Great Spirit agreeably to his mind, and if we do not take hold of the religion which you white people teach, we shall be unhappy hereafter. You say that you are right, and we are lost. How do we know this to be true? We understand that your religion is written in a book. If it was intended for us as well as you, why has not the Great Spirit given it to us, and not only to us, but why did he not give to our forefathers the knowledge of that book, with the means of understanding it rightly? We only know what you tell us about it. How shall we know when to believe, being so often deceived by the white people?

Brother, you say there is but one way to worship and serve the Great Spirit. If there is but one religion, why do you white people differ so much about it? Why do not all agree, as you can all read the book?

Brother, we do not understand these things. We are told that your religion was given to your forefathers, and has been handed down from father to son. We also have a religion which was given to our forefathers, and has been handed down to us by their children. We worship that way. It teaches us to be thankful for all the favors we receive, to love each other, and to be united. We never quarrel about religion.

Brother, the Great Spirit has made us all, but he has made a great difference between his white and red children. He has given us different complexions and different customs. To you he has given the arts. To these he has not opened our eyes. We know these things to be true. Since he has made so great a difference between us in other things, why may we not conclude that he has given us a different religion according to our understanding? The Great Spirit does right. He knows what is best for his children. We are satisfied.

Brother, we do not wish to destroy your religion, or take it from you. We only want to enjoy our own.

Brother, you say you have not come to get our land or our money, but to enlighten our minds. I will now tell you that I have been at your meetings, and saw you collecting money from the meeting. I cannot tell what this money was intended for, but suppose it was for your minister, and if we should conform to your way of thinking, perhaps you may want some from us.

Brother, we are told that you have been preaching to white people in this place. These people are our neighbors. We are acquainted with them. We will wait a little while and see what effect your preaching has upon them. If we find it does them good, makes them honest and less disposed to cheat Indians, we will then consider again what you have said.

Brother, you have now heard the answer to your talk, and this is all we have to say at present. As we are going to part, we will come and take you by the hand, and hope the Great Spirit will protect you on your journey, and return you safe to your friends.

Note: When Red Jacket finished this speech, he went to shake the hand of the missionary, but the missionary reportedly said, "There is no fellowship between the religion of God and the works of the devil, therefore I cannot join hands with them." The Indians politely smiled and went away.

Native American Oratory (cont.)

From Chief Joseph

The earth was created by the assistance of the sun, and it should be left as it was . . . The country was made without lines of dimension, and it is no man's business to divide it . . . I see the whites all over the country gaining wealth and see their desire to give us lands which are worthless . . . The earth and myself are of one mind. The measure of the land and the measure of our bodies are the same. Say to us if you can say it, that you were sent by the Creative Power to talk to us. Perhaps you think the Creator sent you here to dispose of us as you see fit. If I thought you were sent by the Creator I might be induced to think you had a right to dispose of me. Do not misunderstand me, but understand me fully with reference to my affection for the land. I never said the land was mine to do with as I chose. The one who has the right to dispose of it is the one who has created it. I claim a right to live on my land, and accord you the privilege to live on yours.

From Wanigi Ska (White Ghost)

You have driven away our game and our means of livelihood out of the country. Until now we have nothing left that is valuable except the hills that you ask us to give up . . . The earth is full of minerals of all kinds, and on the earth the ground is covered with forests of heavy pine, and when we give these up to the Great Father (the President) we know that we give up the last thing that is valuable either to us or the white people.

From Satanta, Chief of the Kiowas

I have heard that you intend to settle us on a reservation near the mountains. I don't want to settle. I love to roam over the prairies. There I feel free and happy, but when we settle down we grow pale and die. I have laid aside my lance, bow, and shield, and yet I feel safe in your presence. I have told you the truth. I have no little lies hid about me, but I don't know how it is with the commissioners. Are they as clear as I am? A long time ago this land belonged to our fathers, but when I go up the river I see camps of soldiers on its banks. These soldiers cut down my timber. They kill my buffalo, and when I see that, my heart feels like bursting. I feel sorry . . . Has the white man become a child that he should recklessly kill and not eat? When the red men slay game, they do so that they may live and not starve.

Annotated Bibliography

Most of the following books are ones which deal with the American Indian fairly and accurately. Those which do not are indicated as such. They are included here for the sake of education about the inaccuracies and stereotypes within some popular and beloved literature.

Note: The tribe about which the story is written is indicated in parentheses.

Fiction

Dawn Land
by Joseph Bruchac
Fulcrum Press, 1993 *(Available in Canada: Raincoast Pub.; UK: World Leisure)*
Grades 7 and up (mature content)
(Abenaki)

An outstanding and promising young man of his people, Young Hunter knows he has an important task to fill. But when he starts out on his vision quest, he does not fully know what that task will be, only that it will be dangerous and necessary for the survival of his people. Something dark and evil is stalking the land of the Only People, and he has been chosen to save them from a horrible fate. With him he carries a gift that, if used and guarded carefully, will enable him to accomplish his task.

The storyteller, Joseph Bruchac, has called upon his Abenaki roots to take us back into the time of myth making. Based on the oral traditions and history of his people, this book is full of the power of which legends are made. It grips the reader as few first novels do, sometimes with horror and sometimes with poetry. The story is more than one filled with action and daring. It demonstrates and illustrates the values of a people often called "primitive," and it shows the development of a relationship between man and nature. It is a mythical explanation of why and how the world is as it is and an ethical explanation of how it should be. It is a story of how Good and Evil work together to create balance and harmony in life.

The Education of Little Tree
by Forrest Carter
University of New Mexico Press, 1986 *(Available in the UK: Random House UK)*
Grades 7 and up
(Cherokee)

After his mother and father die, Little Tree goes to live in the mountains of Tennessee with his Cherokee Grandpa and Grandma. He is five years old, and in the four years he spends with them, he learns to read the skies and the plants. He learns to listen to the trees and speak to them as well. He learns how corn and running beans are planted by the moon and how love is planted and nourished in the human heart. He learns the art of valuing the best in nature and in people and a healthy disrespect for the phony and the arrogant.

The Education of Little Tree is one of those rare literary experiences which leaves one better than one was before reading it. It is about learning what is true, sharing the good so it spreads out far, and about loving and understanding. At times, it is hilarious; at other times, it is poignant and deeply moving. Often, it is pure poetry. Beautiful and warm, this telling of a Cherokee boyhood in the 1930s is filled with tragedy, humor, and love. It impossible to put down until it has been read cover to cover.

Annotated Bibliography *(cont.)*

I Heard the Owl Call My Name
by Margaret Craven
Dell Publishing, 1973 *(Available in Canada: Doubleday Dell Seal; UK: Pan Books; AUS: Transworld Pub.)*
Grades 6 and up
(Kwakiutl)

Mark Brian is a young Anglican vicar sent on his first assignment to a remote Indian village in British Columbia. What Mark's bishop knows, but Mark does not, is that Mark has only two years to live, and the wise, old bishop knows that this assignment is one in which Mark has the best chance possible to learn what he needs to learn before the time comes for him to die. Mark is not the first clergyman ever sent to this village, but he is different from previous ones. Rather than attempting to impose his own ways on the villagers, Mark works with them and learns from them. He gives to them in any way he can, but he also allows them to give to him in their own ways, and because of his openness and caring, he succeeds in attaining his own kind of vision quest before his time is gone.

This book will grab you by the heart and never let go. Wonderful reading, wonderful teaching, and full of values, this book is a must in every teacher's library.

Morning Girl
by Michael Dorris
Hyperion Books for Children, 1992 *(Available in Canada and AUS: Little Brown)*
Grades 4 and up
(West Indies)

In this book, the reader climbs inside the minds of a young sister and brother, Morning Girl and Star Boy, and looks out with them through loving eyes on their beautiful world. They have the same kinds of sibling rivalries that all siblings have, but they are loved and love in return. They share a wonder at the bounties of nature with all its potential, and they also share a trusting friendliness toward all people. However, the reader knows before the children do how their world will change when the new people who arrive from the sea fulfill their mission. The year is 1492.

Poetic and haunting, this is a book for all ages that can tell us much we need to know about ourselves. The native writer, Michael Dorris, has given us a poetically beautiful book in *Morning Girl*.

Annotated Bibliography *(cont.)*

Red Hawk's Account of Custer's Last Battle
by Paul Goble
University of Nebraska Press, 1992 *(Available in Canada and AUS: 402-472-3584; UK: Academie of University Publishers Group)*
All ages
(Oglala Sioux)

Red Hawk, a fifteen-year-old Oglala Sioux boy from the same tribe as Crazy Horse, tells how his people were camped in one of their favorite camping places by the snaking Little Bighorn River along with six other groups of Sioux and Cheyenne. It was a fateful day in June, 1876. They had just completed their annual joint Sun Dance a few days before and were just awakening in the morning when General George Armstrong Custer and five companies of his Seventh Cavalry swooped down on the still sleepy enclave. The people were at peace, and not expecting to be attacked, had taken no time to prepare for battle. As warriors shielded the "helpless ones" to get them out of the way, others ran to get their horses and weapons to defend their families. Red Hawk grabbed his horse and his bow and arrows and although he had never fought before, he did not hesitate to do his part to protect his people and himself, taking his first coup as he did so.

Illustrated with scenes much like the picture-stories Sitting Bull drew after the battle, this little book puts faces on the people of Sitting Bull, Crazy Horse, and Red Cloud. It is not perfect, but it is human and shows how fear and hate bloodied the memories of one young man "in the time it takes to light a pipe." This book was Paul Goble's first, and while he is not a Native American, his empathies for the Indian, what he felt of the historical injustice done to the Indian, and his fascination with the Battle of Little Bighorn led him to write this very sensitive and historically based little book.

The Legend of Jimmy Spoon
(An Odyssey/Great Episodes Book)
by Kristiana Gregory
Harcourt Brace Jovanovich, 1990 *(Available in Canada: HBJ Canada; UK: HBJ Ltd.; AUS: HBJ Group Ltd.)*
Grades 5 and up
(Shoshone)

Jimmy did not intend to leave home forever. He only wanted a horse and adventure. So when he went to the camp with the two Shoshone boys, he planned to return soon with a horse. But by the time they got to camp, it was a lot farther away from home than he had expected, and he did not know how to get back. Besides that, the old Chief Washakie and Old Mother adopted Jimmy, and suddenly he found himself renamed Dawii with a life as different from the one he had in Salt Lake City as dark is from light.

Based on the true story of a white man in the middle 1800s, this story is of Jimmy and the new life he finds that turns his previous perspectives upside down. Before he knows it, he is going on buffalo hunts and living an adventure unlike anything he has ever known. Carefully researched, the book gives a straightforward picture of daily life as it was lived by the Shoshone in the days of the buffalo. It is an enthralling tale of adventure and coming of age.

Annotated Bibliography (cont.)

The Ten Grandmothers
(The Civilization of the American Indian Series)
by Alice Marriott
University of Oklahoma Press, 1989 *(Available in Canada and UK: Univ. of Oklahoma Press;*
    AUS: E. Web)
Grades 7 and up
(Kiowa)

Historically accurate and beautifully written, this epic of the Kiowa people covers a century from when they live the lives of buffalo hunters to the time the young men go to be warriors on another continent in World War II. The people of Spear Girl and Eagle Plume are painfully transformed from Plains nomads to reservation farmers, and they become very old before our eyes. But deep inside, much stays the same, not only for them but for their children and grandchildren who have never lived in the old ways. The sacred medicine bundles called *The Grandmothers* retain their power to heal and to inspire. This is fascinating reading.

Moccasin Trail
by Eloise Jarvis McGraw
Penguin Books, 1980 *(Available in Canada, AUS, and UK: Penguin Books)*
Grades 6 and up
(Crow)

Jim Keath ran away from home at the age of eleven. After his life was saved by the Crow Indians when he was attacked by a bear, Jim lived with the Indians for six years. During that time, Jim came to think and act like the people who had rescued him from sure death. For some reason, Jim then becomes a "mountain man" for awhile, and while doing this, he gets a message that he is needed by his natural brothers and sister who are on their way to homestead in Oregon. The rest of the book shows his wild "Indian-ness" pitted against the civilized whiteness of his siblings and their friends and neighbors.

"Injun Jim" can do some things very well. He can run fast and swim in the icy cold water during winter. He can track cattle thieves more surely than a bloodhound and get back the stolen cattle without bloodshed. But Injun Jim does not like to work like the white man, and he does not want to live in a house with four walls. He wants to spend his time out in the woods doing the "man's work" of hunting and tracking, but he does not want to do the "squaw's work" of butchering the game. He has a bad influence on his small younger brother and teaches him how to gamble and steal without getting caught. He wears his hair in braids and believes in superstitions like having a medicine bundle and animal helpers to protect him.

The real Indians in the story are even worse than Jim, stealing cattle from the white settlers and making slaves of young boys while all the whites are hard working, courageous, kind, and honest. Of course, you know all along that since Injun Jim is really white inside, he will end up good.

Eloise McGraw tells a good story, and this is no exception. Full of excitement such as chases on horseback and riding the Columbia River rapids on a hand-built raft, this 1952 Newbery honor book goes from one action-packed episode to another. Unfortunately, the entire premise of the book is based on a stereotype which pits the good white homesteader against the "wild Injun," and the story becomes predictable. In the end, Jim cuts off his braids, throws away his medicine bundle, and moves into the house after realizing how much better life would be as a white. Please do not give this book to children unless you use it to teach about stereotyping.

Annotated Bibliography *(cont.)*

Where the Broken Heart Still Beats
by Caroline Meyer
Harcourt Brace Jovanovich, 1992 *(Available in Canada: HBJ Canada; UK: HBJ Ltd.; AUS: HBJ Group Ltd.)*
Grades 6 and up
(Commanche)

In 1836, Cynthia Ann Parker was kidnapped from her west Texas home by Commanche warriors. Twenty-five years later, just before the Civil War, she and her small daughter are recaptured by Texas Rangers and forcibly returned to the home of her biological uncle and his family, whom she does not remember. Her parents had been killed by her abductors, and Cynthia has blocked out all memory of them and the other members of her birth family. The story is dually told from the viewpoint of Cynthia/Naduah and the twelve-year-old daughter of her white uncle.

During her long sojourn with the Commanche, Cynthia has become Commanche herself. She speaks only the Commanche language, and she considers herself one of the People with whom she has lived so long. Her attempts to adjust to living with a white family are filled with conflicts for both Naduah and the family, and she continues to hope to be rescued by her warrior son.

Based on the life of a real person, this book is sensitively written. It is sometimes fascinating as it examines the frequent conflicts which divide the two cultures. Meyer has effectively meshed two different viewpoints in this novel. We see into Naduah's mind to know her confusion, lack of understanding of the white culture, and desire to return "home" to the only life she can remember ever knowing. At the same time, we see her through the eyes of a twelve-year-old who is wise beyond her years and who records the reactions, fears, and prejudices of the other settlers toward this "savage" and her child. No one else can fathom the sorrow which fills the heart of the woman they see only as an interloper they would rather not deal with.

Canyons
by Gary Paulsen
Dell Publishing, 1990 *(Available in Canada: Dell Seal; UK: Doubleday Dell, AUS: Transworld Pub.)*
Grades 5 and up
(Apache)

Fifteen-year-old Brennan Cole, while camping near Dog Canyon, discovers a skull. The skull fills his mind and permeates his dreams until trying to learn its origin becomes an obsession with him. The skull has a bullet hole through its front and back. Who did the skull belong to, and why was he killed? When research indicates the skull was that of an Apache boy named Coyote Runs who was executed by soldiers in 1864, Brennan finds himself mystically linked to that boy in a way which totally surprises him, and he knows he must return the skull to where it belongs, the site of ancient vision quests. To do this, Brennan must run the race of his life, and he cannot explain to anyone why he must make this quest of his own.

Canyons is not so much a story about Indians as it is about a relationship that develops between a modern teenager and an Apache boy killed over a hundred years ago. But it is not simply a ghost story. It is a mystical coming together of two personalities and perspectives. Paulsen is a highly acclaimed writer for young people, and this book is done with great sensitivity. The reader *feels* the bond that grows between Brennan and Coyote Runs. The reader must also feel the pain of a young life cruelly cut off too soon and the peace which can occur only after the boy's remains have been accorded some final dignity.

Annotated Bibliography *(cont.)*

Racing the Sun
by Paul Pitts
Avon Books, 1988 *(Available in Canada, UK and AUS: International Book Dist., 599 Industrial Ave., Paramus, NJ 07652, telephone: 201-967-5810)*
Grades 5 and up
(Navajo)

Life changes in more ways than Brandon Rogers could ever have dreamed of when his grandpa comes to live with Brandon's family. Brandon is a very modern boy who likes modern rock bands played loudly on the stereo and posters of wild rock bonds on his walls. So, it is not easy for him to have Grandpa for a roommate. For one thing, Grandpa comes straight from the reservation, and he likes to chant and sing in bed at night. He smells like sagebrush and cedar smoke, and on his very first morning at Brandon's house he wakes up at 5 AM to tell Brandon it is time to run toward the sun. Grandpa expects him to run that way every morning!

In the few weeks that Grandpa has left to live, Brandon learns from his grandfather some really important things about family and love and being yourself, and for the first time in his life, he learns to be proud of his Indian heritage.

Racing the Sun is a little gem of a book full of understanding and wisdom. Warm, sometimes funny, and always pointed toward the good that life and death have to offer, this book will enrich as it instructs, giving a special glimpse into the values and traditions of the Navajo.

The Light in the Forest
by Conrad Richter
Bantam Books, 1990 *(Available in Canada: Bantam Dell Seal; UK: Bantam Doubleday Dell; AUS: Transworld Pub.)*
Grades 5 and up
(Lenni–Lenape)

True Son was born white in Colonial America, and when he was four years old, he was captured by the Lenni–Lenape and adopted into the tribe. At fifteen, he has learned to hate whites and to love his Indian family, and when he learns that he is to be given back to his white family, whom he does not remember, he is heartbroken. The ensuing months of living inside walls in the town steel his mind against the whites, and he lives only for the hope of someday returning to his Indian home.

Although the book occasionally verges on portraying the Indian as the "noble savage," this is, nonetheless, a good book which explores the many sides of white-Indian relationships during an early period of American history. The cultural differences between the two groups of people is fairly accurately pictured, although Richter comes close to stereotyping both whites and Indians at times. The book could generate some excellent class discussions.

Annotated Bibliography *(cont.)*

Quest for Courage
by Stormy Rodolph
R. Rinehart in cooperation with The Council for Indian Education, 1984 *(Available in Canada and AUS: telephone 303-652-2921 and fax 303-652-3923)*
Grades 5 and up
(Blackfeet)

When Lame Bear was six years old, he was badly injured in an attack by a cougar. As a member of the Blackfeet tribe, the only way for him to gain success and honor is for him to become a respected hunter and warrior, but Lame Bear's injury never healed properly, and it has left him crippled in one leg. When the other boys his age begin going on hunts and learning what they must learn to become men, Lame Bear is left home with his mother doing women's work. Lame Bear despairs of ever gaining the respect he desires until one of the old grandfather chiefs takes him under his wing. The old chief, Fine Bull, leads Lame Bear to a high mountain where he seeks a vision and a spiritual helper. To Lame Bear's great excitement and surprise, his quest is successful, and he sets off on a perilous journey into the land of an enemy tribe in search of a magnificent stallion which no one has ever succeeded in capturing.

This is a very good treatment of the vision quest and the spiritual belief of the Indian that to be whole and complete, a man must have a vision. Not only does Lame Bear succeed despite his handicap, but he returns home as a proven warrior.

When Thunders Spoke
by Virginina Driving Hawk Sneve
University of Nebraska Press, 1974 *(Available in Canada and AUS: 402-472-3584; UK: Academie of University Publishers Group)*
Grades 5 and up
(Sioux)

Norman Tow Bull lives on the reservation in North Dakota with his parents, and he is, in many ways, a modern teen. Yet in this story, Norman finds himself caught between the old ways of his grandfather and the new ways of modern life. Norman's grandfather, Matt Two Bull, lives with Norman and his parents during the winter, but as soon as the weather turns warm, he moves out to live in his tent in the fresh air until the cold weather returns. Norman visits him often. His grandfather has never left the old ways. He wears his hair in two long braids; he tells Norman the old stories. He lives in the past. Norman's mother, on the other hand, has embraced the modern ways of the whites. She is active in church, and she is frightened by the old ways that she considers heathenish and dangerous.

One day while climbing the butte to which young Sioux men used to go on their vision quests, Norman finds a very old stick. He is intrigued by the object after his grandfather tells him what it is. His grandfather warns him not to handle it or allow it to be mistreated because it has sacred powers. Norman's mother is horrified by the object, and she wants to throw it away, but Norman's father refuses. Then, things begin to happen in the Two Bull household which change Norman's life forever as well as his way of looking at the world and himself. Beautifully told, this small book contains a very quiet power which sometimes shows itself most in what it is left unsaid.

Annotated Bibliography *(cont.)*

Soun Tetoken: Nez Percé Boy
by Ken Thomasma
Grandview Publishing Company, 1984 *(Available in Canada and AUS: telephone 307-733-4593 and fax 307-734-0210)*
Grades 5 and up
(Nez Percé)

This little novel is probably the best treatment for young people of the ordeal faced by a young person during the flight of the Nez Percé under Chief Joseph. Soun is the son of Ollokot, one of the chiefs, and the nephew of Young Chief Joseph. Mute since the death of both his parents in a forest fire when he was one year old, Soun has a gift for working with animals by using only sign language. His grandfather, Old Chief Joseph, gives him a colt, and together the horse and boy have many happy adventures until the growing conflict between the Nez Percé and the white settlers leads to war. Soun is forced to grow up quickly when his people must leave their ancestral home. He tries to help the chiefs lead the people safely to Canada.

Simply told and painstakingly accurate as to the cultural ways and traditions of the Nez Percé, this book is worth the extra trouble it takes to obtain it.

Biography/Autobiography

Indian Boyhood
by Charles A. Eastman
University of Nebraska Press, 1991 *(Available in Canada, UK, and AUS: 402-472-3584)*
Grades 6 and up
(Ohiyesa)

Originally printed in 1902, this was one of the first biographies written by someone who was born and raised Indian. The book contains some "contamination" by white values and interpretation since, although the author had been raised in the traditional ways of his native Sioux, from the age of fifteen he lived with whites and received an education which extended into graduation from medical school. Nonetheless, it provides valuable information and insights into the life of the Plains Indian child as it was while the tribe still followed the buffalo.

This book is very easy to read and presents a fascinating picture of life as it was for the Sioux. For anyone truly wishing to understand the beliefs and values of the Plains Indian, it is must reading.

Plenty-coups: Chief of the Crow and *Pretty-shield: Medicine Woman of the Crow*
by Frank B. Linderman
University of Nebraska Press, 1930 and 1932 *(Available in Canada and AUS: 402-472-3584; UK: Academie of University Publishers Group)*
Grades 6 and up
(Crow)

These books by ethnographer Linderman give extremely interesting peeks into the lives and traditions of the Crow Indians. Although not intended as juvenile books, they nonetheless are easy to read and show the life of the pre-reservation Crow from childhood through adulthood in ways no other books do. Surrounded on all sides by enemies, the Crow was the one group of Indians who very early on followed a path of cooperation with the white man in the hope of being able to hold on to their homeland. Many of the young men became scouts for the army, including the 7th cavalry under Custer, and the Crow were the only Indians of the Great Plains who were never at war with the white man.

Annotated Bibliography *(cont.)*

Mankiller: A Chief and Her People
by Wilma Mankiller
St. Martin's Press, 1993 *(Available in Canada: McClleland and Stewart; UK: Macmillan)*
Grades 5 and up
(Cherokee)

She was born in poverty in the hills of Oklahoma. Later, she underwent a kidney transplant, but nothing could stop Wilma Mankiller for long. This fascinating autobiography weaves together the history of the Cherokee people through the Trail of Tears and beyond with the story of an incredible woman's life. In 1985, she was elected the first woman to become principal chief of the Cherokee Nation, and in 1993 she was named as one of the United States' outstanding women. Her story is one of courage, strength, and the triumph of the human spirit. This is a a must read for anyone wishing to learn more about the Cherokee and about themselves.

Other Recommended Reading

Borland, Hal. *When the Legends Die*. Dell Publishing, 1963

Bruchac, Joseph. *Native American Animal Stories*. Fulcrum Publishing, 1992

Caduto, Michael J. and Joseph Bruchac. *Native Stories from Keepers of the Earth*. Fifth House Publishers, 1991

Campbell, Maria. *Halfbreed*. University of Nebraska Press, 1973

Keith, Harold. *Rifles for Watie*. Thomas Y. Crowell Co., 1957

Kreober, Theodora. *Ishi in Two Worlds*. University of California Press, 1961

O'Dell, Scott. *Sing Down the Moon*. Dell, 1992

O'Dell, Scott. *Thunder Rolling in the Mountains*. Houghton Mifflin, 1992

Alternative Responses to Literature

There are many ways in which students may respond to literature other than writing a book report. Each student has strengths which are different in some ways from the strengths of others, and it is important to give students choices which allow them to think critically and to use their own individual strengths.

Here are some generic ways in which your students can show their understanding of and appreciation for a piece of literature other than by writing a report.

- Keep a reader's response journal. Use the journals to record individual responses to the literature. If responses are structured so students must answer certain questions with their writing, and if the journals are treated as having significance, students are likely to respect them and treat them with care.

- Write a newspaper front page which headlines an event in the story. This is also an opportunity to teach about journalistic ethics and dealing with facts. Impress the students with the importance of including who, what, where, when, and how or why in a story's lead, and discuss how facts in a story can be slanted to express a certain viewpoint. This can be either an individual or group effort.

- Produce a pageant about an historical event featured in a book. For example, depict the flight of Chief Joseph and the Nez Percé in *Thunder Rolling in the Mountains* and the Long Walk of the Navajo in *Sing Down the Moon*.

- Design a dust jacket for the book you have read. Illustrate the front cover, write a summary of the book for the back cover, and on the inside flaps write a short biography of the author citing other books by him or her.

- Make a timeline of significant events in the history of Native Americans. You can either begin from ancient times or with the coming of the Europeans to North America.

- Show how political and religious conditions in Europe may have influenced the white man's treatment of America's first peoples or how native traditions and cultures could have influenced native reactions to the white man.

- Write an autobiography of a character in the book you have read. Imagine that you are that person. Tell the story of your life including one or more events which are depicted in the story.

- Compile a book of Native American poetry. Look in the library for anthologies of Native American works in the public domain and choose from them the poems you like best. Illustrate your book and include one or more poems of your own about the story you read or about Native Americans you know.

- Make a video. American Indian art and music are highly prized today, and much is extremely well done. In the library, find a collection of Native American art which you particularly like. Make a video of the art you have chosen and use tapes of Native American music as background for your video.

- Present a speech. Memorize a speech made by a Native American such as the ones by Chief Joseph and Red Jacket included in this book. Present your speech to the class and then tell why you chose to give this speech and what it means to you.

Alternative Responses to Literature *(cont.)*

- Write a history of a Native American tribe or an aspect of Native American life on this continent such as their migration to North America from Asia, a history of the horse in America and the changes it brought to the peoples here, or slavery among the natives.

- Conduct a literary interview. With a classmate, write an interview with one of you portraying a character in a book and the other interviewing that character for a new television program.

- Compile a collection of folktales. Choose a theme for the stories you include in your collection such as the Little People, trickster stories, or stories about the sun, moon, and stars. Illustrate your stories.

- Write a folktale. Write a story to explain something about the world you live in. You might include as your characters supernatural heroes, ancestors, or reasons to explain why an animal has a certain characteristic. For example, you might write a story about why the robin has a red breast, or why the sun and moon are seldom seen next to each other.

- Tell a story. Choose a Native American story which you particularly like, learn it well, and tell it to the class. Use props to help you dramatize the story, such as posters, art work, crafts projects, or music. You might also pretend to be a character from the book telling the story.

- Give a demonstration. Choose something from the book and use it as the focus for a demonstration. You might give a lesson on how to carve a totem pole, how to preserve food for the winter, or how to construct a tipi.

- Make a commercial. Imagine that your book is being made into a movie. Write and perform a blockbuster preview to convince others to see the film.

- Write a letter to a character in your book expressing your congratulations for what he has accomplished or your condolences for a terrible thing that happened. In your letter, tell about the effect the character has had in your own life. Use specific events from the story to illustrate the kind of person that character is and why it is important for you to write to him or her.

- Make a diorama of a scene from the book. Choose a scene which you feel is very significant, and include small-scale models of the characters who were involved. Show the natural surroundings in which the scene takes place.

Culminating Projects

Instead of taking a test, the culmination of an extended unit such as this one may better be evaluated by an individual or a group project. On this page and the pages following are some suggestions of various projects which your students will enjoy and which may give you a more accurate idea of what they have learned than you would get from a comprehensive test. It will also give them a chance to explore new interests in American Indian cultures and allow them to "zero in" on a certain area, thereby gaining a deeper understanding of these very diverse peoples.

Stress to your students that this is a major project intended to take the place of a final exam. If they know what to expect from the beginning of the unit, they can be thinking about it during the course of the unit and have some idea of what they will do when the time comes. Sufficient time should be scheduled for library use.

Most of these projects can be done either by individuals or in groups. Of course, one done by a group would be expected to be more extensive than an individual one.

Culminating Project I: Write Your Own Unit

Choose a Native American group or tribe about which you would like to learn more and then write your own unit much like the sections you have just studied. You will need to provide a section on each of the following topics and include them in your unit.

Social Studies

Research an event in history in which the tribe or group you chose took part; for example, the flight of the Nez Percé in 1877 with Chief Joseph or the Battle of Wounded Knee in 1890. Write an account of it.

Folktale or Legend

Find one or more folktales or legends told by the group you chose and rewrite it, being sure to keep the meaning accurate.

Science

Look through a book of science activities and find one that shows an aspect of Indian life. For example, you might find a wildlife or gardening activity illustrating how the group or tribe you choose would have practiced good ecology.

Math

Think of a way your group's lifestyle might have employed mathematical concepts. Write an illustration of it or present an activity that another student could do.

Arts and Crafts

Learn one of the arts or crafts your group or tribe practiced long ago, such as a special kind of mask for dancing or a special kind of picture they might have made. Write a "how to" on doing it.

When you have finished each of these sections, put them together in a folder you have illustrated.

Culminating Projects *(cont.)*

Culminating Project II: Anthology of American Indian Literature

Compile an anthology (collection) of Native American literature. You might include folktales, legends, myths, poetry, and oratory, or you might limit your collection to one particular genre.

Or, instead of an anthology, consider writing an annotated bibliography of books you have read about American Indians. In an annotated bibliography, you will write brief reviews or summaries of a number of different books. Ask your teacher to let you see the one in this book or another one so you can get the idea of how to do it.

Writing either an anthology or an annotated bibliography will require you to do quite a lot of reading, so plan enough time.

Culminating Project III: Write a History

Write a history of one particular tribe or group. You might begin your history back in prehistory, writing it from the earlier times for which you can find any information, or you might start at some later time.

Instead of writing a history extending over a long period of time, you might concentrate on a major event in history, such as one of the following.

- Battle of the Wichita
- Battle of Wounded Knee, 1890
- French and Indian War
- Sioux uprising, Minnesota
- Battle of the Little Bighorn
- Wounded Knee, 1973
- The Ghost Dance
- Capture of Alcatraz, 1969

Or you might concentrate on one aspect of American Indian history, such as one of the following.

- Reservations
- Indian schools
- The flight of the Nez Percés
- The Lewis and Clark Expedition
- The Spanish in North America
- The rush for gold and the Indian
- Missionaries and the Indian
- Buffalo
- Cochise and the Apache guerrillas
- Government treaties with the Indian
- Indians today and yesterday

You may wish to write a history of another time than the ones suggested, and if you do, check with your teacher for approval.

Culminating Projects (cont.)

Culminating Project IV: Write a Biography

Write a biography of an American Indian who was important to the history of the Native American. Some famous American Indians include those on the following list, but your choices are not limited to these. If you know of someone else you would like to learn more about, clear it with your teacher.

- Dull Knife
- Chief Joseph
- Sacajawea
- Sarah Winnemucca
- Jim Thorpe
- Sequoyah (George Guess)
- Manuelito
- Roman Nose
- Sitting Bull
- Geronimo
- Tecumseh
- Cochise
- Red Cloud
- Pocahontas
- Will Rogers
- Ely S. Parker
- Quannah Parker
- George Bent
- Satanta
- Stand Watie
- Pontiac

Culminating Project V: Build a Model Village

Research the home or lodges of one group of Indians, and build a model village for the group about which you are most interested. Each kind of village not only had a characteristic kind of house or lodge, but the homes and other buildings or structures were set up in a certain pattern in relationship to one another.

For example, when the Plains Indians arrived at a campsite, they did not set up their tipis in just any way. They set them up in circles. You will need to know how the circles were placed and why they were placed that way, where individual tipis were set up relative to the chief's lodge, and the direction in which tipis faced. Other Indian villages followed the rules and customs of their Indian tribe or group.

To make your model village more authentic, indicate the approximate time period during which your village would have been as it is in your model. In various places, place small "people" engaged in activities such as cooking, weaving, or making arrows, which they might have been engaged in at that time.

Culminating Projects *(cont.)*

Culminating Project VI: Make a Model Biosphere

A short distance north of Tucson, Arizona, is a structure known as the Biosphere. In this structure is a group of people who are trying to determine if and how people could live within a small space with a limited number of resources for food, oxygen, water, etc.

Research the Biosphere and learn as much about it as you can. It is possible to visit it if you happen to be in that area, but a great deal has been written about it in the news and various publications. You might write to the people who are there and ask for any brochures or literature available which could be sent to you.

Then, make a model showing the structure of the Biosphere and indicating what is there, how it works, and whether or not more Biospheres will be built in the future.

Explain: How do you think this relates to the study of American Indians?

Culminating Project VII: Make It Artistic

If you are someone who enjoys creative and artistic activities, there are many ways in which you can employ your talents in your study of American Indians. There are few other groups of people who can claim a wider or more talented group of native artists and crafts persons. Your possibilities are almost endless.

Some areas you might explore while you decide exactly what you wish to do include the following:

- silversmithing
- jewelry making
- prints and lithographs
- dreamcatchers
- ceramics
- coppersmithing
- sand painting
- oil painting
- beadwork
- mandalas
- basketmaking
- woodcarving
- leather working

These are only a few areas in which Native Americans excel, and your library probably has many resources for you to use in your study.

Culminating Activity: Indian Powwow

After a major unit like this one on Native Americans, students have a great opportunity to celebrate what they have learned, and there seems to be no better way than with a powwow.

It is thought that the original meaning of the word *powwow* was a term used by certain tribes to refer to a medicine man, spiritual leader, or shaman. Later, it was used to refer to meetings in which spiritual power was requested, such as a Sun Dance or Ghost Dance. Today it has come to mean a large gathering, usually held every year, in which Indians come from a distance, often hundreds of miles, to celebrate with both spiritual and recreational activities.

One of the largest annual powwows is the Crow Fair held every August in Crow Agency, Montana. The Crow name given to the fair is *Um-basax-bilua* which means "where they make the noise." This fair started in 1904 when a government agent, in trying to induce the Crows to become farmers, planned the event as a typical county fair but especially for Indians. He saw it as a way for the Crows to exhibit their produce. He also thought it would encourage them to become better farmers. Women were urged to exhibit their native foods and handcrafts and be awarded ribbons and cash prizes.

To make the fair a social and entertainment event, he relaxed the usual strict policies regarding traditional dances, ceremonials, and singing which had long been banned by the government as "dangerous," and he chose a committee of old chiefs and elders to create a schedule for the fair. The committee quickly scheduled morning parades, afternoon foot and horse racing, and evening dancing, and the agent approved the schedule.

The first Crow Fair was held in an open meadow two miles south of the Little Bighorn Battleground, and the following year a racetrack and an exhibit hall were built. Within a few years, the fair had grown in size to where most of the families on the reservation came to participate. Men showed their produce and livestock, and women brought their native foods, buckskin costumes, and the beadwork they had made during the winter. Children brought pet ponies, calves, chickens, and turkeys to show.

Before long, the chiefs and elders began to take advantage of the agent's relaxation of strict rules, and they scheduled mock battles, reenactments of intertribal warfare, victory dances, public recitals of war deeds (counting coup), and they held gift distributions to clan relatives. By 1920, other activities were added including wrestling matches, tipi-erection races, rodeo events, and dancing exhibitions. During World War I, World War II, and the Great Depression, the fair was canceled, and when it was resumed after World War II, the fair became less agricultural and more festive in nature.

Today the fair is so big and so important to the Crows that it has become known as the "Tipi Capitol of the World" because from twenty to thirty thousand Indians come from Canada and the United States to camp together. Cash awards are given for many events, including various categories within the parades. The daily parades have become spectacular. There are rodeos in which as many as seven hundred Indian cowboys compete, twelve horse races each day, and dancing contests. On the fifth day of the fair is held the "Dancing Through the Camp" ritual when prayers are offered for a good year to come. On the final day, a feast is held, and officers for the following year are chosen.

The Crow Fair today is much more than dancing, horse racing, and "rodeoing," however. It is a giant family reunion where Crows and their Indian friends from other tribes get together to celebrate. It is also a time to display the Crow culture in action and to tell the world the Crow Indians of America have a culture worthy of celebration and emulation.

Culminating Activity: Indian Powwow (cont.)

Your Indian Powwow at school, of course, will not be as grand as the one in Crow Agency, Montana, but it can be a marvelous experience for everyone who participates. It can be as small as only one or two classrooms, or it can involve an entire school. Some of your activities will depend to some extent on the time of the year your powwow is held. An ideal time might be to coordinate it with your annual field day, which is usually scheduled at a time of year when the weather is favorable for outdoor activities. Below are suggestions for activities, foods, and exhibits for your powwow.

Exhibits

- model longhouses
- leaf displays
- fabrics dyed with vegetable dyes
- apple dolls
- charts featuring Sequoyah's syllabary
- Cherokee fables
- models of Seminole summer houses
- corn dolls
- calendars using Indian moons instead of months
- examples of beadwork
- ring and pin games
- model salmon ladders
- button blankets
- sand paintings
- "wooden" masks
- model kivas
- student folktales
- coiled pottery
- God's eyes
- unwoven burlap hangings
- messages written with symbols
- desert dish gardens
- corn necklaces
- Native American poetry
- classroom quilt celebrating differences

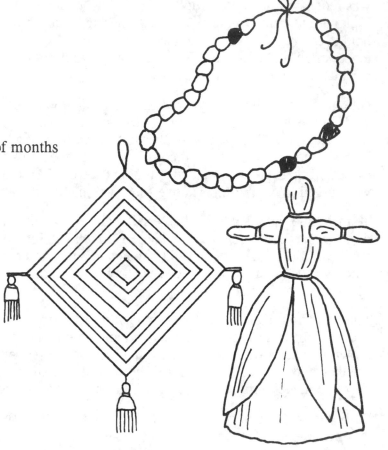

Demonstrations

- oral reports on how the Iroquois Confederacy influenced the makers of the U.S. *Constitution*
- oral reports on how the first Americans have been traced through DNA
- storyteller telling legends to his or her people
- how to play Indian games
- how to make beaded articles
- how the pipe was used ceremonially
- moon illusions
- making God's eyes
- unweaving burlap
- meanings of Indian symbols
- demonstration of how continents were formed
- recitation of Native American poetry
- recitation of Native American oratory
- place of women in Indian tribes
- oral report on native contributions to American life

Culminating Activity: Indian Powwow *(cont.)*

Contests

- foot races
- long jumps
- ring and pin games
- ball games

Foods

Use part or all of the following foods for your powwow, restricting your menu to foods native to North America. Adapt them for modern times and convenience; for example, you might plan on turkey sandwiches instead of roast turkey. Or how about making turkey sandwiches with Indian fry bread? If your powwow is near the end or beginning of the school year, you could use watermelon and fresh corn, but at another time of year you will need to use frozen corn and whatever fruit is available. By the way, when the Puritans first came to New England, they thought the tomato was poisonous until the Indians showed them it was good to eat! What a treat we would have missed if the Indians had not been there to help!

The menu below is made entirely from foods introduced by the Indians. Many of them are now available in many places of the world. You probably can make these foods without using recipes; however, recipes for some other Indian foods follow in case you wish to use them either with these foods or instead of them.

Menu

- sliced, roast turkey
- cranberry sauce
- corn on the cob or Indian corn
- butter or margarine
- fresh vegetable salad
- watermelon or seasonal fruit
- pumpkin pie

Fresh Vegetable Salad

Ingredients:

- 4 large sweet green peppers
- 1 medium onion, diced
- 6 ripe medium tomatoes
- 6 slices bacon
- 1 tsp. (5 mL) red chili powder
- ½ cup (125 mL) vinegar

Procedures:

Cut the vegetables into small chunks and mix well. Salt lightly and let stand 30 minutes. Fry bacon until crisp. Break into small pieces and mix with vegetables. Add chili powder to hot bacon grease and add vinegar. Pour mixture over vegetables and mix. Serve on fresh lettuce leaves.

Indian Fry Bread

Ingredients:

- 4 cups (1 L) white flour
- 2 tsp. (10 mL) salt
- water
- 6 tsp. (30 mL) baking powder
- 1 tbsp. (15 mL) shortening
- cooking oil

Procedures:

Mix the ingredients (except cooking oil) together to make a stiff dough. With your hands, roll the dough into a ball about 3" (8 cm) in diameter and pull the ball into a 6" (15 cm) circle. Do not use a rolling pin. With a knife, slash one side in five places from the center out. Heat 1" (2.5 cm) cooking oil in a skillet and drop in the flattened dough. Brown on each side and serve with honey, refried beans and cheese, or as Indian tacos (below).

Indian Tacos

Ingredients:

- ½ lb. (250 g) ground pork or beef
- ½ small onion (diced)
- 1 small tomato (diced)
- ½ tsp. (3 mL) garlic powder
- ½ small head lettuce (finely chopped)
- 1 cup (250 mL) grated cheese
- 1 tsp. (5 mL) oregano
- ½ can chile beans
- 4 pieces of fry bread (hot)

Procedures:

Crumble the meat and fry with garlic and oregano. Spoon hot chili beans and the meat mixture onto the fry bread. Cover with cheese, onions, lettuce, tomatoes, and chili sauce to taste. Serve hot.

Indian Nachos

Ingredients:

- 1 tsp. chopped green chili or 1 Jalapeno pepper
- 1 large corn tortilla
- ¼ c. (65 mL) grated cheddar cheese

Directions:

Place either the green chili or a small piece of Jalapeno pepper on top of the tortilla. Cover with the grated cheese and broil in the oven until the cheese melts. Serve hot.

Bean Sandwiches

Ingredients:

- 1 cup (250 mL) refried beans
- 2 tbsp. (30 mL) chopped onions
- 2 tbsp. (30 mL) chopped green chilis
- 2 tbsp. (30 mL) chopped sour pickles
- 1 tsp. (5 mL) mustard
- ½ cup (125 mL) grated cheese
- lettuce (optional)
- 4 wheat or flour tortillas

Procedures:

Mix all ingredients (except lettuce and tortillas) and heat them. Spread the mixture on warm tortillas and fold or roll over once. Lettuce may be added, if desired.

List of Museums

The following list contains only a few of the excellent museums, national sites, and heritage centers in North American which feature Indian handiwork and historical exhibits. There are such museums everywhere, including national parks, universities, and even private settings. Wherever you travel in North America, check to see if there is an Indian museum at your destination.

- **Anthropological Museum,** University of British Columbia, Vancouver, British Columbia
- **Aztec Ruins National Monument,** Aztec, New Mexico
- **Buffalo Bill Historical Center,** Cody, Wyoming
- **Canyon de Chelly National Monument,** Chinle, Arizona
- **Casa Grande Ruins National Monument,** Coolidge, Arizona
- **Cherokee National Museum,** Cherokee, South Carolina
- **Cherokee National Museum,** Tahlwquah, Oklahoma
- **Effigy Mounds National Monument,** Harper's Ferry, Iowa
- **Eiteljorg Museum,** Indianapolis, Indiana
- **Gene Autry Western Heritage Museum,** Los Angeles, California
- **Gilcrease Museum,** Tulsa, Oklahoma
- **Glenbow Museum,** Calgary, Alberta, Canada
- **The Heard Museum,** Phoenix, Arizona
- **Little Bighorn Battlefield,** Crow Agency, Montana
- **Mesa Verde National Park,** Colorado
- **Museum and model Miwok Village,** Yosemite National Park, California
- **Museum at the University of Southern Montana,** Bozeman, Montana
- **Native Heritage Center,** Duncan, British Columbia, Canada
- **Pawnee Tribal Reserve,** Pawnee, Oklahoma
- **Pipestone National Monument,** Pipestone, Minnesota
- **Provincial Museum,** Victoria, British Columbia, Canada
- **Millicent Rogers Museum,** Taos, New Mexico
- **The Rockwell Museum,** Corning, New York
- **St. Labre Indian School Museum,** Ashland, Montana
- **Will Rogers Memorial,** Claremore, Oklahoma

The Smithsonian Institution is building a large, new museum dedicated to the American Indian. A temporary building is being used in New York City until a new building has been funded and built.

Bibliography

Arts, Crafts, and Foods

Boy Scouts of America. *Indian Lore.* 1992

Gryski. *Cat's Cradle, Owl's Eye's: A Book of String Games.* Kids Can Press, 1983

Hardwick, William. *Authentic Indian-Mexican Recipes.* Copyright by author, 1972

Milford, Susan. *The Kid's Nature Book.* Williamson Publishing, 1989

Ulmer, Mary and Samuel E. Beck. *Cherokee Cooklore.* Mary and Goingback Chiltoskey Publishers, 1951

Folktales and Legends

Astrov, Margot. *The Winged Serpent.* Beacon Press, 1974. ("Orphan Boy and the Mud Ponies" and "The Image That Came to Life")

Burland, Cotties. *North American Indian Mythology.* Paul Hamly, 1968. ("The Wolf Clan and the Salmon," "Beaver Steals the Fire," and "Raven and the Moon")

Clark, Ella Elizabeth. *Indian Legends of Canada.* McClelland and Stewart Ltd., 1992

Courlander, Harold. *The Fourth World of the Hopis.* University of New Mexico Press, 1971. ("Creation of the Sun and Moon")

Curtis, Edward S. *Indian Days of the Long Ago.* Ten Speed Press, 1975. ("Corn Smut Girl")

Edroes, Richard and Alfonso Ortiz. *American Indian Myths and Legends.* Pantheon Books, 1984. ("Corn Mother," "Little Brother Snares the Sun," "Glooscap Fights the Water Monster," and "Coyote Steals the Sun and the Moon")

Feldman, Susan. *The Story-telling Stone.* Dell, 1965

Gifford, Edward Winslow and Gwendoline Harris Block. *Californian Indian Nights.* University of Nebraska Press, 1930. ("How the Earth Was Made," "The Beginning of the World," and "Thunder")

Grinnell, George Bird. *By Cheyenne Campfires.* University of Nebraska Press, 1971. ("Sweet Medicine Shows His Power," "Sweet Medicine and the Arrows," "Sweet Medicine Foretells the Future")

Hardin, Terri. *Legends and Lore of the American Indians.* Barnes & Noble Books, 1993

Mooney, James. *Myths of the Cherokee and Sacred Formulas of the Cherokees.* Charles and Randy Elder Booksellers and Publishers, 1982. ("How Rabbit Stole Otter's Coat," "Why Possum's Tail Is Bare," and "How Terrapin Beat the Rabbit")

Turner, Frederick. *The Portable North American Indian Reader.* Penguin Books, 1974

General

Adams, Dawn and Jeanie Markowksy. *The Queen Charlotte Islands Reading Series: A Teacher's Guide.* Pacific Educational Press, 1988

American Medical Association. *American Medical Association Medical Encyclopedia.* Dorling Kindersly Ltd., Random House, 1989

Bataille, Gretchen M. and Kathleen Mullen Sands. *American Indian Women Telling Their Lives.* University of Nebraska Press, 1984

Bleeker, Sonia. *Indians of the Longhouse.* William Morrow & Company, 1950

Brown, Dee. *Bury My Heart at Wounded Knee.* Henry Holt & Company, 1970

Calloway, Colin G. *Indians of the Northeast from Facts on File.* International Book Marketing Ltd., 1991

Campbell, Joseph. *The Way of the Seeded Earth* (volume II, part 2 of *Mythologies of the Primitive Planters: The Northern Americas*). Harper & Row, 1989

Clutesi, George. *Potlatch.* Gray's Publishing LTD., 1969

Bibliography *(cont.)*

Culin, Stewart. *Games of the North American Indians* (volume 2: *Games of Skill*). University of Nebraska Press, 1992

Grinnell, George Bird. *The Cheyenne Indians.* University of Nebraska Press, 1972

Hoig, Stan. *The Battle of Washits.* University of Nebraska Press, 1976

Hoig, Stan. *The Cheyenne.* Chelsea House Publishers, 1989

Howard, W.J. *Doing Simple Math in Your Head.* Coast Publishing, 1992

Joseph, Alvin M. Jr. *The Indians Heritage of America.* Alfred A. Knopf, 1968

Kroeber, Theodora. *Ishi in Two Worlds.* University of California Press, 1961

Linderman, Frank, B. *Pretty-shield, Medicine Woman of the Crows.* Nebraska University Press, 1972

McLoughlin, William G., *Cherokee Renaissance in the New Republic.* Princeton University Press, 1986

Medicine Crow, Joseph. *From the Heart of Crow Country: The Crow Indians Own Lives.* The Library of the American Indian. Orion Books, 1992

Powers, Marla M. *Olglala Women: Myth, Ritual, and Reality.* University of Chicago Press, 1988

Rockwell, David. *Giving Voice to Bear.* R. Rinehart Publishers, 1990

Ronda, James P. *Lewis and Clark Among the Indians.* University of Nebraska Press, 1984

Sandoz, Mari. *Cheyenne Autumn.* University of Nebraska Press, 1953

Slapin, Beverly and Doris Seale. *Through Indian Eyes.* New Society Publishers, 1992

Solomon, Arthur. *Poems and Essays of Arthur Solomon.* NC Press Limited, 1990

Sunset Books and Sunset Magazine. *New Western Garden Book.* Lane Publishing Co., 1979

Thomas, David Hurst (et al). *The Native Americans: An Illustrated History.* Turner Publishing, 1993

Utley, Robert M. *Life in Custer's Cavalry: Diaries and Letters of Albert and Jennie Barnitz, 1867–1868.* University of Nebraska Press, 1977

Walpole, Brenda. *175 Science Experiments to Amuse and Amaze Your Friends.* Random House, 1988

Williams, Jeanne. *Trail of Tears.* Hendrick-Long Publishing Co., 1992

Ywahoo, Dhyani. *Voices of Our Ancestors.* Shambala, 1987

Periodicals and Pamphlets

Alexander, Ted. "Muskets and Tomahawks." *Civil War: The Magazine of the Civil War Society.* September-October, 1992

Mastie, David. "Science and Medicine." *San Jose Mercury-News.* San Jose, California, March 15, 1994

National Park Service. "Biological Diversity." U.S. Dept. of the Interior

National Park Service. "Effigy Mounds." U.S. Dept. of the Interior

National Park Service. "Mesa Verde." U.S. Dept. of the Interior

Videos

Note: There are many excellent videos and movies which treat the American Indian and the American Indian experience in an authentic manner. Some are available through the National Park System and others through some of the television networks. This list contains only a few.

Anasazi, the Ancient Ones. A National Park film, Cortez, Co 81321

Ishi, Last of the Yahi

The Native Americans. Turner Broadcasting

The Navajo. Museum of Northern Arizona, 1982

The Real West (various episodes, including "Indian Agents," "Legend and Folklore," and "Flight of the Nez Perce"). Arts and Entertainment channel

Walls of Time: The Rock Art of Canyon de Chelly. Denver Museum of Natural History, 1990

War Against the Indians (various episodes). Arts and Entertainment channel

Answer Key

Page 10: Language Groups of North America

I. Eskimo-Aleut

Eskimo and Aleut (the Aleutians, western and northern Alaska, northern Canada, and Greenland)

II. Na-Dene

   A. Athapascan

     Ahtena, Bear Lake, Beaver, Carrier, Chipewyan, Dogrib, Han Hare, Ingalik, Kaska, Koyukon, Kutchin, Mountain, Nebesna, Sekani, Slave, Tanaina, Tanana, Tuchone, and Yellowknife (the subarctic area of Northwestern Canada and Alaska); Chilcotin and Nicola (the Northwest Plaueau and Western Canada); Hupa and Mattole (Southern Oregon and Northern California); Sarci (the Northwestern Canadian plains); Kiowa-Apache (the Southern U.S. Plains); Apache-Navajo (the U.S. Southwest)

   B. Related

     Haida and Tlingit (the Northwest Pacific Coast); Toboso (in Northern Mexico)

III. Algonquian-Ritwan-Kutenai

   A. Algonquian

     Cree, Magnais, and Naskapi (the subarctic of Eastern Canada); Abanaki, Chickhominy, Delaware, Lumbee, Malecite, Massachuset, Mattapony, Micmac, Mohegan, Nanticoke, Narraganset, Nipmuc, Pamilco, Pamunkey, Passamoquoddy, Pennacook, Penobscot, Pequot, Powhatan, Shawnee, Wampanoag, and Wappinger (the Eastern Woodlands from Nova Scotia to the Carolinas); Illinois, Kickapoo, Menominee, Miami, Ojibway (Chippewa), Ottawa, Peoria, Potawatomi, Sauk, and Fox (the Midwest and around the Great Lakes); Arapaho, Atsina (Gros Ventre), Blackfoot (Blood, Piegan, Siksika), Cheyenne, and Plains Cree (the Plains)

   B. Ritwan

     Wiyot and Yurok (Northern California)

   C. Kutanai

     Kutenai (the Canadian border of Idaho and Northwestern Montana)

IV. Iroquois-Caddoan

   A. Iroquois

     Erie, Huron, Iroquois (Cayuga, Mohawk, Oneida, Onondaga, Seneca), Neutral, Susquehannock (Conestoga), and Tionontati (Tobacco) (the Eastern Woodlands of Canada and the U.S.); Cherokee, Nottoway, and Tuscarora (the Carolinas)

   B. Caddoan

     Caddo, Kichai, Tawakoni, Waco, and Wichata (bordering on the Plains in the Southeast); Arikara and Pawnee (the Eastern Plains)

V. Gulf

   A. Muskogean

     Apalachee, Alabama, Chickasaw, Choctaw, Creek, Hichiti, Houma, Mobile, Seminole, Tuckegee, and Yamasee (the Southeast)

   B. Related

     Atakapa, Callusa, Chitimacha, Natchez, Timucua, and Tunica (the Southeast)

VI. Siouan-Yuchi

   A. Siouan

     Assiniboine, Crow, Dakota Dious (Santee, Teton, Yankton), Hidatsa, Iowa, Kansa, Madan, Missouri, Omaha, Osage, Oto, and Ponca (the Plains); Winnebago (Wisconsin); Biloxi and Quapaw (the Southeast); Catawba and Tutelo (Virginia and the Carolinas)

   B. Yuchi

     Yuchi (the Southern Appalachians)

VII. Utaztecan-Tanoan

   A. Utaztecan

     Bannock, Chemehuevi, Gositute, Kawiisu, Mono, Paiute, Panamint, Paviotso, Shoshone, and Ute (the Great Basin and Rocky Mountains); Comanche (the Plains); Cahuilla and Serrano (Southern California); Hopi, Pima, and Papago (the Southwest); Acaxee, Cahita, Concho, Cora, Huichol, Jumano, Mayo, Pima Bajo, Opata, Tarahumara, Tepehuan, Tepecano, and Yaqui (Northern Mexico)

   B. Tanoan

     Picuris, San Ildefonso, San Juan, and Taos Pueblos (New Mexico); Kiowa (the Southern Plains)

VIII. Mosan

   A. Salishan

     Bell Coola, Chehalis, Coast Salish, and Tillamook (the Northwest Pacific Coast); Coeur d'Alene, Colville, Cowlitz, Flathead, Kalispel, Lilooet, Nisqually, Okanogan, Puyallup, Sanpoil, Shuswap, Spokan, and Thompson (the Northwest Pacific Coast)

Answer Key (cont.)

IX. Penutian
  - **A. Chinook-Tsimshian**
    Chinook and Tsimshian (the Northwest Pacific Coast)
  - **B. Coos-Takelman**
    Coos, Kalapuya, and Takelma (the Columbia River Coast)
  - **C. Klamath-Sahaptin**
    Cayuse, Klickitat, Molala, Nez Perce, Palouse, Umatilla, Wallawalla, and Yakima (the Columbia River Plateau)
  - **D. California Penutian**
    Coastanoan, Maidu, Miwok, Wintun, and Yokuts (California)

X. Yukian
  Yuki (California)

XI. Hokaltecan
  - **A. Hokan**
    Chumash, Karol, Pomo, Salinan, Shasta, and Yana (California); Achomawi, Atsugewi, and Washo (the Great Basin); Havasupai, Maricopa, Mohave, Walapai, Yavapai, and Yuma (the Southwest); Cochimi, Pericu, Seri, Tequistlatec, and Waicuri (Northern Mexico)
  - **B. Coahuiltecan**
    Coanhuiltec, Karankawa, Tamaulipec, and Tonkawa (Texas and Northern Mexico)

XII. Keres
  Acoma, Cochiti, Keres, Santa Ana, and Zia Pueblos (New Mexico)

XIII. Zuni
  Zuni (the Southwest)

Page 30: Migration Math
1. 12, 24, 90, 634
2. 60
3. 39.5 cups or 9.875 L
4. 29 days
5. 58 days
6. 19 deerskins
7. 3159 pairs of moccasins
8. 399 deerskins
9. 12 dogs

Page 31: Garden Math
1. a. 30 people x two ears per day = 60 ears per day for the village
   60 ears per day x 365 days per year = 21,900 ears per year
   21,900 ears divided by 3 per plant = **7,300 plants**
   b. 7,300 plants divided by 6 plants per hill = 1,216 ²/₃ hills (rounded off=**1,217 hills**)
2. a. 183 days x 1 = 183 squashes per person
   30 people in village x 183 squashes per person = 5,490 squashes
   5,490 squashes divided by 12 squashes per plant = 457 ¹/₂ plants (**458 plants** rounded off)
   b. 458 plants divided by 3 plants per hill = 152 ²/₃ hills (153 hills rounded off)
   153 hills = **153 square yards (153 square meters)**
3. a. 30 people x 1 pound (kg) beans per day x 365 days = 10,950 pounds (kg) of beans per year
   10,950 pounds (kg) beans x 1 pound (kg) per bean plant = **10,950 bean plants**

Challenge:
Corn: 7300 plants divided by 4 = corn from 1825 plants
Squash: 458 plants divided by 4 = squashes from 114.5 plants (115 rounded off)
Beans: 10,950 plants divided by 4 = beans from 2737.5 plants (rounded to 2738)

Page 40: Quiz
1. Accept all appropriate responses.
2. Deganawidah conceived of the idea of an Iroquoian Confederacy, and Hiawatha went around to the different tribes advocating adopting it.
3. Accept responses that describe a close family and clan systems with aunts, uncles, grandparents, and cousins all living under one roof.
4. Corn was a central part of their diet.
5. He was a culture hero of the Northeast Indians. He triumphed over the water monster and freed the water for the people. He was able to do superhuman things.
6. You would need to carry enough food, be able to find and kill game, have a water source, have regard for the inability of weaker members to maintain vigorous walking over a long period of time, and so forth.

7. You would need to know how much land each plant takes, how much food each plant produces, how many plants each family member will consume, how to store food for the winter, when the best times for planting each type of plant are, and so forth.

8. Leaves turning their colors are caused by warm, sunny days followed by sudden drop in temperature. The leaves stop manufacturing starches, the chlorophyll breaks down, and the chemicals in the leaves show through.

9. There are many differences, including the facts that then there were few rules to prevent injuries and no referee, and today balls and rackets are usually made commercially instead of by hand.

10. Accept all reasonable responses.

Page 46: Sequoyah and His Syllabary

"Anyone can learn this syllabary of mine in one day and be able to read within one week."—Sequoyah

Page 57: Storing Food

1. **Liters:**
    2 liters per day x 4 persons = 8 liters per day total
    8 liters per day x 30 days per month = **240 liters per month**

2. **Pounds:**
    $\frac{1}{2}$ pound per person per day x 30 days per month = 15 pounds per month per person
    15 pounds per person per month x 4 persons = 60 pounds per month
    60 pounds per month x 12 months = **720 pounds per year**
    Kilograms:
    $\frac{1}{4}$ kilogram per person per day x 30 days per month = 7.5 kilograms per month per person
    7.5 kilograms per person per month x 4 persons = 30 kilograms per month
    30 kilograms per month x 12 months = **360 kilograms per year**

3. **Cups:**
    $5\frac{1}{2}$ cups per person x 30 days per month = 165 cups per person per month
    165 cups = 82 $\frac{1}{2}$ cans
    $82\frac{1}{2}$ cans per person per month x 12 months per year = 990 cans per person per year
    $82\frac{1}{2}$ cans per person per month x 4 persons = 330 cans per month
    330 cans per month per family x 12 months per year = **3,960 cans per family per year**
    Liters:
    1375 milliliters per person x 30 days per month = 41,250 milliliters per person per month
    41,250 milliliters = 82 1/2 cans
    $82\frac{1}{2}$ cans per person per month x 12 months per year = 990 cans per person per year
    $82\frac{1}{2}$ cans per person per month x 4 persons = 330 cans per month
    330 cans per month per family x 12 months per year = **3,960 cans per family per year**

4. **Cups:**
    2 cups per child x 2 children = 4 cups per day
    4 cups per day x 30 days per month = 120 cups per month
    120 cups per month x 12 months per year = **1,440 cups per year**
    Liters:
    500 milliliters per child x 2 children = 1,000 milliliters (1 liter) per day
    1 liter per day x 30 days per month = 30 liter per month
    30 liters per month x 12 months per year = **360 liters per year**

5. **Cups:**
    $\frac{1}{4}$ cup x 2 cups per day per child = $\frac{1}{2}$ cup per day per child
    $\frac{1}{2}$ cup per day per child x 2 children = 1 cup per day
    1 cup per day x 30 days per month = 30 cups per month
    30 cups per month x 12 months per year = **360 cups powdered milk per year**
    Liters:
    60 milliliters x two = 120 milliliters per child per day
    120 milliliters per child per day x 2 children = 240 milliliters per day
    240 milliliters per day x 30 days per month = 7,200 milliliters or 7.2 liters per month
    7.2 liters per month x 12 months per year = **86.4 liters powdered milk per year**

6. **Cups:**
    1 cup per day per person x 4 persons per family = 4 cups per family per day
    4 cups per family per day x 30 days per month = 120 cups per family per month
    120 cups per family per month x 12 months per year = **1,440 cups per family per year**

Answer Key *(cont.)*

Liters:
250 milliliters per day x 4 persons per family = 1000 milliliters per family per day
1 liter per family per day x 30 days per month = 30 liters per family per month
30 liters per family per month x 12 months per year = **360 liters per family per year**

7. **Cups:**
7 gallons x 4 quarts per gallon = 28 quarts per 7 gallons
28 quarts x 4 cups per quart = 112 cups per 28 quarts
112 cups = **112 servings**
Liters:
280 liters = 28,000 milliliters
28,000 milliliters ÷ 250 milliliters = **112 servings**

8. **Cups:**
4 cups per quart x 10 quarts = 40 cups = **40 servings**
Liters:
1000 milliliters per liter x 10 liters = 10,000 milliliters
10,000 milliliters ÷ 250 milliliters per serving = **40 servings**

9. **Cups:**
20 quarts powdered milk x 4 cups per quart = 80 cups powdered milk
80 cups divided by 2 children = 40 cups (10,000 ml) powdered milk per child
40 cups per child x 4 liquid servings per cup = **160 servings liquid milk per child**
Liters:
20 liters x 1000 milliliters per liter = 20,000 milliliters
20,000 milliliters divided by 50 milliliters per serving = 400 liquid servings
400 liquid servings ÷ 2 children = 200 servings liquid milk per child

Page 68: Quiz

1. Accept appropriate responses.
2. Responses should include such elements as the family line passed through the mother, the father was the head of his sisters' families and not his own, there was a clan system, the man went to live with wife's family, and children were not members of their father's family.
3. The head chief was the most influential man in the village. He headed the village council and was in charge of handling local matters.
4. Sequoyah's syllabary was based on sounds in the Cherokee language. One can not write English words with it. If one does not know how to speak Cherokee, one would not be able to read it.
5. Based on skeletal remains, people have lived there at least 14,000 years. However, campfires and artifacts date back at least 30,000 years, suggesting that man was present that long ago.
6. Terrapin won the race by stationing his friends at each ridge of a hill, so from a distance it looked as though he himself was running.
7. Four was most sacred. It stood for the four directions.
8. They were very important. Sports and games were elements often included in stories.
9. Accept appropriate responses demonstrating the knowledge that a Seminole house is open-sided with a thatched roof and a platform floor.
10. Accept all reasonable responses.

Page 84: Buffalo Math

1. 33½ acres or 13⅓ hectares
2. 55.5 million acres or 22.5 million hectares; 333 million acres or 135 million hectares; 555 million acres or 225 million hectares
3. 125,286 buffalo
4. 3,125 buffalo
5. Seven years
6. 29.4 buffalo per year
7. 250 buffalo
8. 6,228 hides.
9. 1,394 hides
10. 30 robes per tipi, 2,460 robes for the village

Answer Key *(cont.)*

Page 85: Prairie Math
1. 52.5 miles or 84 kilometers out; 105 miles or 168 km total
2. 1 second
3. 6 ²/₃ minutes
4. 9 ponies and travois
5. 45 lbs. or 22.5 kg per day
   315 lbs. or 157.5 kg per week
   16,380 lbs. or 8,190 kg per year
6. 15 miles or 24 kilometers per day
   105 miles or 168 kilometers per week
   450 miles or 720 kilometers per month
7. 15 miles or 24 kilometers
8. 100/250 = 350/x
   x = 875 years
9. 43.75 quarts or 45 liters
10. 860 buffalo

Page 96: Quiz
1. Accept appropriate responses.
2. We do not know how many Indians were killed, where and how Custer died, how many soldiers were killed, how Custer's troops were attacked, and so forth.
3. He left Indian Territory to return to Montana with his people. He was caught by the army and taken to Fort Robinson. His people were locked in barracks for five days without food, water, or firewood. They broke out and ran for Montana, eventually getting their own reservation.
4. They scared the buffalo over a cliff.
5. The buffalo were the source of their food, shelter, clothing, and tools. When they were gone, the people had no way to live except by accepting government aid.
6. He was a culture hero of the Cheyenne. He could do extraordinary things.
7. Some of the phrases and their meanings are: "My heart sings" (happiness); "Our hearts floated like breath feathers" (happiness); "My heart stuck in my throat" (fear); "My heart fell to the ground" (great unhappiness or disappointment); "His skin crackled and tore" (old and wrinkled)
8. The effect was catastrophic. The diseases killed many millions, even as much as 90% of the population. The Indians had no natural immunity to the diseases.
9. Indians smoked as part of their rituals, ceremonies, and religions. Tobacco was sacred to them. People today generally smoke out of habit and, often, physical addiction.
10. Accept all reasonable responses.

Page 111: Potlatch Math
1. Women = 119
   Men = 102
   Children = 119
2. Large wooden baskets = 119
   Large baskets = 119
   Blankets = 119
   Small blankets = 119
   Ceremonial shields = 102
   Ceremonial knives = 102
   Bear robes = 1
3. Salmon = 170 pounds or 81.6 kilograms
   Berries = 42¹/₂ gallons (680 cups) or 170 liters
   Bear meat = 113¹/₃ pounds or 54.4 kilograms
   Roots = 680
4. Boat A = 9 trips
   Boat B = 8 trips
5. Salmon = 5¹/₂ pounds or 2.64 kilograms
   Berries = 1³/₈ gallons (22 cups) or 5.5 liters
   Bear meat = 3²/₃ pounds or 2.09 kilograms
   Roots = 22

Answer Key (cont.)

6. Salmon = $1,016.60
    Berries = $1,693.20
    Bear meat = $1,018.86
    Roots = $102
    Total = $3,830.66

Page 112: Fishy Math Problems
1. a. 4,000
    b. 1,200
    c. 360
    d. 900,000
2. a. 300
    b. $5,838 (pounds) or $5,832 (kilograms)
    c. **Helpers:** $600
    Fuel: $450
    Rental: $2,250
    Profit: $2,538 (pounds) or $2,532 (kilograms)
3. 6 hours
4. 30 cans
5. a. 6.5 pounds or 3 kilograms waste
    b. 26 cans (pounds) or 30 cans (kilograms)
    c. $6.50 (pounds) or $7.50 (kilograms)
6. a. $3.50 per week
    b. $15.00 per month
7. 5 hours

Page 124: Quiz
1. Accept appropriate responses.
2. Their natural environment was rich with everything they needed.
3. They did not have an organized religion but rather a belief in spirits.
4. Accept responses showing an understanding of tipis vs. longhouses.
5. They made houses, canoes, clothing, dishes, boxes, and so forth.
6. He or she would prepare great quantities of food and make or obtain many presents.
7. Hatchlings swim downriver to the sea, come back to the mouth of the river from which they entered the ocean, swim up to the spawning grounds where thet were born, spawn, and die.
8. Accept all appropriate responses.
9. Ordinary words need contexts to obtain meanings. Names have specific meanings of their own.
10. Accept all reasonable responses.

Page 141: Vitamin Math
1. a. $3/5$ serving (60%)
    b. 20
2. a. 2
    b. $333\frac{1}{3}$
3. $5\frac{1}{3}$
4. $6\frac{1}{2}$
5. 72,800 IU
6. 5
7. 1,250
8. a. 43,700
    b. 305,900
    c. 15,906,800
9. a. 65,700 mg
    b. 459,900 mg
    c. 23,914,800 mg
10. Answers will vary.

Answer Key *(cont.)*

Page 148: Quiz
1. Accept appropriate responses.
2. It is commonly called "The Long Walk."
3. A kiva is a sunken round room used for ceremonies and social gatherings. See page 128 for a description of its structure.
4. They may have moved because the land was exhausted, for defense purposes, because of drought, or so forth.
5. Archaeologists study them, dig up old ruins, and use radiocarbon dating to date things.
6. Games were sometimes used to decide important matters. They were also used for recreation, gambling, and to develop physical skills.
7. Accept responses showing an understanding of the process described on pages 133-136.
8. Coyote threw the paint pots.
9. Eagle refused because he thought Coyote would drop it or otherwise mess things up. However, after four questions, he relented.
10. Accept appropriate responses.

Page 154: Keeping in Balance
The acrobat can balance because the weight of the coins lowers its center of gravity.

Page 167: Making Math in Your Head
1. a. $87
   b. $193
   c. $157
   d. $223
2. a. $17
   b. $14
   c. $45
3. a. $1.20
   b. $3.75
   c. $1.57
4. a. $36
   b. $35
   c. $79
   d. $19
   e. $24
   f. $4
5. Answers will vary.

Page 173: Quiz
1. Accept appropriate responses.
2. California Indians lived in conical-shaped houses of poles and bark, banked with dirt. A pit was inside in the middle, and tule mats lined the walls. The houses were reasonably permanent, at least for several years. The natives of the Great Plains lived in portable tipis made of buffalo hides and poles.
3. Ishi was emaciated, starving, ragged, and frightened.
4. Ishi was used to walking barefoot and balancing with his big toe. Shoes did not allow him to do this.
5. Captain Jack was not given a lawyer. The decision to execute him was made before the "trial," and a gallows was being built in plain view all the while. He was allowed no appeal, nor was he given the right of due process.
6. Accept all reasonable responses.
7. As far as we know, humans did not originate in North America; therefore, everyone was at one time an immigrant. However, the Native Americans have been there the longest.
8. Two boys in the Sky World are rolling their hoops.
9. They were all one huge continent in the northern hemisphere.
10. Responses will vary based on personal opinion.